A Sense of Self

THOMAS J. COTTLE

A Sense of Self
THE WORK OF AFFIRMATION

University of Massachusetts Press
AMHERST AND BOSTON

Copyright © 2003 by University of Massachusetts Press
All rights reserved
First paperback printing 2006

Printed in the United States of America
LC 2002015644
ISBN 10: 1-55849-574-6
ISBN 13: 978-1-55849-574-6
Designed by Dennis Anderson
Set in Adobe Garamond by Binghamton Valley Composition, Inc.
Printed and bound by The Maple-Vail Book Manufacturing Group

Library of Congress Cataloging-in-Publication Data

Cottle, Thomas J.
    A sense of self : the work of affirmation / Thomas J. Cottle.
        p. cm.
Includes bibliographical references.
    ISBN 1-55849-367-0 (cloth : alk. paper)
    1. Identity (Psychology) I. Title.
    BF697 .C68 2003
    155.2′5—dc21

                    2002015644

British Library Cataloguing in Publication data are available.

For the children

The soul inside me is the last foreign language I'm learning.

Yehuda Amichai, *Open Closed Open*,
translated by Chana Bloch and Chana Kronfeld

The self cannot survive by itself alone.

Emmanuel Levinas, *Face to Face with Levinas*,
edited by Richard A. Cohen

Contents

Acknowledgments

"WRITING a book is a horrible, exhausting struggle," George Orwell wrote in one of his essays, "like a long bout of some painful illness. One would never undertake such a thing if one were not driven on by some demon who one can neither resist nor understand." I think he may be right. I know that George Steiner is definitely right when he referred, as he did recently in a lecture, to the "creative cancer of trying to think."

The question then is why write at all? And while this is hardly the place to proffer a reasonable answer, let me merely submit that for many of us, becoming interested in something seems to lead to a written project. It's the path we take and the best we can do as we attempt to hunt down our prey, and the product of our thinking, the truth.

To be sure, there are some rather glorious moments in the ordeal, but there is another world that sustains and supports us all and most assuredly reduces the struggle and calms the demon: the love and support of our friends and family. And so, before I begin the story that occupies these pages, I wish to thank the following people, the demon busters, the cancer curers. All of them have been thanked before, actually, in my books, but it's never too often, given what they do for me.

I am blessed with many marvelous colleagues and friends. These unusual suspects include Sara Lawrence-Lightfoot, Jerome Kagan, Gerald M. Platt, Barry O'Connell, Daniel Frank, Oliver W. Holmes, Robert Melson, Gail Melson, Gerald Fain, Victor Kestenbaum, Alan Gaynor, Roselmina Indrisano, Rose Ray, Arthur Beane, Donna Lehr, Leroy Clinton, Kathleen Vaughan, Bruce Fraser, Robert Sperber, Joan Dee, Boyd Dewey, Edwin J. Delattre, Patricia and Salvador Minuchin, Anne and Martin Peretz, Anne and Richard Rosenfeld, Brigitte Cazalis and Joseph Collins, and Joan and Robert Weiss, and Ben Steinberg. Professor David Steiner must be singled out on this occasion for his brilliance and utter generosity.

Once again for this volume I have been blessed to have Clark Dougan as my editor and advocate. I hope he knows how grateful I am to him. Nancy Raynor did more than any copy editor should ever have to do, and Carol Betsch shepherded the manuscript with her usual care and thoroughness. A special thank you to Ralph Kaplan as well.

My acknowledgments always conclude with references to my family. Kay Cottle, of course, continues to be its proper head. It's always rewarding to list other family members: Claudia Hinz; Jason E. Cottle and Sonya R. Cottle; number two son, Dr. Anthony Hinz; and our grandchildren, Luke Thomas Hinz, Nicole Kate Hinz, and Anna Carey Hinz. Then there are Judy and David Lahm and, in blessed memory, Eloise and Edwin C. Mikkelsen, Gitta and Maurice H. Cottle, and Leah Weinstock. Talk about a sense of self; these are the ones who give me my own.

PART

I

1 The Act of Affirmation

DURING the week he celebrated his fourth birthday, my grandson, Luke, took me to the tennis court in a park near his home. An all too common Seattle rain had ceased a few hours before our excursion, so it was not surprising to find that small puddles of water had collected in the little depressions in the tarmac. Standing on one side of a miniature pond, I encouraged my grandson to jump across the water, assuring him that there were no serious consequences if his feet got wet. Luke looked at me, then down at the puddle, and said without the slightest hint of emotion, "I'm not a very good jumper." With that, he successfully leaped across the pond and went on his way. Nothing else was said about the matter. I don't even know whether he heard my congratulations, "I knew you could do it!" But he did turn around and smile at me before remounting his tricycle.

One of the several themes I take from this story serves to introduce the topic of this book. Barely four, a child is already making assessments about himself, his talents, his abilities, his capacity to navigate in the world. Not only that, he exhibits feelings about these assessments. In this one instance, I suspect, Luke felt affirmed, not by my words but by his deed, and hence, for the moment anyway, he must have felt something about himself and the Seattle park world in which he spent so much of his time.

In a sense, we are all Luke, all the time assessing ourselves, judging ourselves, sometimes lovingly, sometimes not, often with approval, often with rather harsh criticism. Unlike Luke in this one story—and we come now to the second major theme of the book—we assess the world, the society, the circumstances in which we find ourselves and which, quite frankly, we often create. Eventually, we also end up with feelings about these assessments. By the time we decide whether to jump life's puddles, we have assessed ourselves and our circumstances and in consequence have developed strong feelings about ourselves and these circumstances.

Some psychologists suggest that these assessments and concomitant feelings are precisely what constitute our personalities. Perceptions and feelings, after all, are fundamental ingredients of the personality that are always open to adjustment if not complete transformation. The puddle remains somewhat constant, but our perceptions of and feelings for it, as well as our jumping skills and our sense of selves, can shift in the matter of a heartbeat. "The purpose of poetry," Czeslaw Milosz wrote in *Ars Poetica*, "is to remind us / how difficult it is to remain just one person."

Taking the argument one step further, it might be alleged that these perceptions and concomitant feelings are learned; someone teaches them to us, or we deduce them somehow, from previous experience. Or, we find that they are just there, inside ourselves, really inside our selves; they are, in a sense, "after-the-fact" experiences. Said differently, affirmation becomes defined as a past participle experience: I discover that I *am* affirmed or that I *have* affirmed another, hence we designate these experiences as "after the fact." Either way, they are not born in us as are, for example, our musical, linguistic, athletic, or mathematical talents, along with our temperament.[1] Technically speaking, most of us do not "learn" to be shy or adventurous, impatient or sanguine; we appear to come out of the womb wired in these ways.[2] Thus we speak of our temperament or constitution and differentiate these concepts from our concept of personality.

Someone once remarked that personality is what we are left with from childhood, the residue of our dealings with parents or the people who raised us. These are the infamous culprits, the ones who taught us we are good or bad, capable or inept, able to deal with the world or utterly unable to execute even the smallest jump. Simply put, people and circumstances alike tend to affirm us, cause us to feel that we are acceptable, worthy, and good or that we are not. I doubt seriously that Luke was ever told he was not a good jumper; he merely was hesitant in that instant, perhaps a trifle scared as well. One jump and all that ended. I choose to believe, and here begins our discussion of affirmation, that the power of affirmations deposited in his soul eventually led to his decision to jump, as well as the absence of surprise he evidenced upon successfully navigating the pond.

For the moment, consider that at least three fundamental powers have the potential to affirm us: we ourselves, the people with whom we associate, and the culture in which we live. Any one of these powers can cause us to feel personal disapproval, disaffirmation, or what later we will argue is equivalent to shame and, hence, shape the way we forever perceive our selves and the world. Keep in mind that a child constantly shamed tends to see not only himself or herself in the most negative light but the world as well. Suddenly life is "dog eat dog," the survival of the fittest, a journey of pain and hardship. As Albert Willis and Robert Harper suggest, some people come to exaggerate and "awfulize" their circumstances.[3] Similarly, the harshest of circumstances may break down a person raised with affirmations and constant words of approval. In laying out the requirements of a healthy boyhood, Eli Newberger wrote that every child "needs at least one adult in his life who is crazy about him." Then there is the individual self, affirming itself, celebrating itself, publishing itself, as Walt Whitman once instructed, or, in contrast, retreating, hiding, concealing itself from the world, seeking to make itself invisible.[5]

When Robert Kegan wrote, in *The Evolving Self,* that much of human activity is intended to make meaning of life, which is to say make meaning of circumstances and self, he addressed one of the fundamental issues of both philosophy and psychology.[6] On the one hand, he was alluding to the ancient notion of the examined life, for meaning making—Kegan speaks in terms of "meaning-organizational capacities"[7]—necessarily bespeaks the endless series of internal dialogues each of us undertakes as we attempt to assess our private and public worlds. On the other hand, meaning making refers to psychic conflicts or friendships, the mind engaging itself, affirming itself, presenting itself to others, as Heinz Kohut has written, with pride or with shame.[8] On this same note, Peter Marris offered a word of caution: "Over time, we elaborate and refine structures of meaning for all classes of events and relationships we encounter. We become increasingly confident of these meaning structures as they successfully interpret more and more experiences. But to sustain this confidence, we must . . . avoid situations which would bewilder our understanding."[9]

Beneath all these activities, moreover, is the cultural context in which we survive, for as noted, it too contributes to one's personal affirmations or at least to the dialogues in which one engages with self and others.[10] Just as we keep our selves in mind, so to speak, as we seek to find meaning in our lives, so too do we keep society in our minds, as Emile Durkheim and Freud too, for that matter, described in their classic studies on the nature of humankind.

Most of us are familiar with the common expressions "Life is what we make it," "It's all an illusion, it's all in the appearance, so why not make the illusion positive," or "If you don't love yourself, no one else will." Then there are the more cynical expressions, such as "You might just as well take care of yourself, no one else is going to!" or "If you never have expectations, you'll never be disappointed" (a concept that actually perturbed Ralph Waldo Emerson, who believed that in expecting nothing he was "always full of thanks for moderate goods").[11] Fundamental to each of these expressions is the concept of personal affirmation, or the lack of it. More intriguing, actually, is the degree to which we all require some form of affirmation on a fairly regular basis.

An example of this notion is captured in the famous sociological inquiry revealing what came to be known as the Hawthorne effect.[12] Workers in a Western Electric plant in Massachusetts were studied by Elton Mayo and his associates for their effectiveness, efficiency, and productivity. The results indicated that the workers interviewed showed greater productivity than those who were not interviewed. In other words, just speaking with people, recognizing them, honoring them, barely conversing with them affirmed them, somehow, which resulted in their becoming more productive.

Children in schools and workers everywhere report the same experience: that people's knowing our names, recognizing us or our efforts, makes us feel noticeably better and probably also enhances our productivity and sense of worth.[13] We need to feel affirmed through faith, a force that some argue should exist even in psychotherapy,[14] through communication, through touch, through contact of all varieties. Yet, ultimately, the results of these actions rest on our own personal reflections, our own personal deliberations and considerations. If, as the expression goes, life is what we make of it, then it is our capacity to reflect on our selves, our actions, and our culture, as John Dewey reminded us, that ultimately determines the form and power of the affirmation or the lack thereof.[15] In the absence of reflection, we may not even recognize when we are being affirmed.

Self-reflection, what may well turn out to be an essential action of self-knowledge,[16] as Aristotle believed, is what Luke undertook when he reached the temporary conclusion that he was not a good jumper. Not so incidentally, Hazel Markus labels self-knowledge as *the* critical component of personality, although as Jung reminded us, self-knowledge may be forever elusive.[17] Luke's reflections, presumably, changed as a function of his single little leap, which puts me in mind of this observation about adolescents from Jean Piaget: the adolescent believes "that the world should submit itself to idealistic schemes rather than to systems of reality . . . the proper function of reflection is not to contradict but to predict and interpret experience."[18]

This in turn raises the question, Just how much do we reflect on our selves, our individual actions, no matter how insignificant they may seem, and our culture? How often do we stop long enough not merely to smell the proverbial roses but also to take inventory of who we are, what we say, what we think, what we feel, what we determine is fate, what in truth is the product of our habits of the mind and heart, and what we might do to alter our lives so that we ourselves and, just as important, others too feel affirmed?

In these few pages, I have laid out what will become the themes in the book. My fundamental concern is the notion of affirmation. What really is it that we experience as affirmation, and what are the ramifications of affirmation or its lack in the leading of our lives? For that matter, what case can be made for affirmation being such a valuable concept in the first place? It may help to explain how I came to think about the concept, one that has been intensely researched by social scientists in many cultures.

Years ago I confronted a physician with this question: "If there is one thing people can do to benefit their health, what would it be?" He paused not even a second and answered: "Regular exercise." Granted, he added that he would like to see people stop smoking, cut their cholesterol levels, reduce the stress in their lives, and get regular checkups. But his initial answer was quick and to the point.

Then suddenly he turned the tables on me. "What one thing," he wondered, "would *you* say is the best thing parents can do for their children?" It was a reasonable inquiry for which I was totally unprepared, although his question revealed how superficial my own question to him had been. But then, without giving much thought to my answer, I said parents should read to their children every night of the year, starting whenever they think their children will listen and lasting for as long as the child will tolerate it.[19]

Truthfully, I have no idea from where that answer sprung; it was just there and may not be valid, but it did cause me to wonder why I had even thought of it. Reading, I concluded, does several things. First, at very least it brings parent and child together. I imagine the two people cuddling together, the child needing to find that special resting spot next to the parent, touching but still able to see the pictures, of course. Second, reading causes the child to think, imagine, wonder, make sense of words, what Selma Fraiberg in her classic study calls "word magic,"[20] as well as discover a world that exists apart from everyday "experience," which Jerome Bruner defines as meaning "a categorizing, a placing in a syntax of concepts."[21] Third, reading is a way into the self,[22] or what Harry Stack Sullivan called "the self-system." All the actions of wondering and meaning making begin not only to find their way in to the child's self but also may be part of what ultimately forms the child's self.[23] Heaven only knows what the child is thinking and feeling in response to his or her parent reading a story, perhaps the same story night after night after night, although a recent report confirms our suspicion that what children need is parents who will talk to them, play with them, and read to them as part of their everyday routines.[24]

Two more things about this nighttime ritual of reading—although daytime reading is just as wonderful. While spurring the mind to action, reading also appears to calm the child before he or she falls asleep. The notion seems almost contradictory: why would all this mental activity help the child fall asleep? Wouldn't it be better to minimize the cerebral stimuli before bedtime? Surely television viewing before bedtime has many ill effects on children, especially the younger ones.

The only explanation I have goes this way: If bedtime signals anything, it is the end of the day, the commencement of sleep. More to the point, it marks the moment when children, often in darkness or dimmed light, are about to descend into themselves, really into their selves, until sleep overtakes them. These, then, are the moments when children confront their own being, their own unique capacities, their minds, their ideas, their feelings, the stories they have just heard, without anyone around and, unlike at any other time of the day, with the knowledge that they are about to be transported into a totally different state of mind: unconsciousness, sleep. Something mystical is about to happen that actually causes some children to be frightened. These little ones seem to dread the psychological move to the "next place." What is going to happen when not only the room but also their mind gets darker and darker and darker? What will visit them during sleep in the form of dreams? Will they wake up? Will they be themselves tomorrow? Will they be tomorrow? For that matter, what is tomorrow other than the time "after this sleep"? "Surely the child feels most vulnerable," Brian Hall wrote, "when slipping under in the darkened room."[25]

It is amazing, given all these possible contemplations, that parents anywhere can get their child to fall asleep at a reasonable hour. On the other hand, it is not all that amazing that so many parents are awakened by children so many times during so many nights. One conclusion to be drawn from this description is that the mind of the child is profoundly rich, even at the youngest ages, even before the development of formal language. I am not certain that anyone yet knows of what children's minds are capable from the very start, although the psychoanalyst Paul Federn broke slightly with Freud's notion of psychic structure and suggested that the ego was present in the child at the commencement of life.[26] Which means that no one can say with complete assurance what the child is thinking about in connection with his or her own self and state of being. I do know that parents everywhere are constantly stunned by the remarks and observations made by their children and that the word "precocious" is used rather often to describe their sons and daughters, which suggests that every day we awaken to the realization that we have underestimated children's capacity to reflect on the world as well as themselves.

For me, in my unthoughtful response to the physician, reading to the child makes this possible. Or, if this notion seems too extreme, for surely children develop a sense of their self without people reading to them, then reading enhances the intellectual and emotional engines that ultimately fire up the furnaces of self-reflection and self-expression. Which means, furthermore, that what the child has committed to memory, learned "by heart," as the expression goes, serves as foundation of the self as well. Memorization of words, facts, conventions, rules, and stories from an oral or written tradition also fills the mind of the child and provides a sumptuous fuel for developing the contours of the self.

Something about reading to the child, however, not only intensifies his or her ability to reflect, focus, deliberate, wonder about the material at hand, the story of the night—as if most of us as parents in the early years ever got away with reading only one book—but also enriches the child's conversations with himself or herself. Stories become a source of sustenance, carrying us through the day, defining it in part, and most assuredly carrying us through the night, or at least that part of the night when, alone in bed facing only sleep, we undertake our self-examinations and reflections and practice and elaborate our various dialogues with self and others.[27] Perfectly alone we find ourselves auditioning for our selves, performing our dress rehearsals, checking our notes, for we are forever playwright, director, and actor— probably audience as well—preparing for tomorrow's opening or another matinee performance.

External and internal dialogues seem always to go hand in hand. The parent reads the story, and the child eventually tells the story back to the parent or "reads" along with the parent. Or perhaps the next day the child performs an entire theatrical production for the parent around the themes derived from the previous evening's tale. Which means that the child is also telling the story to himself or herself. Which means that children are constituted of these stories. Their very selves, or their earliest conceptions of their selves, are in part beginning to take the form of stories, and hence, much of the meaning making they undertake involves constructions of stories.

One thing more involves that matter of calming a child before bedtime with stories even of monsters and ogres and things that go bump in the night. I suspect that what I originally meant to be the significance of the reading, along with the obvious intellectual stimulation and activity—not to mention the introduction in a child's life of the sacred object known as a book—is the presence of the parent. Mother sits on the bed or lies alongside the child. Her voice alone is comforting, and she speaks words very different from those she speaks during the day, expressing herself in tones unlike those the child normally associates with her. A story is being told, a story on which both parent and child must focus. During these precious moments neither reader nor listener must be distracted by anyone or anything; neither can tolerate interruptions, especially the child.

From mother to child, and to no one else, a story is being read. It is their own secret moment together. Two people, perfectly undistracted, are being connected by a story, drawn together into that story, a teller and a witness, with characters only they know about and appreciate: two people, two selves conjoined in and through the words of another, the ideas of another, the self of another.[28]

It is more than a miniature schoolroom they have constructed; I suggest that in these moments the child is being affirmed. Indirectly, of course, the child is being told that there are stories in the world, many of them your own, and they are good and legitimate stories that make you who you are, and I am here to read some of the stories and, equally important, ratify the stories that you will tell to me and to your self. I am here to ratify our story-reading sessions, for the two of us are bound together in part by the story and all that it delineates and creates in us. I am here to ratify your mind, your being, your self. As Rollo May wrote, "It is only through discovering and affirming the being in ourselves that some inner certainty will become possible."[29] And one more very important matter.

Before the parent leaves the room, he or she must complete the bedtime ritual. "Tomorrow we will have more fun and do good things together," the parent says softly. And tomorrow night, the parent pledges, we will read more stories, which means that the parent will return to the child the next night before sleep once again overtakes the child. The pledge, however, also implies that there will be a tomorrow, that the child's self will be "there" tomorrow, "within the child," stories and all. "Sleep well," the parent whispers, relieving a bit of the fright that may be associated with falling asleep (for no one believes in rising to sleep, unless they are alluding to death). "I'm here if you need me," for all parents know that their child must be reassured that Mommy or Daddy is close by, within the sound of a voice or a cry. "Pleasant dreams," the parent adds, which implies that more stories may come to you when you are asleep, and I hope that they will be good ones, for they come from you and only you, which means that if they are pleasant and good, you too are pleasant and good. "I love you," the parent concludes, kissing the child and stroking the child's face. "I love you more than the *whole* world."

To a certain degree, the bedtime-reading ritual reveals precisely the manner in which intimate relationships are sustained by individual identities being affirmed by members of that relationship, although one rarely thinks in terms of reading to a child as a contribution to the child's consciousness and thus his or her emerging identity. Similarly, we may not automatically think of the bedtime routine as a ritual even though an argument for just this position could be advanced.

Two features of a ritual, for example, are, first, that participants employ the ritual to preserve their collective identities,[30] and second, participants make certain to separate the so-called sacred components from the customary or profane ones.[31] Parents learn that they cannot merely read anywhere or in any manner; the place and the performance must follow a prescribed (ritualized) routine. On the other hand, as Gloria Mays and Carole Lund point out, there are occasions, known clearly to book readers and listeners, when the so-called normal, pedestrian routine must be affirmed for the sacred part of the ritual to flourish and be maintained.[32] The simple, uncomplicated practice of reading to the child is constantly being affirmed and celebrated by both parent and child, and in this manner, in these affirmative actions, the bedtime reading habit becomes not routinized, exactly, but ritualized.

Putting all these ostensibly unthinking expressions and these almost automatically executed components of the ritual together, the parent has affirmed the child, affirmed the child's self or, more accurately, the emerging sense of self as the child experiences it. For children, it could be alleged, are not merely the collectors, listeners, or witnesses of stories but *are* stories; they are in their way living fables, *homo fabulans*. During the reading ritual, storyteller and witness also are one. All the components, then, are part of the affirmation package, with the ultimate statement being, I forever take responsibility for you.

In the end, I imagine this is what the reading ritual comes down to and what caused me to offer up that one response to my physician friend. Both symbolically and literally, a parent reading to a child captures for me the repeated act of affirming the child, an act that is rarely if ever articulated. Parents do not necessarily announce, "I am here to take responsibility for you." They do say, however, "I'm here if you need me, and tomorrow night we will read more stories." They say as well, "I will never let anything bad happen to you," which, although a promise that obviously cannot be perfectly kept, at least suggests that they will give their life for their child; they will never knowingly harm the child.

The promise represents a form of indebtedness to the child which lives within the child's self as part of her or his own being. Neither the parent nor the child have made any pledge, agreed to any contract, or probably even thought all that much about the ritual, other than that it absolutely must take place on a nightly basis and that a palpable absence is felt when something untoward occurs and the ritual is not enacted; both parent and child expect to be reunited the following evening through the ritual of the book. Without a stated agreement, parent and child merely discover that an affirmation has been made; it happens almost passively. The affirmation lives within the child's self as if it were already there, put there at the time of birth, and as I will argue later in the book, it may just have been put there at that time, or even earlier.

To summarize these points, all of which are elaborated in various chapters of the book, I have outlined at least three different components of the reading ritual and, more significant, of the concept of affirmation. First, there is a *story*, a communication from self to self, from self to itself. Second, there is a *reflection*, a self-reflection stimulated by the story and the bedtime ritual, and hence, in some mystical way, the story and the child's reactions to it become part of the child's own self. Conventions in this context, Eliot Turiel suggests, actually serve as affirmation of the rules of the ritual.[33] Thus, the story reader also becomes part of the child's self. As some have remarked, we are, perhaps, little more than the stories we tell and, at bedtime, the stories read and told to us. Finally, there is the sense, often never articulated but a part of the story nevertheless, that the teller who is taking *responsibility* for the story is also another person, another person taking responsibility for the child. Thus, the affirmation comes to be formed and internalized.

In more general terms, the reading ritual opens our mind to at least four potential categories describing the act of affirmation, categories in which one discovers a great deal of intriguing and highly provocative research. First, there is *psychic activity*. What really is going on in the mind as the child hears the story and from it develops, allegedly, a bit more of his or her personal algebra of self? What is the nature of the self-reflection undertaken by the child? What is the experience, in other words, of focusing one's self on one's self? As Erich Fromm reminded us, "Man may be defined as the animal that can say 'I.' "[34]

Second, there is the person, child or adult, attempting to *mediate* his or her experiences of self with (and within) the social world. This opens for us the complex matter of assessing the world of others, those known to us and those we only imagine knowing, like characters in a children's book, as one seeks to define the nature of one's self and then attempts to strike some sort of balance between one's self and one's environment.[35] This too is part of the affirmation, an affirmation, presumably, that one confers on one's self.

Third, and possibly the heart of the investigation of affirmation, are *relationships*. The bedtime reading habit, our prototype for the affirmation ritual, is essentially a relational experience; it does not take place unless both parties are present (to and for each other). As Martin Buber wrote, "All real living is meeting."[36] A significant moment is marked when the child begins to read alone prior to falling asleep and therein discovers what James Carroll reminds us "is the purest act of intelligence," although one suspects he or she carries intense memories, traces of the original reading ritual.[37] In great measure, the relational aspect of affirmation involves the shaping of self by dint of the actions of others. Intimacy, caregiving, and group affiliation emerge as vital components of this category, along with actions psychologists describe as being "pro-social," meaning that they enhance the life of someone, affirm life to some extent.

Finally, all these categories devolve to the nature of *theories of the self*, a concept defined by William James as the "sum total of all that he can call his,"[38] and the notion of allegedly inborn psychological needs all of which are fundamental to the healthy growth and development of the individual and all of which in some manner touch on the concept of *affirmation*, a term meaning "to make firm" or "to strengthen." Who is to say that reading to children does not strengthen them as much as the other nutritious foods they hopefully will be fed.

I BEGIN the following review of research on affirmation with a word of caution: the studies and theories below are hardly intended to represent an exhaustive survey of the relevant social scientific and philosophical literature. More important is that the reader begins to derive a sense of the avenues one may explore in hunting down the meaning to a person of being affirmed or failing to be affirmed. In the end, an investigation of affirmation and necessarily disaffirmation as well becomes an investigation of the self or, to be more accurate, the self encountering another self and from this encounter forming a new definition of itself, a new attitude about itself, a new understanding of itself. Eventually, these encounters produce a firm,

strengthened sense of self—firm and strong being at the heart of the definition of affirmation, along with the idea of presenting one's self as "fixed."
Conversely, an infirm, weakened, or disaffirmed sense of self, which, as discussed in later chapters, predisposes the person to living a life characterized
by shame and perhaps violence to self and others as well, may be defined as
presenting one's self as unfixed, broken.

THOSE KNOWING the client-centered therapeutic theories of Carl Rogers
are not surprised to discover the concept of affirmation replete in his work.[39]
Much of Rogers's theory stresses tasks performed by the therapist and client
together around the issue of what properly can be called affirmation, which,
in the therapeutic context, turns out to be a form of feedback from therapist
to client.[40] In one study, for example, in which investigators examined a
particular session between Rogers and a client known as Miss Mun, we learn
of five such tasks.[41] Among them are the role of self-reflection on feeling;
working with what Rogers calls the "inner critic," which is the self judging
itself; and, significantly, the role of empathy and affirmation, particularly on
those occasions when a person appears vulnerable. Affirmation, in other
words, is employed almost as a curative procedure, available to a person
when the self (or therapist) senses itself to be available to this sort of strategy.
The intervention, however, is predicated on a form of self-reflection, the self
of the client being asked to reflect on itself by the therapist. "It's all right,"
the parent comforts the child, communicating that the child is all right, that
the child's self is intact, firm, strong. In this manner, an affirmation through
self-reflection has been rendered.

   In research conducted by Jeff Stone, these same roles of self-reflection
(the self telling stories to and about itself) and self-affirmation come together in a most intriguing manner.[42] At the root of this work is the question
of how the self assesses a piece of behavior or derives meaning from it.
Stone's research suggests that after performing some task or behaving in a
particular fashion, if a person can purposely focus (the self) on the positive
results of the behavior, the self will find itself willing, as it were, to drop any
need to justify that particular act or piece of behavior; it can simply accept
itself, one might say, for what it is and what it does. In more general terms,
a dissonance between what I have just done and what I think and feel about
what I have just done (self-reflection) is significantly reduced by disciplining
the self to reflect on the positive features of the behavior. In a sense, this
represents an act of self-affirmation,[43] or what literally could be called self-
notification.

The common notion of thinking of the proverbial glass as being half full as opposed to half empty is what Stone is attempting to describe during those occasions when we struggle—that is, our self struggles—with itself in a disaffirming manner over some recent behavior. "Focus on the good things of life," we counsel friends. "What's done is done." "Think good thoughts," we tell our children before they fall asleep. "Pleasant dreams."

In a therapeutic setting not unlike that described by Rogers, work was undertaken around the issue of assisting patients to feel and accept the emotional pain they were experiencing. Pain, Leslie Greenberg and Sandra Paivio explain, can be imagined phenomenologically as a state of "brokenness" (of the self), what we call disaffirmation. So the question becomes, how does the self integrate itself, put itself back together and mend the brokenness?[44]

Greenberg and Paivio outline several techniques to achieve this self-integration, including mobilizing unmet needs and overcoming one's natural tendency to avoid certain issues that evoke the original pain. In the end, however, the technique of self-affirmation proves to be as powerful as any. The self appears to mend itself, right itself, by affirming itself, no matter how this action is defined. The sense of brokenness, therefore, is countered by the sense of a self repairing through the stories (of self) it tells itself. In the stories and accounts (and accountings), in other words, the self fashions a renewed version of itself which it can now tell itself and others as well, if only these others will listen.

In a similar fashion, the work of the psychoanalyst Hans Loewald frequently focused on dealing with a patient during those moments when he or she appeared most vulnerable, "broken" in Greenberg and Paivio's terms.[45] What concerned Loewald was the patient who might actually feel broken by the rigors of the psychoanalytic process itself. Careful not to overstep the boundaries imposed on the relationship between analyst and analysand, and most especially looking out not to destroy the nature of what Freud originally coined the "transference" (of feelings of the analysand onto the analyst), Loewald sought to detect ways the patient might feel affirmed when he or she appears especially vulnerable, particularly when the ego attempts to defend itself from what he called the loss of reality and what David Winnicott labeled "the unthinkable anxiety."[46] Accordingly, Loewald advocated affirming techniques even when these techniques might appear to the outside observer to be exaggerated, a procedure that years later other psychotherapists would actually come to support.[47]

In the same vein, in examining the nature of the self-object differentiation, generally a significant dynamic in self psychology, Mark Sehl spoke of the importance of the patient recognizing the feelings of the therapist, even feelings of anger.[48] Allegedly, this perception of the therapist's emotions leads to an affirmation of the patient's individual identity. Taken together, these last studies reveal to us a moment when the self, feeling itself to be on precarious ground, requires the strength made possible by the affirmations of another.

In the realm of holistic psychology, as the concept of the self comes to be elaborated and more finely etched, the role of affirmation assumes even greater significance. Although I am focusing on the so-called psychological activity of affirmation, note that studies of affirmation derived from therapeutic encounters ineluctably involve the presence of the other, notably the therapist or counselor.

This point is illustrated in the work of holistic psychology in which a strong emphasis is placed on the moment-to-moment examination of what is transpiring in the therapeutic setting. Mind, body, spirit—all are open for observation and consideration, if one will allow that traces of the mind and spirit are available for observation. Consider, for example, the work of Michael Robbins, who emphasizes what he calls "the presence" of the two selves together in therapy.[49] The self for Robbins, and other theorists too, for that matter,[50] is essentially organized around the notion of intention: what is it I intend to do? For the self to understand itself, it must first be mindful of itself and all that it does, intentionally that is, to detract from its allegedly authentic nature and purpose. The inauthentic self, therefore, can never discern meaning that it itself can determine to be valid. Simply put, if I constantly lie to myself about my self, there is no way in the world I can either know or understand my self.

The self must be made aware, therefore, through educational interventions such as therapy, of what it does or intends that yields it an authentic understanding of itself, as well as what it does to trick itself, deceive itself into believing things about itself which at some level it "knows" not to be true. But notice that part of this action of self-reflection or self-understanding rests on the existence of the other person being present. Said differently, part of my recognition that I am acting falsely is your being there and witnessing the story (of self) that I am telling.

Although some of this reasoning may sound abstruse, we all recognize those moments when we present our selves to another or even privately think about our selves in ways that we know full well to be false. A judging or observing (aspect of) self, in other words, is listening to the self speak to itself, it saying at times, That's a nice story you're spinning, but it has no basis in truth, and you know it! How can you intentionally tell this perfectly lovely person such a disingenuous tale! Wittingly committing an immoral act is another example of the self acting in an intentionally false manner. "You knew better than to do that," we admonish our child, and quite often he or she *does* know better.

If some of the above material seems confusing or even paradoxical, then perhaps I may borrow from the literature of Zen Buddhism and suggest that these paradoxes, termed koans by the Zen Buddhist, are actually intended to help a person attain the stage of satori, or "enlightenment."[51] Indeed, Zen training often requires the student to experience the sorts of koans which in part are purposely meant to throw the self against itself, as it were. In a sense, this is what Martin Heidegger and Rollo May call the realm of the *Eigenwelt*, the world of the self thrown against itself.[52] It is the world of self-reflection, consciousness, and identity, the world in which one seeks to discover the meaning of oneself (one's self) in part by using the presence of others to assist them in the process—Heidegger and May call this realm of being with others the *Mitwelt*, the "with" world.

In *The Couch and the Tree*, John Suler and Anthony Molino have gathered together a series of essays that describe the sort of paradoxes which may yield insight into the self, that is, insight gained by the self about itself.[53] As such, these paradoxes involving self-reflection further help us to understand not only what may transpire in the therapeutic context—the merging of the realms of the Mitwelt and Eigenwelt—but may begin to define as well the fundamental nature of the therapeutic enterprise.

If psychotherapy is intended to create transformations of the self's definition of itself and the nature of the social world and hence transformations in how the self feels about itself and the social world, then koans contribute to the self's understanding of what ultimately it defines as reality. Koans define as well how the self presents itself to others and itself, how it literally turns back upon itself to appreciate its meaning as well as the meaning of the social world (classic self-reflection), and, most significant, what the influence of self-affirmation is on these other dynamics. For, ideally, the purpose of these paradoxes purported to help the person reach the state of enlightenment is to find the meaning of self and the social world and thereby experience one's self as having been affirmed.

But perhaps we should turn the argument on its head and claim that when we affirm our selves, we find, or at least imagine that we have found, personal meaning (in the realm of the Eigenwelt) and the meaning of being with others in the social world (the realm of the Mitwelt). Either way, we

begin to understand that the concept of the affirmation takes us simultaneously into the realms of the personal self and the self in the presence of
others, the self engaged with others, its definition now being affected by the
presence of others. In this context, Kathleen Hirsch offers this lovely description of "presence," replete with its interpersonal and mediational tones:
"Becoming present to the very rooted, particular reality of my own life and
that of my child has opened me to concerns about mutuality, responsibility,
community. I find myself 'in' the world more than I ever have been and
discover in this a profound convergence between my deepest individual
yearnings and those of the society in which I am challenged to live."[54]

Clearly, the self must navigate in both these worlds, its own and the world
of others, often finding that it must mediate between the two realms much
in the manner of Freud's ego mediating between the urgings of the id and
the inevitable realities of the external world imposed on it through the structures of the ego and superego.[55] Not surprisingly, the concept of affirmation
plays a highly significant role in the research on the development of the self.

ONE ENTRY point into the second realm of research involving affirmation,
that of affirmation as mediator of the self and the social world, is the act of
caring for the environment, surely one way the self involves itself with the
social world. Altruistic behavior, generally, represents another example of
what psychologists might refer to as behavior requiring mediation between
the self and other. One researcher, E. S. Geller, established a so-called mediational model to explain how the "actively caring" self, what he called an
aspect of altruism, takes responsibility not only for itself but also for the
environment.[56] Geller argued that it is in part the action of self-affirmation
that makes possible this brand of altruism. My acceptance and protection of
my self, in other words, becomes translated into my acceptance and caring
for you as well as the natural world in which we both survive. As Terence
Wilson's research suggests, acceptance becomes an active process of self-
affirmation; it need not be viewed as passive resignation or mere acceptance
of the power of fate.[57]

Two points about Geller's research might be stressed. First, affirmation
sits alongside self-esteem, a concept I will discuss later, and personal control.
In caring for my self and taking control of my self, I discover that I am able
to care for the environment, "take control" of it in an altruistic but not
dominating fashion. In the same manner, I can speak of taking control of
my children to mean not directly orchestrating every facet of their lives or
arranging for various outcomes but making certain to care for them and look

out for their well-being. Second, affirmation for Geller and those testing his hypotheses is tied to the notion of claiming responsibility for self and other (which includes the natural environment) in the same manner as Markus outlined in her conception of a self-schema.[58] I will later return to this theme to formulate a fundamental definition of affirmation.

Consider a second illustration of how affirmation plays into the self seeking to mediate itself with the environment, in this case, the human environment. Reminiscent, perhaps, of the social psychological studies on cognitive dissonance, a series of studies is performed to understand why it might be that when threatened—psychoanalysts might call the process "narcissistic assault"—the self seeks to compensate for the threat or the sense of having been wounded by casting a positive light (a "positive spin") on itself by almost automatically comparing itself with others. Involving affirmation, the comparison somehow helps the person reintegrate the pieces of self wounded by the threat.[59]

In this context the work of Joanne Wood, Maria Giordano Beech, and Mary-Jo Ducharme, appears elegant in its simplicity and in the end tells a lovely story.[60] Subjects in their experiments are selected on the basis of having exhibited high self-esteem. These are people, presumably, able to affirm themselves (their selves) through one means or another. In one experiment, these people with high self-esteem fail in a task and are allowed, if they so choose, to compare their behavior and performance with those of others. It turns out that they opt to compare themselves with others over the issue of what they consider to be their strongest attributes. When their weakest attributes are up for consideration, the number of reported social comparisons drops off substantially.

Not surprisingly, a second experiment revealed similar findings. When a subject succeeds at a task, he or she is very likely to make comparisons around the issue of his or her strongest attributes. When failing at a task, however, subjects preferred to make their comparisons with others around the other's corresponding relative weaknesses.

Here now is the punch line: when I fail at a task or believe myself to have failed, if I compensate for the failure with self-affirmation, I tend not to compare myself with anyone. Affirmed by itself, my self is able to mediate between itself and the social world in such a manner that it *imagines* it has been successful; it feels sufficiently good about itself. I need no further comparisons to confirm anything about my self. Most likely, I am able to move on and face the next challenge generated either from the social world (Mitwelt) or from my self (Eigenwelt).

A form of mediation also is observed in research performed by Martha Dore, Lani Nelson Zluplco, and Eda Kaufmann, with third- and fourth-grade children in an urban school setting.[61] All the children participating in this study were selected because of their family's involvement with substance abuse. The question confronting the researchers was what were the so-called workable strategies these children might learn to better manage the difficulties encountered in such family circumstances.

Two fundamental findings emerged from the investigation. First, children seemed to be helped by learning how to predict situations, thereby making the conditions they regularly encounter appear less frightening. Second, and more to the point of our concerns, teaching children how to use the group—what we have called mediation—to affirm themselves appears to reduce the strain of having to confront family members engaged in drug use. In fact, Dore and her colleagues were able to document perceptible increases in conceptions of self-worth as a function of the various group learning strategies employed.[62]

A similar study conducted by Dusty Humes and Laura Humphrey, this one involving drug-dependent adolescent girls, indicated that the parents of these girls tended to communicate almost contradictory messages.[63] On the one hand, the daughters were condemned for their drug use; on the other hand, they were offered affirmation. Interestingly, daughters tended to follow the lead of their parents in condemning (disaffirming) or affirming themselves.

Mediation seems also to play a role in a study conducted by Gloria Mays and Carole Lund in which male caregivers were asked to offer their perceptions of the work they performed with mentally ill relatives.[64] Their findings suggest an answer to the age-old question of how it is that people can sustain themselves while undertaking such psychologically draining work.

Three categories of responses emerged from the Mays and Lund data. First, and predictably, the men spoke of the physical and psychological burdens inherent in their work. Second, they spoke of the depth and duration of their commitment to their realities, the source of which is not revealed in this particular investigation. Third, they spoke of the affirmations they received not, they suggested, for the people they are as much as for the role they perform. Not surprisingly, it was the role of caregiver as much as themselves (their selves) as caregivers that required affirmation. With proper affirmation, presumably, I can commit myself to a task as well as extend the tenure of the task, perhaps even indefinitely as in marriage and parenting, two other forms of caregiving. Sometimes, apparently, I need you to tell me that I am worthy. Other times, even in moments of burdensome toil, I need only for you to assure me that the *work* I undertake is worthy. I will then make the connection to my self as worthy.

At still other times, as the work of Nathalie Des-Rosiers, Bruce Feldthusen, and Oleana A. R. Hankivsky indicated, I need you to affirm the fact that what has happened to me is wrong.[65] Des-Rosiers and her colleagues found just this position in a study on the survivors of sexual violence who took their cases into civil court. Not unexpectedly, these people seek financial compensation for the wrong that has been committed, but money often turns out to be an insufficient compensation. More significant, the litigants report a need for a public affirmation of their suffering, something inhibited by the adversarial nature of the legal system.

Married couples, according to the work of Joseph Veroff and his associates, also must balance or mediate between affirmations given to the self by itself and affirmations derived from one's partner.[66] Needless to say, there is often great tension about this issue; who, for example, is supposed to affirm whom at a particularly delicate moment? For couples to report satisfaction in their marriage, the researchers suggest, there must be some affirmation of individual gender roles as well as affirmation of each individual. Like the caregivers in the aforementioned study, people apparently need approval of role as well as self, each form of approval clearly enhancing the other.

The seven Cs of marriage, the magical concepts allegedly defining a satisfying and enduring relationship advanced by Gary Birchler, Diana Doumas, and William Fals-Stewart, further our appreciation of the role of affirmation in mediating between the self and the social world.[67] Although the authors do not actually mention this notion, affirmation becomes a vital component in the first C, character, just as it does in the formation of the fourth C, commitment. Not surprisingly, the authors have assigned affirmation to the fifth C, caring, where it plays a logical role in support, understanding, and the display of affection.

The Birchler research dovetails with work on affirmation within couples conducted by Sandra Murray and her associates.[68] Their work indicates that an individual discovers virtue in his or her partner only when that partner finds virtue in them. Representing a finding that tends to confirm the defense mechanism Freud labeled "projection," people designated as revealing low esteem reacted to situations arousing self-doubt by turning around and doubting the regard in which they imagined themselves to be held by their partner. In contrast—and this too reflects what we are calling a mediational process—people exhibiting high self-esteem react to situations in which self-doubt is aroused by becoming even more confident that their partner holds them in high regard.

By examining this work, we begin to see that at any point in a relationship, people can perceive the relationship as a source of strength and affirmation or weakness and disaffirmation. Yet underlying these perceptions is a more fundamental sense of an affirmed self or disaffirmed self entering a relationship and then perceiving all three entities, one's self, the other's self, and the relationship itself, in accordance with the original sense of personal affirmation or disaffirmation. Either way, affirmation plays a profound role in the perpetuation of the relationship, not to mention the satisfaction members derive from it.

If the perception of virtue derives from affirmation, so too does a sense of dignity. For as Harry Moody discussed in his article about older adults, when people find dignity within themselves (their selves), surely a form of affirmation, the self experiences this affirmation as transcendent, a call to freedom, as it were.[69] This finding, in turn, causes us to question the various social roles the self maintains and the forms of behavior it employs in mediating these roles. With similar research intentions in mind, The Jungian therapist Jane Pretat explored the ways in which people generally discover affirmations in order to make a more gentle transition into what she called their "croning years,"[70] or what Constance Rooke described as the "winding-up" phase of the life cycle in which affirmation plays a significant role as a person confronts continual losses and the specter of death.[71]

Shifting our focus for the moment, we assert that there may be no better illustration of the notion of a self mediating between itself and the social world than that of an eating disorder. In the terminology of self psychology, food represents a selfobject, something simultaneously "in here" and "out there." Literally speaking, the self confuses itself and others with food. Early on, it is speculated, children reveal this same confusion: the self and its nurturance come to be one and the same. Thus, to regulate food intake is to regulate the self or at least to allow one to imagine that the self is somehow being regulated and, hence, under (self) control.[72] This means, however, that for me to be nourished or affirmed, I rely not only on my food intake but also on those people who provide me this nourishment, and thus my self may tend to confuse itself, its nourishment, and ultimately the providers of this nourishment.[73]

Following this theoretical line of reasoning, it is alleged that people with eating disorders, notably anorexia nervosa, are impaired precisely because the original nourishment they seek—something we might call "symbolic affirmation"—in selfobjects such as food, is found to be defective, literally inedible. The act of eating, an act that seemingly mediates the social with the personal and the external with the internal, is viewed as a way of managing or controlling the very concept of the self.[74] If I control food and body weight, then I have convinced my self (or tricked it into believing) that I have also successfully controlled not merely my emotions but all aspects of my self.[75]

In addition to this line of reasoning, the research of Bill Thornton and Jason Maurice indicates that women with eating disorders tend to affirm attractiveness as an ideal for the self.[76] Notice that the self is not idealized; rather, it is the publicly agreed-on conception of attractiveness that comes to be idealized. Accordingly, those women in the Thornton and Maurice investigation who appeared to affirm their own body types, women, that is, revealing low self-consciousness, exhibited less of what the authors called "physique anxiety."

As a final statement on the notion of affirmation and its role in the mediation of self and the social world, consider one aspect of the extraordinary writings of Carl Jung. Readers of Jung recall his concern that the creative richness and almost infinite expansiveness of what he termed our "collective consciousness" are constantly under assault by the more dogmatic institutions of the culture, religion being one of those institutions.[77] The assault is so intense, moreover, it produces what Jung called a "psychic emergency," a phenomenon serving to drive the self toward what he envisioned as a spiritual rebirth.

In her work on classical Jungian archetypes, Marie-Louise von Franz instructs us on how Jung believed we manage this potentially overpowering dilemma of the assault on the collective consciousness and what really is the nature of the psychic emergency Jung had in mind.[78] Briefly stated, nature and body, on the one hand, and matter and spirit, on the other, are reintegrated by the self essentially through the act of affirmation of self and other, so that eventually the self emerges in a new form, one conjoining its own being (self) with nature, the quintessential feature of the social world.[79]

2 The Relational Aspect of Affirmation

WE ARRIVE now at the heart of the mediational aspect of affirmation, namely, the shaping of the self by the other, a phenomenon anticipated in several of the studies mentioned in chapter 1. One place to begin in a vast psychological literature on this subject is in the realm of what psychologists have called the "Michelangelo phenomenon."[1]

Predicated on interpersonal relationships, the Michelangelo phenomenon represents an attempt by social scientists to describe how the individual self is formed by the perceptions of it of some significant other, as well as by the behavior of this significant other. The essence of the phenomenon rests on the notion that the more the self is affirmed by the perceptions and behavior of the other, the more the individual self "moves" toward its own conception of an ideal form. Simply put, the more you affirm me in word and deed, the more I imagine that I have begun to reach an ideal form of (for) my self. Conversely, the fewer affirmations you provide me, the less likely I imagine being able to attain an ideal version of my self.

Support for the Michelangelo phenomenon is found in research conducted by Tanya Scheffler and Peter Naus in which the investigators sought to learn the effects on a young woman of her father's affirmations of her or lack of them.[2] On the basis of questionnaire data, some sixty university women indicated that when they believed their fathers demonstrated unconditional positive regard to them—something akin to what I am calling affirmation—they reported higher personal self-esteem as well as a greater comfort with their own sexuality and sense of womanhood. Once again, feeling that the words and deeds of another affirm me, I imagine I am reaching an ideal of my sense of self and definition of being.

Similar results are found when young men, university students in one instance, are the objects of the research. In work undertaken by Peter Naus and John Theis, a positive correlation was discovered between the degree of a father's affirmation of his son and the son's self-esteem, his security in intimate relationships, and a general contentment with his "masculinity," irrespective of how that term was defined by the young men taking part in the study.[3]

Considering the results of the Scheffler and Naus study as well as that of

Naus and Theis, we might ask whether the Michelangelo phenomenon can be turned upside down. That is, can people interpret and thereby refashion the words and deeds of others merely to give confirmation to their sense of worth and goodness? Research undertaken by Keith Beauregard and David Dunning argued for just this position.[4]

To reach this conclusion, the researchers, employing Scholastic Aptitude Test (SAT) scores, utilized the device of either threatening or bolstering the self-esteem of experimental subjects. As it turned out, when their self-esteem was threatened, subjects tended to evaluate the scores of others negatively. When their self-esteem was raised, this negative relationship appears to dissipate. Once again, those young men whose esteem had been threatened exhibited a far greater contrast in their judgments of others than did those subjects whose esteem was enhanced. Interestingly, this same pattern holds true when the topic of the investigation shifted to abortion and in another study when the focus turned to evaluating members of a stereotyped group: those persons who are previously affirmed tend to stereotype far less than those who lack not adequate information but adequate personal affirmation.[5]

Another illustration of the social world shaping the nature of the self, or at least the self's perception of itself, is found in work conducted by Susann Hill and Toni Tollerud in which the purpose of the research was to enhance the (felt sense of) dignity in students.[6] More specifically, Hill and Tollerud wished to learn whether people would alter their sense of self as their basic needs come to be met and others enhance their personal sense of dignity. Not surprisingly, the research indicated that the more others meet our needs and generally affirm us—the investigators used the word "empower"—the more empowered and dignified we hold our selves to be.

Even more to the point is the work Anne Sved-Williams conducted with daughters of mentally ill mothers.[7] Predictably, therapeutic sessions with these adult women yielded expressions of hatred of self and mother; difficulties in their own parenting chores; a sense of isolation, especially from certain family members; and a generalized belief that they were, somehow, stigmatized by their mother's illness. Interestingly, while all the women perceived themselves as "troubled" or "disturbed," their comrades saw them as strong and resilient. Thus, by affirming one another, the women tended to lose a bit of what we might call the social psychological inheritance of their mother's illness and come to perceive positive ways to handle the isolation and stigmatization concomitant with the illness, in the same way that grieving patients can be affirmed in group or individual settings by therapists who fundamentally affirm the emotions associated with the original grief event.[8]

If a self is formed in part through its relationships with other selves, thereby forming what self psychologists call "selfobjects"—recall that this is the realm that Heidegger and May designated as the with-world (the Mitwelt)—then nothing, theoretically, can be as damaging to the self as the destruction of the original relationship.[9] Not so incidentally, Lev Vygotsky alleged that "all the higher functions originate as actual relationships between individuals."[10] According to Lauren Lawrence, this destruction, caused by separation, divorce, and death, even finds its way into dreams, many of which depict in highly realistic fashion the circumstances surrounding the original dissolution of the relationship.[11] Not so incidentally, dealing with those who have experienced separations and death, what Lawrence calls "splitting experiences," is made somewhat easier when we appreciate the role of affirmation among those persons grieving for lost love objects.

To understand better the aforementioned notion of selfobject and its relation to affirmation, recall that self psychology generally perceives the self as striving to reveal itself to the world, as well as to itself, as cohesive, integrated, and regulated.[12] In theoretical terms, this is the overriding motivation of the self. In other words, the self employs objects partly to affirm itself. Objects to which the self becomes attached or with which it actually becomes literally confused, the so-called selfobject, represent the need of the self to develop and regulate itself.[13] Additional needs of the self include the well-known phenomenon in self psychology known as "mirroring," which turns out to be a form of self-acknowledgment and affirmation, idealization, protection, and the development of a positive and cohesive sense of self. It includes as well something self psychologists call "twinning," which is also akin to affirmation in that it involves a belief that not only can one share one's self with another but also that, in some essential ways, these two selves are alike.[14] For Heinz Kohut, the "fragmented" self requires affirmation, or what he called a merger with a powerful other, in order to reintegrate the parts of the self.[15]

The role of affirmation in this context of relationship of self and other is exemplified best, perhaps, in the work on attachment theory conducted by John Bowlby.[16] It was Bowlby's contention that the nature of the original relationship between mother and child creates security, insecurity, or a complicated form of ambivalence the child tends to reveal for the rest of her or his life. As background for these assertions, Erik Erikson had written that identity "begins way back when the child first recognizes his mother and first feels recognized by her, when her voice tells him he is somebody with a name, and he's good. Already he begins to feel that he's somebody, he's an individual."[17] It is not difficult to conclude, therefore, that Bowlby and, later on, his colleague Mary Ainsworth would designate the nature of the (maternal) attachment to be a central feature in the development of pathology.[18]

One such example of this speculation is found in the research of Pat Sable, who employed Bowlby's theories to explain the emergence of the so-called borderline personality in adults.[19] The essence of the borderline personality reflects Bowlby's original typologies of attachment. In one moment, the borderline personality seeks intense closeness with significant others, only to reveal in the ensuing moment an avoidance, even a dread of closeness with the other.

While early trauma and an inability to regulate emotions are alleged to play a role in the development of the borderline personality, the therapeutic treatment of the borderline case presents a serious challenge to the therapist, inasmuch as the nature of the therapeutic alliance (yet another selfobject paradigm for the patient) may be as significant for healing as any technique the therapist may utilize. Here affirmation of the patient by the therapist plays a prominent role in the therapy as the patient must develop sufficient trust and security in the relationship with the therapist so that he or she may be able to engage in a discussion of the self differentiated from others (including the therapist) and not feel terrified. In more theoretical terms, the self must be able to define itself comfortably both in relation to another self (the selfobject) and apart from another self (the self as object to itself). This ability is made possible by the act of the therapist genuinely seeing the patient and the patient imagining that he or she has been seen by the therapist exactly as the common expression suggests: "Has anyone seen you about this matter?" Sable's research suggests that affirmation of the self by the other makes both these formidable actions possible or at least less daunting, as well as less likely to lead to pathology. Said differently, it may be that the original pathology itself is caused by the lack of affirmation of the self by the other, a position also taken by Michael Basch and John Pardeck, the latter arguing that affirmation ought to become a core concept for therapists, generally, as they seek to diagnose and treat their patients.[20]

In more theoretical terms, Lorna Benjamin took this idea one step further by challenging the early psychoanalytic concept suggesting that defense mechanisms prevent people from becoming conscious of their own thoughts and emotions.[21] By affirming people, Benjamin argued, one increases the likelihood that particular behavior will become associated with what she called "attachment effects." In this regard (and affirmation again plays a central role) behavior that some observers would automatically consider abnormal or maldevelopmental may actually prove to be beneficial for growth and understanding.

Coming from a psychoanalytic self-psychological tradition, Basch argued that a healthy sense of personal power and an unhealthy sense of destructive power, forces akin to Freud's original life instinct (Eros) and death instinct (Thanatos), derive from a common genetic trunk. In the beginning, Basch and others asserted, the child experiences what has been called "infantile grandiosity"—in cognitive terms it is called "solipsism." All the world revolves around this little being who in some primitive sense believes that he or she is capable of everything, even immortality.

Ineluctably, however, the external world enters the drama (really the child's sense of self) in the form of affirming and disaffirming actions. The child's grandiosity, therefore, comes to be either confirmed or rebuked. The child accordingly feels pride or humiliation. As John Dewey wrote, "There is nothing more spontaneous, more 'instinctive,' than praise and blame of others."[22] In Erikson's terms, he or she feels either autonomy or shame and (self) doubt.[23] Where pride yields a growing sense of confidence and probably the capacity to affirm others as well, humiliation and shame eventually yield, Basch argues, a nihilistic conception of the world in which customary moral and religious beliefs are debunked or trivialized. In addition, the person experiences a felt sense of a purported death force in which he or she not only engages in (self) destructive behavior but also acts as though he or she has no regard for the well-being of self or others.[24] In the social realm, not surprisingly, this posture tends to inhibit any capacity for empathy.

Although I will further discuss the notion of a "death force" extant in the minds of so-called disaffirmed individuals, I want to mention here that Freud's original concept of the death instinct appears relevant to these notions of affirmation and disaffirmation. Yet just as we are prepared to capture a definition of the death instinct, the work of Gunnar Karlsson opens up the possibility that Freud's monumental essay "Beyond the Pleasure Principle" contains two totally distinct meanings of death instinct.[25]

Briefly stated, Freud's thesis was an attempt to understand behavioral and psychic phenomena that could not be explained by employing the concept of a pleasure principle.[26] If the "philosophy" of the id was to seek pleasure and avoid pain at all costs and urge the ego to fulfill its rapacious wishes, then how did one interpret clearly destructive, even nihilistic behavior? Karlsson argues that a form of "binding energy" of the self takes an individual beyond the pleasure principle and actually stands in complete contrast with the original notion of a so-called primordial death instinct constantly striving, according to Freud, toward death. For Karlsson, this binding energy beyond the pleasure principle is purported to correspond to Freud's original notion of a death instinct and actually serves to *affirm* the existence of the self (hence the reason I include his work in this discussion).

As complicated as the argument may seem at first, understand it to mean simply this: If I decide that, because I have to die, there is no reason to value life or any of its institutions or moral strictures, then why not assume a nihilistic posture and let the chips fall where they may? Why have children, and why be concerned about anything? In this regard, my sense of self would appear to be driven by what one might call a "negative death force." In contrast, if, upon recognizing and accepting the idea of my finitude, I determine that I shall use this acknowledged final end point as motivation to value everything about life and the few years constituting my own life, I then proceed to affirm my self, others, and life itself and, hence, exploit a "positive death force" as a motivation to do good. In the former example, I act in terms of what I have called disaffirmation; in the latter example, I am using death as a touchstone for affirmation. In many of her poems, some of which have led various critics to contend that she may have been obsessed with death and dying, Emily Dickinson communicated much the same sentiment: there can be no authentic or courageous affirmation of life without a deep consideration and appreciation for the existence of death, thus, a positive death force.[27]

Interestingly, Kohut offered a similar vision when he spoke not about a death force, precisely, but the death of an idealized figure: "The realization of the death of the parent, of the disappearance of an idealized figure, can have two results: It can bring about rebellious destruction. . . . Or it can bring about a surge of independent initiative: after the integration of the parent's values and goals has been accomplished, the youthful minds of the new generation penetrate further into the regions that the ancestral efforts had made accessible."[28]

For Viktor Frankl, the confrontation with death or, more precisely, the recognition of the transitory nature of existence became a paramount feature of his logotherapy, the combined root "logo" meaning "word," "speech," and "discourse."[29] From this recognition of transitoriness is derived an individual's sense of responsibility. Frankl argued that to the very instant of death, one must affirm existence; it is the only posture to assume in the face of one's finitude. Nihilism, in contrast, remains unacceptable. Understand-

ing this defining principle, an example of what Frankl called a "life boundary," provides meaning for the self as it confronts any life situation, the most
momentous, clearly, being that of death.[30] In fact, Frankl suggested that it
was the affirmation of boundaries—the defining principles—that not only
brought into consciousness ways for the self to act in the presence of some
powerful force but ultimately allowed for the self to be liberated.

If Frankl spoke of principles of existence, then most psychologists and
psychoanalysts speak of fundamental universal needs of the self which are to
be distinguished from wishes in that they cannot be repressed. Granted, a
wish unfulfilled leaves a person unhappy, but a need unfulfilled leaves the
self in structural disrepair. Developing distinctions between needs and
wishes, Salman Akhtar lists six basic needs that he claims are essential for
the development of the self as well as for the self's ability to engage in relationships, both activities that involve acts of affirmation.[31]

Three of Akhtar's needs seem especially relevant to the thesis here. First
is the need for recognition, identity, and affirmation. Second is the need
for the emotional availability of the loved object, yet another aspect of affirmation. Finally, Akhtar suggests that the self maintains a need to have its
love objects respond with resilience under what he calls "special circumstances."[32] In other words, in times of extreme stress or outright terror, the
self asks that the other grant it some leeway, some flexibility so that it may
find its way toward (self) understanding and liberation. Joy Dryfoos offered
a similar observation in her discussion of adolescents at risk: "Consistency,
caring, encouragement, and maintenance of contact through childhood and
adolescence are all important factors of resilient youth."[33] In the end, Akhtar's notion of "resilient responsiveness" stands as a rather lovely by-product
of affirmation. Surely it captures the essence of the relational aspect of an
affirmation.

I RECALL one evening in a university class when my students finally determined two things. First, they agreed that the self was really both my "me"
and my "I," by which they meant their public presentation and their private
sense of who they were; self and mind, in other words, were one and the
same. Second, they agreed that thinking about these matters was utterly
exhausting and they begged to go on to another topic.

Appreciating the complexities involved in attempting to understand what
philosophers and psychologists have written about the self and recognizing
that I am about to simplify highly complex notions and formulations, let
me assert the idea that my self, just as my students recognized, has some-

thing to do with who I am on the "inside" as well as on the "outside." But note that I find myself compelled to place these words within quotation marks because already a bit of a problem exists. When it comes to deliberating about the self, does it not seem as if everything eventually comes to reside inside me? That is, when I think about me, am I not by definition working "inside" of me? And when I think about you and our relationship, am I not in part also working inside me?

Perhaps the best I can do is appreciate that I can never get inside your head, as a common expression goes, as much as I believe that I can. I may imagine that I know what you know or feel what you feel and thereby know your self, but I may just be deceiving my self. In fact, even utilizing all the empathic powers I possess, it is sometimes very difficult to distinguish the boundary line separating my (sense of) mind or self from that which my mind is perceiving. Perhaps I am always at some distance from the so-called external world, your world, so that whereas I imagine I genuinely know you, it may be that my "knowing" is actually a bit dreamlike. The old chestnut about whether a tree falling in an unpopulated forest actually makes a sound reminds one that it is often very difficult, if not impossible, to have my perceptions of the outside world wholly confirmed. It just seems as though the self looking outward is able only to approximate the external world it perceives. I think you like me, I really *feel* as if you do, but there is always that shred of doubt stemming not from any personality disorder but from some intuitive knowledge that I cannot be completely certain of your love. The best I can do is make an approximation, which I do when I say, alas, I must trust you. In this same context, Erikson wrote: "To a considerable extent, adolescent love is an attempt to arrive at a definition of one's identity by projecting one's diffused self-image on another and by seeing it thus reflected and gradually clarified. This is why so much of young love is conversation."[34] And Joseph Adelson and Elizabeth Douvan expressed a similar sentiment: "Characterized by mutual trust,[friendship] permits a fairly free expression of emotion; it allows the shedding of privacies (although not inappropriately); it can absorb, within limits, conflict between the pair; it involves the discussion of personally crucial themes; it provides occasions to enrich and enlarge the self through the encounter of differences."[35]

The next problem involves that interior work of knowing my self. Do I engage this work alone (Eigenwelt), or are you part of that work as well (Mitwelt)? Said differently, do I first establish some boundary between my self and your self, and second, do I use you, somehow, in creating a sense of my self? And if I do, then what, precisely, am I "using"? What you say about me? How you treat me? Or how I imagine that you treat me or feel about me? To consider my self, therefore, I probably do consider you, but just how "accurate" is this consideration of you when I have acknowledged that genuinely knowing you is but a conceit?[36]

As complicated as these matters appear, they raise in us the sense that what we determine our selves to be may or may not be true, which opens another Pandora's box. So let me change the wording and suggest that we tend to recognize aspects of our selves that we imagine to be real, authentic, true; we choose to stand by them; they emerge as the staples of our selves. Then there are those aspects of our selves which at some level—a level implying that a part of our selves views other parts of our selves and makes judgments about these other parts—we know to be untrue, inauthentic, false. Thus, many of us walk around with our so-called true selves and false selves that we display both to our selves and to the exterior world. All these components, the interior and exterior, on the one hand, and the true and false facets of the self on the other, comprise what we think of as our identity. I imagine who I think I am, just as I imagine who I think *you* think I am. I even shape part of my identity on the basis of what I think you think I am. And if I am uncertain about the former, then I am highly uncertain of the latter. George Berkeley's famous line is worth repeating at this juncture: "To be is to be perceived."[37] One begins to see why my students that one evening grew so fatigued and so quickly.

"Self-consciousness," Charles Rzepka wrote in his remarkable book about Wordsworth, Coleridge, and Keats, "requires the presence, real or imagined, explicit or implied, of another."[38] Which further suggests that I am forever vulnerable to the assessments (affirmations and disaffirmations) you make of me. I have no control over how you perceive me; I do, however, maintain control of which of your impressions I choose to incorporate as part of my self or concept of self, along with how I feel about those impressions. We may well be able genuinely to see each other for what we are, as the expression goes, which means that either you understand the nature of my self, I choose to believe that you do, or we may not be able to see each other for what we are. Similarly, as Rzepka also suggests, I may or may not make my self accessible to you, which further complicates my sense of self, at least in your presence and evolving identity which normally demands that I make certain that you see me, or at least meet my eyes. At very least, I imagine that you are willing to see me, recognize me, affirm me. That is, if I have been affirmed, I *imagine* that you are willing to see me and recognize me. I must learn, as Parker Palmer instructs, "that my sense of self is deeply dependent on others dancing with me *and* that I still have a self when no one wants to dance. . . . I must take a solitary journey into my own nature *and* seek the help of others in seeing myself as I am."[39] If I have not been affirmed, then I will imagine you have little or no interest in seeing me, or recognizing me; thus I shall always dance alone. Even more, I may imagine that no one in the world is willing to see or recognize me. Or I them, for that matter.

As I discussed above, there appears to be a boundary line demarcating my self from objects exterior to it. At times this boundary seems utterly distinct, at times indistinct. According to some theorists, the more blurred the boundary, the more blurred the essential conception I maintain of my self.[40] In his family systems theory, for example, Salvador Minuchin places great stress on this notion of boundaries that delineate people and systems within families.[41] The blurred boundary, moreover, yet another product, I would argue, of the self having been disaffirmed, makes it more difficult, if not impossible, for the self fully to differentiate itself from the exterior world. Although it requires the exterior world to form itself and develop something called an "identity" with which it is sufficiently content (surely essential components of affirmation), the self nonetheless must be able to differentiate itself from that same exterior world and the (self) objects within it. I need you in order to become me, but I must not imagine that you *are* me or that I can become you. That affirmations tend to make the original boundary line distinct, less blurred, allows me to imagine (or more easily convince my self) that I am presenting a true self to you, you being one of the people who made it possible for me to develop this sense of a "true self" in the first place.

To render these notions more concrete, think only of the small boy whom Arthur Jersild might have described as cutting a figure "in the eyes of others" and about whom we say, he sure is his own little man.[42] In fact, if we could engage this child in philosophical discourse, we might even discover that he feels this sentiment as well. But our argument here is that he has been affirmed by others; that is, his self has been affirmed such that he can now present his self, as his own little man, to the very people who helped him achieve this state of mind, this state of consciousness of self. "The adolescent," Piaget wrote, "wants to surpass and astound [adults] by transforming the world."[43] Having been affirmed, moreover, he is less likely to fear a loss of self, actually a disintegration of self, as he deals with his exterior world. He is confident, proud rather than humiliated, as Basch might suggest; autonomous, rather than self-doubting, as Erikson might say. What we denote as his sense of self has to do with his seeming comfort with who he is, along with his recognition that there are others in the world who live apart from him but who, in the natural leading of their own lives, furnish him a sense of self-definition.

Then, finally, there is the matter of affirmation playing a role in teaching him who he is, shaping, in other words, what Patricia Cameron, Carol Mills, and Thomas Heinzen call "crystallizing experiences," in which people come to understand their own talents and competencies—their research was performed on academically talented sixth-and tenth-grade students—which presumably lead to heightened levels of esteem and more finely etched conceptions of self.[44]

In contrast, the disaffirmed self gobbles up everything from the outside—the boundary line having been blurred—and lives a life of solipsism or narcissism, forever believing the exterior world ought to be defined strictly in terms of how it treats (although ultimately fails to form) his or her own private self. The disaffirmed self seems almost incapable of receiving any form of genuine recognition; he or she cannot see it, hear it, or accept it. "How is it that you don't know how good you are?" we inquire of the disaffirmed person. Typically we say about this same person that he or she appears withdrawn, not fully engaged, and in a sense this is an accurate reading. For the disaffirmed self does indeed withdraw into itself if only to gain a modicum of recognition or protection from an exterior world that in his or her mind constantly looms as threatening. And because no amount of public affirmation can compensate for the original damage done to the self in prior disaffirmations, this form of affirmation is the only one he or she receives. This is what Basch means when he speaks of the grandiose self of the child having been too regularly humiliated or shamed.[45]

Following on this line of reasoning, we return to a question dating back at least to Descartes: how does the self know itself? Can it truly be conscious of itself, or is it only conscious of its various perceptions?[46] Moreover, if there really is something that I determine to be my self, is it anything more than a collection of momentary sensations that seem to disappear the instant I imagine I have focused on or identified them? Is my self, in other words, the perceiver or the perceived?

Kant answered these questions by suggesting that the self is a form of consciousness that we experience essentially when we reflect on it.[47] Said differently, our self makes itself apparent to us; it is not anything that can be called "embodied," even though such philosophers as David Hume argued that our (sense of) self is pretty much like a body living within our body.[48]

I would further argue that it is precisely the constant affirmations of self and, more significant, the original affirmations experienced during childhood that render it apparent to us. Affirmations allow me to engage in self-reflection, thereby giving birth to self-consciousness, which in turn, if Kant is correct, allows me a sense of my identity. Without self-reflection, implying as it does an acknowledgment of my self (what we call self-consciousness), there can be no sense of my having an identity.[49] (And, as Mihaly Csikszentmihalyi said, "To know ourselves is the greatest achievement of our species. . . . If we don't gain control over the contents of consciousness we can't live a fulfilling life, let alone contribute to a positive outcome of history.")[50] All this is what we imagine we observe in small children who appear to be their own man or own woman. They actually seem to be reflecting on themselves, and their identity. They appear, in other words, to be self-conscious in the best sense, and we, their affirmers, are partly responsible for what they now present to us as their being.

The process of self-reflection leading to a sense of identity—again, Heidegger's and May's Eigenwelt—occurs, moreover, because I imagine my self as embodied in the eyes of another; I believe these others genuinely have seen me, that my actions have caused them to see me, and this also arises in my consciousness (of self) as a fundamental aspect of affirmation. Disaffirmation, on the other hand, appears to yield just the opposite effect: the self has denied itself; it fails to render itself apparent, which in turn reduces the possibility of it engaging in self-reflection. The disaffirmed self imagines it is not embodied in the eyes of others, and hence it struggles in its efforts to carve out a workable, acceptable, coherent identity; one might say that it struggles to see itself, recognize itself. Without the recognition of the other, the disaffirmed self can neither regard itself nor offer regard for itself, just as it cannot regard or offer regard for another. If I cannot make sense of the world, if it is beyond any capacity I possess for making meaning of it or finding logic in it, if I can discover nothing that I consider to be a solid, stable reality in the world outside my self, a reality that others are *supposed* to confirm for me, then I cannot possibly make sense of my self; I discover no logic in or about my consciousness.[51] Accordingly, my identity, such that it is, is at best inchoate and probably disjointed as well.

Affirmation, as I will elaborate later on, surely aids in my making sense of the world. It is precisely what is at stake when Joseph Goldstein, Anna Freud, and Albert Solnit suggested that a child needs an average predictable environment.[52] It is the predictability, or felt sense of it, that allows my self to imagine a logic and coherence about the world, which then allows me entry into my own consciousness; I do not linger long anywhere in the exterior or interior worlds where things (selfobjects) do not make sense to me. Is this not part of what we imagine we detect when we say that a little boy is his own man? Does he not seem to exhibit a sense of the world, a feeling about us and himself that is coherent, logical, complete? Does it not seem, moreover, as though he genuinely understands what is happening about him, as well as within him? Once again, the words of Parker Palmer: "Acknowledging our gifts is difficult for many of us, either because we are modest or because it is risky to stick one's head up."[53] This little boy seems willing to take the risk. His head is up; his eyes are on us, as our own are on him.

In contrast, does not the notion of disaffirmation begin to describe the child murderer who we reflexively label "sociopathic," the very child who stands before the judge seemingly unable to reveal even an ounce of contrition or remorse? What is it about this child that he cannot seem to grasp what is going on about him or what has been happening in his life? Why can't he provide us the slightest clue to what might have gone on in his mind when he committed this heinous crime? Has he nothing at all to say?[54] Has he no sense of himself (his self)? And what really do we mean when we claim we can begin to understand both his actions and his reactions to them by referring to him as a victim of trauma?[55] Might disaffirmation play a role in the emerging consciousness and identity of this child, such as they are?[56] Might it be the case, moreover, that when we allege that he committed his crime to gain a moment of attention or recognition, we now may better understand what lies beneath his need to be seen, to have others' eyes fall on him or, more likely, to avert the gaze of the other? Aware of it or not, we are constantly under the gaze of the other, a gaze, I will later argue, that provides the true commencement of the act of affirmation.

In the end, believing there is a self, embodied or not, "residing" within us, what John Locke called the "little man in the big man," may all be illusory, nothing more than fantastic speculation.[57] Indeed, all the above considerations may turn out to be just that: mere considerations. "We can see from (the five sense organs and their objects)," Mark Epstein wrote, "feelings, perceptions, mental factors, and consciousness, but we would have a hard time putting our finger on 'self.' . . . This self is certainly not nothing, but is it something that we can imagine? Can we even be justified in using a noun like 'it' to designate it?" And from Robert A. F. Thurman: "You become like a dog chasing its own tail. Because you are the self, you feel like a unity, but when you look back for that solid unity of self, you don't find anything."[58]

If it is the case that we cannot accurately pinpoint a palpable self, how possibly could we ever certify a palpable identity much less something called a true or authentic self? Perhaps Descartes was right; perhaps the best we can do is make our little inferences and judgments about our selves, and others and take as a matter of faith and trust that the products of our deliberations have some merit. If all the self-work undertaken in the realm of the Eigenwelt is little more than fantastic speculation, then of course we have doubt about our selves. The very nature of self-consciousness necessarily bespeaks self-doubt; who among us doesn't know this? Who can claim with authority that they know themselves completely? It is the examined life that counts, not the settled life.[59]

The presence of the little boy who seems to us to be his own man lingers in our minds. He is remarkable precisely because he seems sufficiently content with the products of his deliberations and self-reflections; he actually appears confident that his deliberations of self have validity, qualities that naturally attract our attention. It is as though he understands "the game," which may be that if the self is but an appearance to itself, a tantalizing apparition, then it may be nothing more and nothing less than its appearance to others, hence the common expression, "What you see is what you get." For what makes the child in question so appealing is that with words and gestures he is able to communicate to us this understanding of self as well as a (consequent) self-assuredness, a self-assuredness that has no resemblance to what we normally think of as cockiness. (It is the bully, after all, who marches before us wanting us to believe that he has won the game of self-knowledge when in truth he battles a persistent sense of disaffirmation. It is the bully who emerges as the bellicose one, literally demanding that we look at him, recognize him, affirm him. For he is not, after all, his own little man.) This, in turn, makes possible our ability to respond to him, assure him, attempt to reason with him, and, hopefully, affirm him. If what he is doing, as Basch and Erikson point out, is seeking some form of recognition, by gosh he is going to get it from us, at home or in school, either in the form of an affirmation or a disaffirmation.[60] No, this is not wholly accurate. He has already received our affirmations or disaffirmations; they live within him as "after-the-fact" experiences.

Thus we argue that it is the affirmation that reduces his doubt of self, ultimately making him and us believe that he possesses and exhibits a unique identity and sense of self that are not at all illusory. As a patient once told Dr. Rachel Naomi Remen, "Somewhere deep inside there is a sound that is mine alone, and I struggle daily to hear it and tune my life to it. Sometimes there are people and situations that help me to hear my note more clearly."[61] We all agree that the boy we described as being his own man reveals a sense of self that is absolutely real, palpable. He is not deceiving himself, we further imagine; there is a very real self that lives within him and with which he is in constant contact. There is a depth, we claim, about this child. Nothing at all of his inner self is hidden or secretive; he reveals it to us all the time as part of his gazing upon us. Paraphrasing from Jean-Paul Sartre, this little boy "owns his self."[62] Our presence surely makes his psychological posture possible, but somehow he convinces us that he is free of any external constraints that will in some fashion disturb his emerging conception of self and identity; he is on track. We literally believe we have witnessed in this child the little man in the big man. Or is it the big man in the little man? Either way, his presence connotes affirmation writ large!

IN THIS next part of my argument, I suggest that affirmation underlies the concept of "empathy," a term suggesting having feeling or compassion for another, something the Dalai Lama has claimed occurs only between equals.[63] Similarly, for Kohut, empathy signifies a moving toward another, although Akhtar's earlier notion of "resilient responsiveness" also captures the action and spirit of what we normally think of as empathy.[64] Given what we have already stated, we now allege that the affirmed person is by definition empathic if only because he or she has derived a sense of self, self-consciousness, and identity in part from the presence of others whose gaze is not only accepted but also desired, cherished. Only naturally do I have feelings for those people whose perceptions and evaluations (that I imagine) of me I incorporate as complex variables in the algebra of my self. I almost cannot search for my inner self (Eigenwelt) without relying on the world I share with others (Mitwelt). You and I are hardly interchangeable, but we are utterly dependent on each other in the establishment of our unique identities. More precisely, the emergence of our inner worlds, the site of our mind fields, is dependent on the public affirmations (and, alas, disaffirmations) each of us offers to the other.[65]

Our selves develop in a social context, in a world of others;[66] it is the nature of our existence no matter how much the distractive forces of popular culture may attempt to instruct us otherwise. That I can even write these words and assume that you can read and understand them, agree or disagree with them, confirms the notion that the contents of my inner world—even a world of madness—draw a significant portion of their meaning from a public world, one about which there is at least some consensus. As I noted, although you cannot fully know me, nor I fully know you, and although our perceptions of our shared reality cannot be perfectly coincident, that these notions are even understandable by the two of us once again suggests we both inhabit a world that provides us meaning and ultimately makes possible the development of both our unique selves.

All the same, a bit of a chicken-and-egg question emerges from this: what comes first, a sense of self that allows me to understand the existence of other selves, or a sense of other selves that allows me to develop my own personal sense of self? Not surprisingly, many psychologists and philosophers lean toward the second option, and I position myself among them. There is a point in the developmental history when children must learn, first, that they are not that object, their parent, who sustains them and, second, that they are not anybody but themselves, no matter how powerful the influence of all the people who circle about them. Somewhere along the line, the child must learn that it is his or her developmental task to develop a sense of self and, hence, an identity; the external world appears to demand it. More precisely, somewhere along the line, the child must become aware that he or she has already developed a sense of self and thus an identity. So the child learns early, perhaps earlier than we ever imagined, that she must look at herself, look at others, look at herself looking at others, and look at others looking at her. The famous looking glass self of Charles Cooley, who perceived the self as a collection of roles, has suddenly been transformed into a veritable hall of mirrors.[67] This notion puts one in mind of Thoreau's insistence that "we do not worship truth, but the reflection of truth." Perhaps I should say, therefore, that one observes not one's self but only the reflections of one's self.[68]

As such thinkers as Freud and Merleau-Ponty have asserted, that child we perceive as being his own man may be seductively intriguing, but without having first internalized the other—Freud coined the term "introjection"—or more likely some mental representation of the other—for example, the father in Freud's conception of the development of the superego—there will be no such appealing sense of self being communicated to others.[69] Indeed, there will probably be no integrated, coherent, consistent sense of self the child imagines can ever be rendered comprehensible. Without taking in (introjecting) the proper psychic nurturance (affirmation), the argument goes, I can develop no competent sense of self, no sense of my own competence, and, even more, no sense that the world is out there to help me, be recruited by me, as Kegan suggests, to any appreciable degree.[70] Over time, as part of my self-reflective endeavors, I become aware that part of my self-assurance, or lack of it, was born in the Mitwelt, in the world with others (selfobjects all) whose foods (and selves) I ingested. In cases of disaffirmation, however, I fail to learn; perhaps I have expelled or rejected those particular foods (and persons) and now go to great lengths to rid my body of any trace of them. Or perhaps I never ingested them in the first place; my self remains malnourished.

Combined, these actions and perceptions (of the self) represent the data, the building blocks, really, of primitive self-consciousness and identity. The child's self necessarily contains the admonitions and counsel of others if only to the extent that it understands the concept of expectation. People expect me to do this or to be that, and I must either oblige them or explore what happens if I do not, something we regularly observe with two-year-olds who clearly are developing a sense of self and corresponding identity, although we call it, often in somewhat pejorative terms, their "will." Thus begins a most complicated series of negotiations between the self and the external world typically culminating in a full-blown revolution during adolescence when the young scream at us such things as, "You won't let me be the person I want to be!" Or, "You haven't the slightest idea of who I really am!" Or, "I'm sick and tired of being the child *you* need me to be!" One cannot be certain, as Erikson suggests, whether this brand of anger represents the stretching out of the self toward a new identity or simply the guilt felt by adolescents as they shift the focus of their love from parents to friends.[71]

Truth lurks, nonetheless, in every one of these laments. Who can say whether any of us fully knows what the other thinks about or expects of us, or whether the person I am with you is truly the person I am alone with me, or whether the person I am with you is somehow a better person than the person I am alone with me. Besides, how come you just don't seem to get who I am? How come you miss all the clues and do not come close to appreciating my self? The world's just not ready for me. And don't call me crazy just because *you* don't understand who I am! *You* may be the crazy one, you know.

The essence of the interpersonal nature of the self's development and its association with the concept of affirmation comes to life in these words of Paul Ricoeur: "My existence for my self depends utterly on this self-constitution in the opinion of others. My self—if I dare say so—is received from the opinion of others, who consecrate it."[72] Interestingly, as Rzepka points out, there is a growing theoretical literature suggesting that even the unconscious is formed in great measure from the unrecognized wishes and expectations born in the self from contact with others.[73] What more intimate contact could there be between the Mitwelt and the Eigenwelt! Jacques Lacan, as readers of his work know well, has argued that the unconscious is all about the other and the sorts of dealings, successful or not (affirmations and disaffirmations), one experiences with others.[74] Extending this idea, one might argue that our entire identity, our entire self-consciousness, is formed from our involvements with others, thereby making the concepts of affirmation and disaffirmation even more significant than ever we imagined.

These, then, are the themes to be developed in the final sections of the book; surely they warrant a richer examination. For the moment, however, let me anticipate the ensuing chapters.

Part II, accordingly, is devoted to a discussion of the concept of affirmation, how it seems to be born in us and how it shapes the nature of our selves. In Part III I conclude the discussion of affirmation by focusing on the nature of the family and the individual and generational bonds in which affirmation resides and is either perpetuated or extinguished.

I THINK it fair to say that little Luke shared a piece of his self when he admitted to not being a very good jumper. In the end, it may be the greatest gift one can receive, this piece of another's self, this scheme one lives by, this trace of the so-called inner world. It is a palpable piece of trust and attachment, recognition and intimacy, often a proof that self-reflection has been undertaken. It may also be a hope for affirmation, offered by society or by the self to itself, that there is purpose and reason for merely being alive. There truly is something we sense and call a "life force," as Diane Ackerman actually describes it in a discussion on spirituality, wherein people experience a "sense of belonging to the pervasive mystery of nature, of being finite in the face of the infinite . . . and feeling surrounded by powerful and unseen forces."[75] At the very least, our attempt to develop some sense of self becomes a trial, an experiment—once again, a jump. Frequently we refer to it as a momentous leap of faith, although at times it appears to be no more than a leap across some rainwater on a Seattle tennis court.

PART

II

3 The Gaze of Affirmation

AT ONE level, to affirm a child makes that child a part of our selves. In contrast, to allow that child to live in what we clearly recognize to be an unjust circumstance is to make certain, in our minds, that the child never becomes a part of our own selves, a part of our own consciousness.[1] What can *I* do about those children living in wretched conditions? we ask, denying the fact that our mere knowledge of the existence of these children has already rendered them part of our selves. For to deny that we were part of the origin of their circumstances, or even that we can do little about them or their circumstances, in effect is to deny our selves of our selves. It is to turn away from the truths of what we know our selves to be, although let it be said from the outset that we do not, we cannot know the origin of the self. Like the birth of any character of fiction, it derives from sheer mystery, heaven itself; we may never have a language to explain it.

Reality, the philosopher Emmanuel Levinas alleged, is not always defined by the known. We are, in other words, deceiving ourselves, tricking ourselves in the same way, Freud postulated, the ego attempts to trick the id. A defense mechanism, after all, is really a conceit the mind plays on itself, "knowing" all the while that the id, theoretically the source of all psychic energy, always maintains power over it. We deny that because we see these certain children, all children actually, we cannot *not* know about them, we cannot *not* affirm them. We affirm them, however perversely, merely by recognizing their existence and our connection to them. Merely to hear their words, their accounts of experiences, which essentially are accounts of the self (encountering experience), means that they are now part of our lives, part of our consciousness, whether or not we choose to focus attention on them or, really, focus them in our selves.

Well, this is not wholly true, for never do we truly know another person. For that matter, as the woman, Graca, asks in V. S. Naipul's novel *Half a Life*, "How can anyone say who he is?"[2] What we do know about others is only that which we are given by them, what philosophers call their "otherness." One might say that the rest of what we "know" about them we have made up in our imaginations or called up in our reminiscences. We may deceive ourselves in believing that we know another, that we can feel what he or she feels—walk in one's shoes, as the expression goes—but this too is merely a conceit. At times, moreover, particularly in the absence of genuine affirmation, we tend to "devour" people. The term is apt if not slightly melodramatic and probably relates most significantly to children who, for one reason or another, we sometimes tend to believe have barely integrated selves and thus do not really know who they are or where the extensions of their identity end and our identities commence.

In believing that we know another, we feel as if we actually have become the other, a process resembling the psychoanalytic concept of identification. The child about to play catch with his friend proudly announces, "I'm Ken Griffey Jr., who are you?" He does not say, "I'm *like* Ken Griffey Jr., who are you like?" (Ironically, it is one of the only times in modern American culture that the omnipresent term "like" is *not* heard in a child's utterance.) In this moment, through the process of identification, the hero becomes the object of the child's attention and hence, in a way, devours the object or in turn feels the palpable sensation of being devoured by it. The idea, and it is only this, of devouring or being devoured by another remains one of the most primitive of all human fantasies. Let no one imagine that the story of the big bad wolf's attempt to eat Little Red Riding Hood—a tale replete with colorful illustrations—is the child's first encounter with the notion of devouring or being devoured.

A similar type of devouring process occurs when, assuming we know all that needs to be known of the other, we claim the right to speak for another or say all that needs to be said for another. It happens when we write narratives of and life studies about another, attempting as best we can to bring only the true facts to the light of day, only to discover that the objects of our accounts feel they have been grossly misrepresented.[3] The occurrence is almost inevitable as people seemingly object to representations of themselves, claiming this is not the true story, this is not our true visage; surely this cannot be what I really look like (we often experience this while studying photographs of ourselves). The point is that in genuinely affirming other persons, we are not only honoring their singular and ultimately inexplicable being but also intentionally and publicly claiming we have no right or capability to speak for them or even adequately represent them because in a sense they have not given themselves to us; we (imagine we) "possess" only small traces with which they have been willing to part.

Ironically, affirmation makes it impossible to give oneself to another, for an affirmation really does little more than convince the other of his or her own singular identity and integrity of self—what psychologists might call "ego integrity"—and hence the impossibility of being another or the same as another. When I affirm you, I essentially give you the right to be (you). I ratify your being there and my being here; there will be no devouring of anyone, especially you, on my watch. You are safe with me and with yourself. And, incidentally, beneath the skin we are also uniquely different from each other, which must be recalled as we contemplate the notion of identity. Even in a world of organ transplants, we are never a mere collection of interchangeable parts. (We'll just have to see how cloning technology alters this perspective.)

For the reader who would perceive these notions as esoteric or purely academic, consider for the moment the child who cries at night, desperately reacting to a nightmare. We might even imagine he fears he is being chased by a witch or wild animal that seeks to consume him. Now, what does the parent do in this delicate moment? Cite Kant? Freud? Levinas? Or, best of all perhaps, John Mack's insightful volume on night terrors?[4] No, the parent is summoned and arrives at the bedside. Let us not overlook this significant interaction: the child calls out, the parent comes running. Only one purpose is on the line: the parent is about to reconfirm his or her pledge to take responsibility for the child and thus call into being the concept of ethical behavior wherein both parent and child discover the essence of their relationship. As Levinas insisted, the ethical must always be present: "Even though we are ontologically free to refuse the other—one's own child in this case—we forever remain accused, with a bad conscience."[5] So the parent arrives at the child's bedside, hugs the child, assures him that everything is all right and no one is going to harm him. In the embrace and through the words, but most especially in the action of the parent volunteering to take care of and responsibility for the child, the child is affirmed. His being is restored; from a state of terror, his sense of self is magically put back together.

The response of the parent represents more than mere comforting. The child is not going to die; someone else apart from him will protect him from that or, more likely, from the thoughts of death and tragedy in this one moment. In this manner, the mother comforting the child, rescuing him from the pangs of the night terror, almost like the soldier running back to fetch his wounded comrade and carry him to safety, affirmation in its broadest strokes is revealed. For what affirmation accomplishes is the preparation for the self to begin to recognize its own being. Affirmations bring us to the point where we can begin to inquire of ourselves about our own being. Without some form of affirmation, I cannot reflect on my self; I remain distracted and without an identity. My self is diffused.

In this one regard, genuine affirmation is simultaneously the act of the most rational being, although it may be driven by something primitive in the state of nature; other animals appear to do the same thing. They, too, rescue; they, too, temporarily pull an offspring back from the clutches of tragedy. The difference, for I have no understanding of whether animals possess consciousness, is the degree to which the animal, unlike the human being, then integrates this affirming experience into the very formulation of its definition of self. Does it, in other words, deliberate on such matters? How much does the rescued being, the affirmed being, incorporate the intermittent rescues and perpetual acts of others taking responsibility for it into its consciousness? Is it possible that animals of a certain level of cognitive development are connected to their parents precisely because of the constantly affirming role of their parents? Is it possible that affirmations become the glue of genuine familial involvement? Might affirmations be at the root of what Heidegger and May called the Mitwelt, the world with others, the realm of being in which one absorbs, integrates, incorporates the being of another, or at least the conception of the other—again, that part of otherness offered by another—and transforms these incorporations into bits of one's own self? Freud called the process "introjection," and it remains one of the fundaments of the object relations school of psychoanalysis; the pieces of others we bring into ourselves (by devouring them) become the introjects with which we live. It was May, however, who wrote that "man is the particular being who has to be aware of himself, be responsible for himself, if he is to become himself." In this same regard, Louis Breger warned of what he called a "profound narrowness of viewpoint," the inability, in other words, to conceive of oneself as otherness.[6]

Without the affirmation, one may argue, there can be no genuine incorporation of the other, no making parts of the other the same as I. Affirmation stands as the public announcement that I am available to you; you may avail your self of me by incorporating (introjecting) my otherness into your being, which you will do when you genuinely feel affirmed by me. Once again we ask, Is this but esoteric theorizing? Consider those nights ages years ago when, for reasons we could not explain to another or to our selves, we finally revealed parts of our selves (our otherness) to someone else and felt the touch, literal and symbolic, not only of *their* being but also of their affirmation of *our* being. Just their saying in reaction to one of our treasured revelations, "I know exactly what you mean," caused us to feel a thrill, a momentary sense of personal completion and wholeness. In those moments, we imagined that we discovered the mind of the other as well.

The experience is erotic in the sense that life or some mysterious life force has been affirmed. We are not defective; someone else reports knowing these same private thoughts and sensations; someone else possesses stories similar to our own; someone exterior to me has assured me I am normal to contemplate such thoughts, deliberate with my self as I do, and then recount my narratives. I am different from others and the same as others. I am different from what I was before this night and, at the same time, precisely what I was. Tonight, through this one encounter, I am less scared. For one erotic instant, (the dread of) tragedy has been suspended. Weren't these the nights we felt as if we were actors in a movie, somehow suspended in real time and real space? And doesn't it also seem as though the affirmation that one night supplied or supported our personal life force?[7]

The affirmation supported something else as well: our ability to deal with another free of prejudgments about him or her. In general terms, Levinas believed that in confronting another we are assimilating new information, which means, as Nietzsche and Piaget also suggested, locating the new information in older or preexisting schemes. Levinas referred to this action as "making equal what is new." For Levinas, "knowledge has always been interpreted as assimilation."[8] Knowledge, therefore, and this is essential for this discussion of affirmation, is a denial of difference. Said simply, when I know something, it is no longer alien; it is familiar. When I know someone, he or she is no longer a stranger. When I am known by another, I am no longer a stranger to my self. Not only that—and affirmations create just this phenomenon—when I know you I make you a part of my self, but not by possession of you, only by knowledge and recognition of you. For if I possess you or even imagine that I can, I have done little more than try to make your self my self, which means that I have silenced you, objectified you. One hears this very expression during lovers' quarrels: "You may love me, but you don't *own* me!"

The discovery that someone else thinks as I do implies that I have believed they thought differently from (and about) me, which suggests that I have made judgments about them, about their "differentness," really; I have had mistaken intuitions about them.[9] I have limited them, somehow, to (my) categories of thought and have therefore rendered them unequal to me. As a consequence, I have denied them their humanness, something that ought not to occur in authentic affirmations. Levinas calls this action "totalization" and perceives it as an act of violence, for in truth I do damage to others by believing things about them merely because it is convenient for my reasoning about them. As Erik Erikson also suggested, the intolerance of people who appear to us as different represents a defense against our identity confusion, an act often leading to our exclusion of others.[10]

One of the fundamental purposes of narrative research is to remind us that all people have a history of their own being, a time they call their own, as Erikson suggested, as well as a way of recounting this self-understanding to themselves and others. In common language, we claim that everyone has a story to tell—some of us, with grandiosity, even believe it comes forth as an epic, the proverbial great American novel—a story, one imagines, that relates each of us to everyone else, past and future, while it stands as a piece of one's self that represents only our own lives.[11] I am always part of the world, a piece of all time, and part only of my self. You may know my face, but to the world I am faceless, a stranger. Thus, I am at the same time always known to the world and anonymous, always an (imagined) celebrity and a stranger. The narrative, accordingly, ought to reveal traces of both my accounting of the world (to the world and to my self) and my accounting of my self (to the world and to my self). It ought to reveal my face as well as my facelessness.[12]

Acknowledging the story of the other or, said properly, genuinely affirming the storyteller begins with the presumably simple requirement to listen to the words of the other. (T. S. Eliot once remarked that the first encounter with any poem ought be nothing more than experiencing the jingle of the words.) Listening, in the words of Paul Ricoeur, really affirming the other through listening, is always a face-to-face rather than side-by-side affair.[13] In affirming the other, be he or she a stranger or not, we truly *hear* the other, *see* the other; we do not merely *overhear* the other or, in the language of television, "see" it reported. Unlike the nightly news reports, the reports we always imagine of the "real world," storytelling and witnessing, the essential actions of the narrative, become interpersonal acts requiring us to respond, not merely receive; we listen to the teller as well as the witness.[14] In Levinas's terms, the words of others, really their gaze, constitute the domain of concrete existence.[15]

The words of others contained in narratives are meant to remind us that none of us wishes to be a mere representation of some population, ideology, or disorder. Although at times we imagine we speak for others, we are never quite certain. Nor do we wish our narratives to be mere representations of our selves. Only politicians, it appears, dare to speak for us; at least they claim they can. Affirmed or not, we forever remain the authors of our own discourse. We are forever the curators of our own voice, if we have been freed (by affirmation) to experience it. We wish to be seen and heard, not reduced to some state of representation wherein we feel defaced. A mere representation of us, already a violation of the narrative, violates us by eclipsing us, leaving us behind; it is quintessential disaffirmation. In affirmation, conversely, we are placed in front, left *ahead*. The narrative reminds us that we do not know the worlds and minds of others, only the worlds and minds we create for others and then label "otherness"; it is now time to rethink, reknow the other.

In creating disaffirming circumstances, dehumanizing platforms for human encounter, we violate others, disaffirm them by making *their* stories *our* stories. We do not have to buy their books or take options on their screenplays to possess them. By creating a parasitic relationship with the other, disaffirmation automatically assures us psychological ownership of the other; it represents a form of tyranny we observe in homes, schools, communities, and entire nations. (In some corners of society, we predicate entire social and economic scaffolds on our constructed categories meant to define—and perhaps to possess—the lives and narratives of those for whom we claim responsibility.) "Well, you know," a man grouses, "the trouble with women . . ." The violation has already begun. Or how about the common expression from the world of politics: "What the American people want at this time . . ." Somewhat cynically, this last line tends to confirm Gary Sasso's contention that "in large measure, politics is the process of creating reality, even when overwhelming logical evidence suggests an opposite factual basis."[16] As nobody knows the stories of the American people, the violation inherent in the disaffirmation has already commenced. Policies ought never be written without looking in the eyes of those for whom the policies are intended. It is the essence of what John Rawls called the "veil of ignorance."[17] Would I write that same policy if I were the intended object of its rulings? Ideologies notwithstanding, we are each different from the other, our stories interconnected but never interchangeable, our eyes familiar but never identical.[18]

What, then, is the antidote to the toxicity of what Levinas labeled "totalization"? Levinas prescribes the concept of "sensibility," suggesting that in this passive form (unlike the active form of reasoning) we simply move toward the other, as we also do in Heinz Kohut's concept of empathy.[19] Levinas speaks of "comporting" oneself toward another, thereby finding the enjoyment of the other. We live (the affirmed) life with the other, filled with the sensations initiated by the contact with the other, and hence, we feed off the human environment. For Levinas, the sensations constituting sensibility form the foundation of the self, a happy and selfish self most likely, a self able to contemplate the world of the so-called extramental but an initial self, nonetheless, and surely one created in great measure by the act of affirmation. As I noted earlier, the baby begins to learn she is neither the food she eats nor the milk she drinks. In her happiness, ultimately in her satisfaction of needs caused in part by these early affirmations, she begins to draw a sense of (the boundaries of) her own self. Affirmations, therefore, influence the birth of what psychologists speak of as self-awareness, the consciousness of consciousness.[20]

What the affirmation makes possible is, first, the capacity to bring from the outside into the inside the original sensation of another being present to (and in) me. I do not invent the affirmation; it has not just sprung up in my mind from whole cloth like any idea. Moreover, I am dependent on another to provide me affirmations. That thing, that being in the world, Levinas suggests, which I really want to enjoy comes to me in the form of the other person affirming me. Best of all, perhaps, I come to learn that in the affirmation not only am I not consumed by the affirming person but I am not able to consume him or her. So there really is a person "out there" and a person "in here." Levinas writes that the other person is felt as a weight that I encounter pushing against me. I prefer to see the other person as a weight that stays solid, thereby allowing me to push against it. Either way, it is a weight existing *in my behalf*, constantly refusing my atavistic desire to become one with it or devour it.

The second "gift" of affirmation is the ability of the mind to distinguish between the self and the source of self-satisfaction. Just as I am not the food that brings me satisfaction, I am neither the body nor the being of the other that affords me satisfaction; I am also not the person who reads to me before I fall asleep. Physical reality, apparently, is not simply the product of my imaginings or mere linguistic and social constructs. Thus, in a sense, the affirming person, the one assuming responsibility for the other, possesses the power to transcend any categories of thought the other person might conjure up about the affirming one. This important notion reminds us that others do not exist purely for our self-satisfaction; our narratives are hardly produced for others' entertainment. If we were to believe this, if we actually determined that others are meant to be either the source of our satisfactions or the legitimate objects for our violent impulses (themselves stemming from constant disaffirmation), then we would believe in the objectification of the other, the very phenomenon we recognize in sexist and racist ideologies and behavior.[21]

Violent acts, all acts of injustice for that matter, are acts of devouring; they are acts of self-satisfaction brought to the point of disavowing the fundamental commandment to take responsibility for the other inherent in affirmation. They are acts indicating that, spiritually blind, the violent one perceives his prey not as being but as thing. In this regard, the psychoanalyst Joel Kovel coined the term "thingification."[22] However, once I see this other not as thing but as being, a perception predicated on my own self having been affirmed, it is axiomatic that I will take responsibility for the other and therefore protect rather than harm him or her. In disaffirmation leading to my failure to consider the other, I logically fail to be considerate of the other.

In affirmation, I have not reflected on the imperfection or inadequacies of the other; I have not rendered the other a subspecies, inferior to me and thereby warranting no ethical response to its being. In genuine affirmation I have neither conceived nor reasoned out anything about the other; in a most passive manner, I have merely found myself in the place of the other. In disaffirmation, an act, we recall, that disavows both *my* being and *yours*, I automatically perceive others as nonbeing. I have rendered others objects or things; I have "thingified." In this regard, I may well be reacting to the sense of loss that the original disaffirmation represents. Without having been affirmed, my self is left to die. Freud stated this position in the following way: when the ego perceives itself having become threatened beyond any capacity to cope with the terror, a feeling akin to the original disaffirmation, it "sees itself deserted by all the forces of protection and *lets itself die.*"[23] In not taking responsibility for the other, therefore, I have already committed an act of violence. These others are a priori nonexistent in my mind as beings outside myself; they have no freedom, will, or any inalienable claim to just and ethical treatment. My final act of violence only confirms and concludes my original conceptions and perceptions of them.

Although it would seem that violence is instinctive and the product of nonreasoned action, it now may be alleged to be the product of disaffirmation, what D. J. Flannery, M. I. Singer, and K. Wester in a 2001 article refer to as the exposure to trauma of one sort or another or what in simplest terms we hold to be the experience of shame.[24] The capacity to respond, unwittingly, to the look of the other is more likely what we deem the instinctive act. Recall Dewey's earlier words regarding the instinctive nature of praising and blaming others. He then went on to say, "Morality that makes much of blaming breeds a defensive and apologetic attitude; the person subjected to it thinks up excuses instead of thinking what objects are worthy to be pursued."[25] Aware of it or not, violence, the child of disaffirmation, is learned. It is born in the personal doubt and repudiation felt as an emptiness created by the receding of the life force itself created by the cessation of affirmations in a person's life. In their article of 2001, for example, R. F. Valois and colleagues point to dissatisfaction with life circumstances and with one's self as correlates of violence. Children reporting such dissatisfaction become either the violent ones or, interestingly enough, the victims of violence.[26] In hollowing out the self, disaffirmations automatically create nonbeing in the self. To kill that which is considered to be a nonbeing, therefore, is essentially to aver a redundancy. How can I kill that which is already (in my mind) killed? All violence, therefore, which includes all acts of injustice, is by definition premeditated. For at some point in my life I have determined the nonbeing of others; I have determined that I shall take no responsibility for others, both "rational" conclusions not only "allowing" me to act unjustly and kill but also "causing" me to act unjustly and kill. The deer as pet is unkillable; the deer as object of the hunt, fair game.

In this last example, I have defined the status of the other; I have given it a face or, conversely, defaced it. The same is true for the enemy soldier: I enter battle having concluded my determination of his or her nonbeing. Without that determination I must conscientiously object to soldiering, no matter what the ideology undergirding a particular war may be. I offer no interpretations of the ideology, only my commitment to affirm the other and thereby take responsibility for him or her. I shall not kill! Shoot when you see the whites of their eyes? Not a chance!

An important refinement of this notion seems in order. When I allege that all violence is premeditated, I mean only that at some level, nonbeing is premeditated for (the consciousness of) nonbeing arrives in the form of a perverse dividend as part of the disaffirmation package. Feeling a need to avenge some act, most likely the act of having been disaffirmed, the disaffirmed person may well decide that tonight he or she is going out to kill someone or, more likely, discover that he or she has killed someone. This would be the classic example of premeditated violence. On the other hand, just as we discover that we have affirmed someone, so does a person recognize, consciously or unconsciously, that he or she has not been affirmed. This is passively comprehended as well. Thus just as disaffirmation "lives" within the person as part of his or her consciousness and attending sense of a death force, so too does the act of violence emerge in his or her consciousness as a fundamental component of it.

Taking the argument one step further, we allege that it is perfectly reasonable to imagine that a person having committed a crime, a person having violated the commandment not to kill, can stand before us, look us right in the eye, and literally proclaim that he never planned the crime, he never schemed or intended anything. What is more, he claims never to have thought about the consequences of his actions. It now makes sense to us when he reports that he *found himself* having committed the crime; he *found himself* standing over the body or running from the scene of a crime as if he were an amnesiac until those fateful moments. The tense of his language, the notion that, ostensibly, nothing reached the state of his consciousness until the criminal action was completed, becomes comprehensible in the context of disaffirmation being something someone only discovers has occurred. It represents yet another past participle or "after-the-fact" experience.

Granted, much of the above argument could also be made employing the notion of the well-known psychological phenomenon "dissociation," a state of mind in which one cannot conjoin an act with its so-called appropriate emotion or cannot remember the act in the first place. The argument here, however, is that affirmation and disaffirmation are after-the-fact experiences. Moreover, inasmuch as they shape the nature of consciousness and identity (the main constituents of the Eigenwelt), they necessarily shape the manner in which internal and external events are experienced, remembered, and adjudged. Which means that life itself, like the self itself, is experienced as past participle, after-the-fact impressions. The very consciousness of an individual, therefore, becomes a compendium of after-the-fact experiences. Furthermore, because the mind of the disaffirmed is programmed to travel the interior and exterior worlds partly in nihilistic fashion, as Basch has theorized, in this same regard acts of violence are premeditated.[27]

In Robert Kegan's language, the act of affirmation allows me to recognize the difference between the interpersonal relationship and the interindividual relationship wherein one honors the other's being as an entity unto *it*self forever apart from *my* self.[28] That I can contemplate life without any of my needs being fulfilled means I know that I am not identical to other people who, in part, satisfy my needs. Ultimately, genuine affirmations reveal to me that there is never complete sameness with another and that the debt of human responsibility for the other is never fulfilled, never paid back. As Levinas claims, it extends to eternity. And let us also be reminded in this context of the words of Jacques Derrida: "We did not choose this responsibility, *it imposes itself upon us.*"[29]

In genuine affirmation, we merely look at the newborn's face or listen to the words contained in a narrative, experience the sensations called up in us, and seek to analyze nothing. The face of the other comes to us, Levinas writes, as a "resonance of silence that resounds." We live life, Levinas further alleged, we do not understand life.[30] In affirming the other, we live (with) the other, we do not seek to understand the other. We comfort the child awakened by night terrors, but we do not analyze the contents of her dreams. One might even argue that a complete analysis of something is at one level an attempt to become one with that other or to make the other the substance of our knowledge: "I know that woman so well it seems as if she no longer exists on her own, free of my analysis of her; I don't even need to speak to her to know what she is thinking."

The ages-old erotic utterance, "I know exactly what you mean," comes from sensation, enjoyment, connection with the other, quintessential Levinasian sensibility. For an instant living off the other, literally deriving nourishment from the other and along with it, Levinas suggests, deriving my energy and my strength exactly as the mother does with her newborn, although we rarely contemplate the mother's dependence on the baby—the mother's affirmation of the baby, that is—we are filled to the brim with sensations. And we say, as Levinas would predict, I feel more alive, stronger, and more vital in these moments than in any other moments of my life. If affirmation creates what Levinas calls "sensibility," then disaffirmation contributes mightily to the creation of what he designates as "totalization."[31]

The media, I believe, often confuse these forms of affirmation just as they blur the distinction between *inner* lives and *private* lives. To obtain through interviews what is essentially gossip is often advanced as an "up-close" glimpse of the inner world, but it rarely is. Gossip is but a thin slice of the otherness we are willing to impart to the other, but it has nothing to do with who we genuinely are.[32] Gossip is a form of parasitic coexistence; one hardly need mention that my digging up gossip about you never constitutes genuine affirmation. In fact, at some level, it is probably meant to reveal precisely that (part of your self) which you wish *not* to reveal. It is a form of outing and thus may be motivated by a desire not to take responsibility for you but instead to demand that you take responsibility for your self. Ultimately, it is an attempt to shame you. No one genuinely sees another in gossip; gossip denies the gaze and precludes affirmation.

I am tempted to suggest that affirmation from another, a form of human interaction akin to what Levinas calls *taking responsibility* for the other, is an action temporarily forestalling the felt sense of tragedy. Gossip, in contrast, tends to incite tragedy or the felt sense of it. A child cuts her finger and runs to Mommy, who kisses the boo-boo. The medicine and Band-Aid turn out to be mere addenda to the affirmation; the kiss and caress constitute the authentic affirmation. The bleeding has stopped, but this is the easy matter. More profoundly, Mommy has warded off tragedy. The child is okay; life, which surely has come to a complete halt at the first sensation of pain or sight of blood, may once again resume. For the child in the child care center, however, it may be that being and time are put on hold until the end of the day when Mommy's or Daddy's kiss brings the young prince or princess back to life. Do we not often feel in times of despair or terror that in some way we have been cursed and require some magical, well, affirmation to break the evil spell and resume our normal lives, which means the lives we have come to know as being our own?

In a sense, one could argue that in listening to narratives it seems inconsequential to analyze what the other person is speaking about, manifestly or latently, as if we could ever truly know, although we recognize these are not accounts of gossip. The important matter is that their words cause us to attend to them, face them and therefore face up to them and, by extension, imagine them, strangers all, facing up to us in every meaning of the phrase. By listening to the words contained in a narrative, in listening to people's expressions of self, expressions of people seeking truths about themselves or at least what they feel they may genuinely know about themselves, we discover that we have had called up in our selves our own words (in reaction), and hence, we have reexamined our own definitions of self, otherness, relationships, and human connection.

Merely listening to these words, therefore, becomes a form of affirmation. For at one level affirmation means facing the other, attending to the other, or at least the other's narrative, which in some cases is all we have of the other. Most significant, the self cannot be itself without the presence of the other. Levinas describes it this way: "I am defined as a subjectivity, as singular person, as an 'I,' precisely because I am exposed to the other. It is my inescapable and incontrovertible answerability to the other that makes me an individual, 'I.' "[33] Thus, it is not merely that I have been introduced or exposed to the other, Levinas instructs. Rather, when the other looks at me, "his responsibility is incumbent on me."[34] "With the appearance of the human . . . there is something more important than my life, and that is the life of the other."[35] Affirmation of the self, therefore, is impossible without the presence of the other.[36] As Paul Tillich might argue, there is no I without Thou, a notion Erikson captured as well when he observed that the so-called clarified self-image "is the affirmation of the self by means of the Other or the presence of the Thou."[37]

In more extreme terms, if Edmund Husserl is to be believed, my entire sense of the meaning of your words, your being, comes down to my interpretation of your words, your being, which essentially means that you are in great measure the product of my mind work just as I am the product of your mind work. This perspective surely complicates the meaning of my being present with and for you. Nonetheless, the mother comforts the child: "Don't worry. *I am here now*, so nothing is going to happen to you." *My* presence, the result of *your* summoning, automatically commences the ritual of affirmation. Nothing yet has been said, done, or even imagined. We are merely gazing at each other, attending to each other, acts that do more than simply reveal one's self to the other, inasmuch as the other is allowing his or her self to be revealed to us. (Literally speaking, we find our selves gazing at each other.) These become acts that *oblige* us to reveal our selves to our selves. Affirmation is captured in words like "summon," "face," "gaze," and most assuredly "assume responsibility for."

It seems appropriate to close this chapter by revisiting some of the notions prominent in the writings of Emmanuel Levinas, inasmuch as they form the basis for my argument in this and forthcoming chapters. Born in 1906, Levinas emerged as both philosopher and commentator on the Talmud, though no one could make the case that he was truly a theologian. Scholars such as Maurice Blanchot, Martin Heidegger, Gabriel Marcel, and Jean Wahl all became significant intellectual figures in his life, although for political as well as philosophical reasons he broke from Heidegger. On the one hand, Heidegger, he argued, was too concerned with ontology, the philosophy of being, and not enough impressed by the ethical nature inherent in human relationships, what Martin Buber would call the I-Thou relationship. On the other hand, Levinas departed from Heidegger when he learned that Heidegger had sympathies with the Nazi movement.[38]

If one had to reduce Levinas's work to a single line, it might be, as Denis Donoghue has written, that ontology, the philosophy of being, and epistemology, the philosophy of knowing, must inevitably take a back seat to something far more significant, even sacred: the nature of the relationships between and among human beings. In Donoghue's words: "It follows that Levinas's aim is to displace the priority of knowledge by the priority of faith: not faith in God but in the sublime existence of other people than oneself. Not faith in their mere bodily proximity on the street, but in their mode of existence as persons for whom I hold myself responsible."[39] How ironic these words seem in the present argument, which, on the heels of Levinas, posits that the development of the self is predicated on a philosophy itself built on interpersonal rather than ontological elements. It is built, moreover, on elements of faith and ethics rather than knowing and thus flies in the face of the traditional Platonic ideal that our fundamental duty as human beings is to know.

The significance of this position is that every act undertaken by the individual must be perceived in the context of justice. In turn, the very concept of justice and, hence, ethical action imply taking responsibility for the other. Levinas himself cited the words of Alyosha in *The Brothers Karamazov*: "We are all responsible for everyone else, but I am more responsible than all the others."[40] This concept of responsibility, moreover, is based not on reason or even duty but remains the elemental, rudimentary, yet most profound ethical act we can commit, or fail to commit. Again from Donoghue: "The primary act is the spontaneous one by which I address another person as 'you.' *I ground my own mode of existence solely upon that act.*"[41] I cannot, therefore, become me, develop my own concept of self, without acknowledging you and taking responsibility for you. In this way, finally, societies come to be formed, for in a sense they are nothing more than the "gathering together of those who speak and listen."[42]

Granted, there is much with which to argue in the writings of Levinas, as, for example, the ways in which he fails to deduce ethical laws, as Donoghue points out, but can only posit them. One can also take aim on the most obvious principle in his writings, that being the foundation on which he rests almost his entire argument, the very argument I have borrowed for constructing many of the ideas contained in this volume. It is evident that what he demands of us is the leading of an ethical life. It derives from him and thus comes to us almost as commandment. In his writings it appears as though Levinas desires to lay these words at the foot of God. Still, he argues to the end that ontology, being, is preceded by at least one life force, be it a motive, a drive, an impulse, a primordial sense of "proper" human action—namely, one must derive a sense of self from the life one leads with another and the responsibility inherent in being held hostage by the other. Without this life force there cannot emerge a genuine knowledge and sense of self. Nor can there be anything in the society resembling genuine justice.

4 The Miraculous Stranger

THE PSYCHOLOGIST Robert Kegan once remarked that as one of his or her many capacities, the healthy child exhibits the ability to elicit the sort of help he or she may require.[1] It is an intriguing observation for the student of affirmation, because it suggests that prior affirmations of the self, acts initiated by the gazer, not the one who receives the gaze, make it possible for the self to request further affirmations, further ratifications of its being. Those of us in the academy often hear the lament, "Oh, I wouldn't ask my professor that question. She doesn't even know who I am. Besides, who am I to raise that matter with *her*?" Plaintive expressions, surely, but also symptoms, perhaps, of a self made defective not just by destructive conversations held by the self with itself but also by a lack of public affirmations. In and of myself, I am not sufficiently significant to address someone on my own behalf. I may well be able to address you in someone else's behalf, but not my own. I am, presumably, not even visible to these momentous figures. The experiencing of affirmations, apparently, not only makes me comfortable with my own being but also makes me believe that I am present, real, worthy, visible.

Is it any wonder, therefore, that in many sectors of our culture we take especial precaution *not* to look into the eyes of the person we pass on the street or sit next to in the café? To look at them, after all, may imply speaking to them, which means running the risk of conversing with them, which means running the risk of engaging them, which means running the risk of befriending them and hence rearranging our entire structure of self. Best to avoid the encounter altogether if only to avoid burdening our selves or even harming our selves, as the meaning of the word "risk" implies. Better to seek forms of entertainment and distraction than confront our selves, or at least those parts of our selves that (we imagine) would be summoned in us by the mere presence of this new person, the mere looking at us by this stranger. "Thou shalt welcome the stranger in your midst," the Bible reads. But as Levinas reminds us, if we welcome only those we know, we have not welcomed strangers; we have affirmed no one. If we first know the other then respond to his or her summons, we have not acted ethically. We affirm before knowing, even before reasoning. The philosopher Roger Scruton warns of this same matter when he insists that the so-called good citizen must both recognize the obligations to strangers and then act on them. Furthermore, as Douglas Sears reminds us, Scruton included in his definition of strangers people of past and future generations.[2]

Through their very familiarity, friends and acquaintances make us believe—in yet another trick the self plays on itself—that we need summon up nothing at all. We need not affirm or disconfirm (our selves or others) but merely remain comfortable in our old ways and well-worn conventions. In this manner, we choose the presence of friends, equals most likely, who, as Aristotle instructed, never look to gain advantage from one another. Strangers, in contrast, call up in us the sensation of strangeness and alienation (from our selves and others). How do we know that the stranger will return our look or respond to our summons? How do we know he or she will not harm us? "If only she would just once look at me," we said a million times during high school. The risk of looking and not having the look returned, the risk of proffering affection and not having it accepted, seems too great to take. Said differently, how many parts of my otherness am I willing to just give away? And if I just give them away, as Trevor Griffiths questioned in his play *The Comedians*, are they even worth having?[3]

Affirmations not only provide me confidence to seek counsel in my own behalf, as Kegan suggested, but the act of affirming another also serves to endorse my belief in my own (sense of) healthiness. The blood appearing on the child's cut finger convinces him tragedy is but moments away. Mommy's words, "It's nothing, you're fine," instantly remove the child from harm's way and return him to life.

In genuine affirmation, we neither control nor judge, for control of the other, as Erikson pointed out, yields doubt and shame, not to mention serving as an exemplar of objectification of the self of another.[4] We do, however, exhibit self-control. For just as we constantly struggle to control our passions, so we also seek to assume responsibility for our actions and, hence, our authentic character, which, Aristotle counsels, inevitably affects our perceptions and our treatment of self and other. This as opposed to the formulation of purely modeled caricatures of self derived in great measure by practicing distraction, many of which are formed through irresponsible action.[5] Self-constraint, Goethe noted, becomes an art, and the affirmed self may be said to be artistic, as opposed to the self of the disaffirmed, which could be described as "artful," as in "crafty." In their self-doubting and self-distrusting manner, the disaffirmed appear to engage life as artful dodgers of the external and internal worlds, as opposed to artistic explorers. As Erikson noted, although he did not use the term, affirmed ones, at some level, feel both external and internal realms of their being to be friendly, receptive, accepting, trustworthy. The disaffirmed, in contrast, tend to have bad or wrongheaded intuitions about others essentially because of their lack of trust of the external world. Erikson warned that shaming children for their actions or scolding them for their failures might well lead to self-doubt.[6] "Whatever matters to human beings," Sissela Bok wrote, "trust is the atmosphere in which it thrives."[7] Most especially, the disaffirmed run from people who they fear cast moral judgments on their life. In addition, perception for them is too often supplanted by projection. "You know you want this!" the date rapist proclaims.

Similar distinctions come to us from a different venue through the work of Lawrence Broer.[8] Examining various themes in the writings of Kurt Vonnegut, Broer distinguished those themes and characters expressing bitterness and despair from themes and characters wherein despair appears to be balanced by a degree of optimism and a sense of genuine possibility for human growth. Whereas the former orientation seems coincident with what I call disaffirmation and the latter with affirmation, Broer calls the latter orientation an affirmation of old values that advocate for self-reflection and progressive alterations in the culture.

Self-control bespeaks as well the ability to contain emotion—Aristotle used the word "continence." One expects the affirmed to be comfortable with self and all it produces and, hence, comfortable with intimacy and expressing feelings. In contrast, one would postulate that disaffirmation breeds either the explosive (inappropriate or uncontrollable) expressions of feelings—incontinence for Aristotle—as in intemperance, or conversely the inability to express feelings altogether, what psychologists call "psychic numbing."[9] The issue here is that the disaffirmed lose control of the self because they feel overwhelmed by sensations or stimuli and thus feel a primitive sense of helplessness they have always experienced in such circumstances. Once again, the distinction, as Socrates taught, is between whether desires follow reason or reason follows desire. Can the self, through internal dialogue, reason, self-soothe, control the flood of feelings emanating from itself and thereby elicit aid? "Grab a hold of yourself, man," we cry out to a friend who appears utterly helpless while exhibiting behavior the sociologist Erving Goffman called "flooding out."[10] "Pull yourself together," we beg him as he decompensates in front of our eyes, wittingly or not alluding to the psychoanalytic notion of the unintegrated ego or Plato's unharmonious soul.[11]

Self-indulgence looms as a concomitant of disaffirmation inasmuch as it suggests a self unable to approach itself (as in self-reflection or self-analysis) in any authentic manner. Rather than define or contain the self, the disaffirmed one merely feeds it, as if any amount of narcissistic gratification could ever bring the disaffirmed self to the point of contentment or satisfaction.[12] In disaffirmation, there is no end to desires, no possible way to satisfy even a small percentage of them, despite expecting all the world, seemingly, to devote itself to working for us on just this one monumental project. Do we not observe parents indulging their children, providing them satisfaction of every whim and desire all the while withholding affirmation, the one nutrient they genuinely require?

The self-indulgence of the disaffirmed takes one of two forms. In the first, the self is overwhelmed by its own perpetual appetites and desires, need for personal gratification, sensory preoccupation, or what Piaget called "sensorimotor egocentrism." Anna Freud's harsh words to describe adolescents generally are perhaps better applied to the disaffirmed: "Adolescents are excessively egotistic, regarding themselves as the center of the universe and the sole object of interest, and at no time are they capable of so much self-sacrifice." Disaffirmation leads a person, moreover, to focus on immediate circumstances exactly as John Dewey described the unselfreflective individual. For in the absence of self-reflection, literally a disregarding of the self, the self is left with nothing but appetite; reason and thoughtful self-regard seem to be nowhere in sight. "Flight from self, from home," William Deresiewicz wrote, "is futile, and only results in the obsessive repetition of the same self-blinding, self-revealing gestures."[13]

The second form of self-indulgence is the inhibition of appetite, the disinterest in immediate circumstances whether they reside in the self or the external world. This describes the persons we observe seemingly empty of emotions or desires, persons uncomfortable with intimacy. Nothing fazes them, we comment, nothing appears to get to them. They are, perhaps, the "cool" ones, but there is something unsettling about their opacity. In psychological terms we call them depressed, people who have apparently lost interest in life and in themselves; neither reason nor appetite motivates them. Aristotle employed the word "insensibility" to describe them, but they fit well the more contemporary psychiatric descriptions of clinical depression or even psychopathy. Even more, they remind us of Freud's notion of anaclitic depression—anaclitic meaning "to lean"—a form of depression caused by the loss of a prized object, like one's mother (on whom one may lean). In fact, if affirmation is predicated on the taking of responsibility for another, then disaffirmation is born in the reality of having no one to lean on, no one to affirm us. To lose the prized object may be for some to lose the one and only source of affirmation.

Addressing himself to adolescent development, Erikson theorized that the sense of identity forming at this point in our life is in great measure founded on the understanding of how others judge us, how we judge others, and how we judge the judgments of others.[14] In the present argument, none of these dimensions gains salience in the experience of genuine affirmation where judgment (by the prized object) is absent. In genuine affirmation, we neither dominate nor allow ourselves to be judged, much less subjugated. By definition, genuine affirmation is a just encounter, a just discourse; we merely reveal ourselves to the other. As Levinas writes, "In his face the Other appears to me not as an obstacle, nor as a menace I evaluate, but as what measures me."[15] In this same manner, the act of affirmation is intended for both of us; I affirm my self as I affirm your self. The act ought to yield a form of love, perhaps the true form known to us as unconditional love, the very term bandied about so cavalierly in the discourses of popular culture.

The constant usage of "unconditional love"—in one respect a redundant phrase as love ought never to involve conditions—bespeaks the persistent need of all people for affirmation. Too many moments of one's life, even as an adult, are exemplified by the familiar scene of the parent helping the child to ride a bicycle. Parents hold us aloft, they encourage and uphold us, they run with us offering a few final words of support until at last they let go and we find ourselves riding on our own! Now, tell me that the first bike ride free of support, free of otherness, is not the sensation of living life itself! This is quintessential autonomy, the felt sense of unconditional love. Surely it comes close to Benjamin DeMott's description of parachute jumpers: "Man diving is alive; the ecstasy is that of non-connection—the exhilaration of sinking the world to nothingness, or at least to stillness, and thereby creating the self as All."[16]

Why, then, might we continually hear that ostensibly illogical term "unconditional love?" I suspect it may be an expression, albeit an imperfect one, of genuine affirmation. At very least, it connotes a felt sense of affirmation. At some level we all recognize that love arrives with no strings; we either love or we don't love. We add the word "unconditional," perhaps, to suggest some primitive understanding, some primitive felt sense of affirmation. We "know" there is something that resides within us, or ought to, that allows us to accept our selves, love our selves, be our selves, that goes even deeper than love. It is that "thing" that lives within us, a life force that assures us we are who we are and that we are good enough. Unfortunately, we cannot perfectly articulate it, just as we cannot wholly locate it within our selves. We only sense it is there; we lean on it to become our selves, but it seems almost impossible to touch it or describe it. The misused "unconditional love" suggests that we have no language to describe it. Imagining that it is a form of superlative love, we throw in the word "unconditional" and let it go at that. We assume others will know what we mean, and most of them, the affirmed ones, do. The "thing" in question, of course, is affirmation.

Unconditional love or not, my experience of my self ultimately and ineluctably must be an experiencing of you as well—Heidegger suggested that we do not *have* relationships as much as we *are* relationships—or at least that part of you which you are free to share, for I cannot know you, much less own or possess you. All I have access to is that which philosophers call your "otherness." You are still there, out there in some exterior space, forever apart from me. The parent does not own the child, the lover does not own the lover. They imagine they become one, it surely feels this way, but ultimately sameness is but a conceit, an act of wishful imagination, or the felt sense of the trace of the other left in us after the encounter. Affirmation, one likes to conjecture, prevents this form of (unrealistic) self-ownership, just as it enables individuals to differentiate themselves (their selves) from one another in order to become genuinely attached.[17]

In genuine affirmation, one is assured that moral behavior and just conduct will proceed. For to punish you, own you, destroy you, would be to punish me. Again from the loving, affirming parent, we hear, "Take my life, not my child's." We hear as well the sentiment of parents not being meant to bury their children, surely the ultimate act of failing to take responsibility for the child. Employing Levinas's formulations, it could be argued that it is the act of affirmation that forever assures you that I shall not destroy you. Your self is safe in my presence. Indeed, for the child, it is my presence that renders this felt sense of safety, this refuge from tragedy. In philosophical terms, affirmation underwrites being or, more likely, the felt sense of being. In architectural terms, affirmation represents shelter, sanctuary.

Affirmation in these terms, precisely as Levinas suggested, also implies a debt that is infinite. Not only must we conceive of it going on forever, that is, the account is never closed, but we must think as well that one keeps depositing into the account, for it can never be filled up. This is truly the basis of the old line, "What have you done for me today?" With affirmations, moreover, there are no quid pro quos, no appeal to all that one has contributed to another in the past. It is said that a parent's work is never done, but neither is a child's. Which raises the question, If I see in your eyes that you are willing to take responsibility for me, how do I pay you back? Especially in the case of parents and children, is not the debt asymmetric to the point of the child not being able to reciprocate?

Reciprocity is always possible; repayment never is. It is the gaze that keeps alive the opportunity for reciprocity, but not for symmetry. The child can "pay back" the parent through numerous affirming acts. He can say, as many of us did to our parents, I will pay you back by taking responsibility for my own children as you have taken responsibility for yours. She can say, I will pay you back by taking responsibility for you when you reach an age when you can no longer take responsibility for yourself. Significantly, for those motivated by guilt to pay back, Roy Baumeister, Arlene Stillwell, and Todd Heatherton suggest this may not be all bad inasmuch as guilt, assumed by many always to produce negative results in relationships, may actually prove to enhance them.[18] Indeed, they contend that guilt actually represents a symbolic form of affirmation, a notion, one suspects, that would deeply trouble Levinas.

These are obvious courses of action. Consider now, however, the following observations about the family and ultimately a definition of family formulated by Felton Earls and Mary Carlson. I offer these observations for a variety of reasons, only one of which is to exhibit perhaps the most profound form of the nature of reciprocity in the work of affirmation.[19]

Throughout the animal kingdom—for primates surely are social animals—the family provides its offspring their initial emotional and material supports and resources, although one doubts seriously that other animals define their sociability in terms of what Levinas calls their "being-for-the-other." Without this "being-for-the-other," however, there is nothing resembling socialization, much less viability, and, hence, little opportunity for the offspring to emerge as competent citizens of the community. Seemingly every day the offspring feel what Erikson called the epigenetic forces of development: the (felt sense of) pushing toward the world from the individual's unique genetic code, as well as the world pushing back in the form of norms, values, and social and cultural constraints.[20] At every moment the individual and culture are transmitting something to each other, the individual advancing his or her state of being, the culture responding with the dynamics of social arrangements and codified meanings of communal life and the agreed-on outlines of what we have called life and death forces.[21]

This is an important matter to keep in mind not merely because of the interaction of what we commonly call nature and nurture. More to the point, it suggests that the work of affirmation, the taking of responsibility for the other, the original response to the gaze of the other, teaches the other that ethical behavior is binding (even without a written contract demanding either reciprocity or symmetry), because essentially it is not called up in us; it is brought into us from the exterior. It is brought into you through my response to genuinely seeing you. My responding to your look transports to you the seeds of the ethical life and with it, perhaps, a sense of universal laws of conduct.

If Kant is correct, I eventually reach the point in my reasoning where I act as though my behavior were formed by some preexisting universal moral laws. I can teach ethics to you all I want, this theory suggests, but studying alone cannot render you an ethical person even though an ethical paradigm inevitably exists in the context of human relationships. Without the original affirmation, therefore, the sense of ethics fails to take root. If the will can be guided by reason, Kant instructed, then the highest principle we can achieve is moral law—a free will to be certain, but one that lives under moral law.

Even granting the self free will and thus the right to choose the moral or immoral path—the will for Kant being the motor of morality as the id for Freud was the motor of the intrapsychic engine—I argue that attaining this highest principle requires affirmation of the self, an act that transcends any fundamental law of the natural environment. The state of the newborn is more than merely a collection of drives and instincts. Morality offers freedom, which in turn means that affirmation, born first, perhaps, in the look between mother and child, finds its final resting place in the self as freedom. "Whether we admit to it or not," Dana Wilde wrote, "almost all of us have a sense of fairness or justice, and this means we have a moral sensibility. We have the idea that some things are fair and some aren't." But as C. Eric Lincoln reminded us, "Freedom implies power, the power to be responsible." Not so incidentally, Erikson too subscribed to this notion, warning that adolescents in particular tend to take freedoms that are not secured by appropriate demonstrations of responsibility.[22]

Something else may also be discerned in that first look between child and mother: namely, the barest outline of the divine. Is it possible that what emerges in early childhood in the original gaze between the child and mother as an idealization of the parent,[23] and what frequently breaks through in adolescence as the deidealization of the parent, a form and intensity of love and later a reaction to it transcending anything that might be rationally based or expected, is a belief on the part of both participants that they have detected the trace of God in the face of the other? If God is within me, the child might well deduce, it has been put there in the look of the other or, more precisely, in the other's willingness to respond to my gaze. Which means there is something godlike within me and about me; someone is *looking* out for me. Perhaps this too is part of what people mean when they employ the term "unconditional love."

Possibly the most important question addressed by Earls and Carlson goes this way: How do you meet the needs of children in a constantly changing society when the needs of children never appear to change? Even when parents' roles necessarily shift from nurturing the fundamental needs of the very young to nurturing the aspirations of the growing child, the formation and stability of the family must constantly be addressed. Making matters even more complicated is that economic, political, and social structures regularly reveal unstable conditions even as the parent seeks to render stability to the child. The individual affirmation may become even more complicated as it comes to be played out in a wavering world characterized by inconstancy. What, then, sustains this child, this parent, this parent-child relationship, this family?

Earls and Carlson suggest that it is the capacity of the adult to commit to the child, which in our vocabulary means affirming the child, taking responsibility for her or him. Ideally, this capacity provides the child the strength not only to make it through his or her own generation—Earls and Carlson describe it as the capacity to "outlast" any one generation—but also to feel the desire, furthermore, to re-create life, thereby establishing the (life force for the) next generation. (In this idea of responsibility for a generation we see the notion of affirmation transcending any simplistic concept of mere loyalty of the sort one finds in the philosophy of communitarianism.)[24] Not so incidentally, the desire for relationships to endure into the next generation, not to mention the creation of the next generation, serves as yet another example of "paying back" the (Levinas) debt of responsibility. Of course single parents and homosexuals desire to parent children; they too long to affirm the other and endure. My parenting provides you a foundation for your parenting, for in taking responsibility I pledge to love again and again and again; we therefore call the debt of affirmation settled or determine we will never conceive of our relationship in terms of any forms of debt. This arrangement might also be part of what Erikson referred to as the "effective remnants" of childhood.

Not surprisingly, Earls and Carlson assert that this facet of the debt can never be resolved through sex education or parent training courses but only through the earliest experiences of parents and children being together, what we have called the experiences of the original gaze, or the affirmations of being; it is at the root of socialization. In a different context, J. C. Nyri wrote: "What does the mind see? It sees ideas, forms, 'characters' that are, as it were, 'stamped' upon it."[25] Affirmation provides the psychic bed in which the so-called stamping action of socialization is consummated; the family, one presumes, provides the bedroom.

From the outset, cooperation and reciprocity must be established in the family; everything developmental, seemingly, is captured in the totality of relationships. This is a fundamental position of the modern family systems movement.[26] It has to be this way from the standpoint of family inasmuch as no one can ever genuinely know the individual being of another, only the (felt sense of) mutual attachments of otherness that underwrite the family constellation and its individual subsystems. The best I can do is know slightly something of you and something of our relationship. The rest I must trust to the enduring powers and work of affirmation.

If the task of the (moral) child is to comprehend and incorporate the values of his or her culture, the task of parents is to "teach" these values, which they accomplish in part through the affirmation of and by taking responsibility for the child. If I assume responsibility for you, I necessarily teach you moral character. If I renounce my responsibility for you, I literally let you run wild, which is to say, permit you to be amoral. I may justify my actions as permissiveness, but it remains, nonetheless, a renunciation of the gaze and lives in you as the felt sense of disaffirmation.[27] All the "teaching," by definition, occurs within the relationship, within the connection of our mutual otherness, and thus it lives in a remarkable zone conjoining the physical and metaphysical worlds. My mother teaches me what I should and should not do, but she inculcates in me as well the idea of the ideal, for this too is part of the taking of responsibility for the child. Freud's superego, normally taught to the child, Freud alleged, by the father, although in modern times by both parents surely, is known to us as the source of the conscience, the moral way. But Freud wisely placed the ego ideal, the ideal self, in the realm of the superego as well, thereby indicating his recognition of the connection of the moral and the ideal being.[28] I learn how to be good just as I learn the concept of goodness. I learn what I am good at (competence) just as I learn that I am good (at being me). It all arrives with affirmation.

Significantly, at any instant, this "social" learning can be extinguished. The disaffirmed child may have more important things on his or her mind than doing good or maintaining some ideal notion of the good or the moral. Said more precisely, the felt sense of the disaffirmed child's self is no longer available to the sort of social teachings he or she previously may have experienced. Disaffirmation causes the inhibition of pro-social learning if only because inherently it teaches antisocial learning and, hence, violence. Affirmations instill cohesiveness; disaffirmations, in contrast, perpetuate social disintegration, a collapse of a sense of moral responsibility directed at anyone, including one's self. Disaffirmations destroy the gaze, annul the summons; they blind the eye. As Rzepka says, they are taken away from themselves by the eyes of the other.[29] Thus there can be no relationship with others, the world or anything resembling a life force, and hence, the capacity to be moral is diminished. Affirmation permits tolerance and reconciliation, disaffirmation yields intolerance and dogmatism. The quality of the relationship, the quality of the affirmation, therefore, looms as significant for social learning as the content of the so-called family curriculum.

In affirming acts of socialization, parents demonstrate their capacity to attend to social cues, the slightest shifts in behavior, gestures, and vocalizations. In the first weeks of life, Earls and Carlson suggest, parents necessarily focus on the facial expressions of the child, which means that essentially they fixate initially on the gaze of their baby. These acts are rendered successful in part by an underlying motivation of the parents to instruct the child about his or her social behavior and, hence, his or her sense of being, a sense, we recall, that remains intimately tied up with the child's notion of family. We are speaking here not merely of *having* family but *being* family, since it is in the context of the family that so much of this individual sense of one's unique being is formed. The cohesiveness of social relationships comes to be translated by the child as cohesiveness (or integrity) of the self. As the others cohere, I cohere. As they disintegrate, my (sense of) self disintegrates. In the family context, or the "family crucible," as Augustus Napier and Carl Whitaker described it, my sense of self is threatened by my weakness in any relationship in the system, even relationships in which I do not directly participate; when my parents quarrel, my self is diminished.[30] Politically incorrect perhaps, the phrase "broken family" may be an apt one. How else does one conjure the sense of a family's roles having disintegrated and with it a sense of the self as unraveling! As the promise of affirmation breaks, the family breaks, our spirit breaks, our self breaks.

Along with the summons to assume responsibility for the other, the act of affirmation tends to carry with it an implied interest in the other, a genuine motivation to be with and for the other, as well as a wish to allow the other to become part of one's self. I make no bones about it, you are a part of my life forever! You exist in my mind forever as an end in yourself, never as a means to some end—Kegan called this the "interindividual relation-ship." In Levinas's words, I will forever be held "hostage" by you, a word that at first pass seems rather harsh, but intriguingly, the word "hostage" derives from the words "lodging" and "pledge." Precluding any chance of my enslaving you, the affirmation makes me responsible for you, and *I* remain in *your* debt forever, but again, as neither slave nor subject. In this manner, each of us is called on to give (the meaning of being) to each other.[31]

The work of affirmation, therefore, represents social as well as personal (psychic) activity; it signifies a motivation to assume interest in and learn about the other and then become indebted to the other, three critical components of the presence of self offered to the other. In affirming you, I bring all my senses, along with my powers of intuition and analysis, to our mutual presence. All my being becomes part of my response to the summons, my response to infinite debt. For in the summons I become aware of what is essentially human in me and in you. It is just that too: a summons, not a contract to which we agree to affix our signatures. There is nothing unusual about it; these notions live in the wording of almost every version of the marriage vow.

Note, however, that much of the experience of being held hostage is primitive, inchoate. Indeed, the phenomenon lends credence to the very definition of experience as put forth by Theodore Roszak, who argued that experience may be thought of as "knowledge before it is reflected in words or ideas: immediate contact, direct impact, knowledge at its most personal level as it is lived."[32] Thus again we recognize the absence of a language to describe so much of our being, just as we recognize the weight of these so-called after-the-fact experiences. Be definition they are merely felt, not artic-ulated, not yet lifted up to the status of idea or concept available for com-munication to others or even to one's self. We know they are there, we know we are held hostage, we know someone has taken responsibility for us, but most likely we cannot find the words to describe these experiences until well after they have settled in and become part of our ongoing history and per-sonal narrative. Even more likely, we recognize them primarily in the ac-counts of others. Suddenly, something is evoked in us, the felt sense of the inarticulated experience, and we respond, Oh, I recognize that; something there feels terribly familiar. The experience, then, is called up in us through words, our own or someone else's. Either way, we now are able to reflect on something whose presence we previously barely detected. The sensation has always resided there as part of the phenomenon of having been held hostage.

It is transformed into an after-the-fact experience only upon applying words to it. But it has been there all along.

Inasmuch as every act of affirmation is by definition mutual, I affirm my self just (and justly) as I affirm your self. I anticipate and empathize with your needs through the acts of recollection of my self and my motivation to move toward you. Recognizing I cannot truly know your needs and desires, I must infer them from the realm of our connection and the realm of my own being, to both of which I maintain access essentially through affirmation. Then again, as David Steiner writes, "too much nonsense can result from endless pedagogic exercise in learning to feel each other's pain, as opposed to learning how to judge the universal claims made by strangers on oneself and the polity."[33]

It is my contention that so-called disaffirmed children lose access to these realms of being and thereby lose the capacity to anticipate the needs of others, empathize with others, or outright choose to neglect the potential consequences of social actions, especially those taken *against* another. (Or is it that only upon our questioning do they recognize they have neglected the consequences of their action? Said differently, might it be that disaffirmation renders the ability to anticipate the pain of another impossible?) In retreating from us, these certain children turn their eyes away, renouncing any commitment to moral responsibility. Probably they also close their eyes to their own unique being or more likely discover, in yet another after-the-fact experience, that their eyes have been closed. In their solitude, in loneliness, and in mourning the assaults to their self, to their very sense of being, they are devoured by the death force.[34] One can see, therefore, how it could be that any family member might violate the commandment inherent in the gaze and abuse or kill any family member.[35]

The punch line for the student of affirmation lies, however, in the definition of family proffered by Earls and Carlson. Granting the obvious ethnic, cultural, religious, and, probably too, social class variations, these authors define family as the outcome of strategies employed by all family members to satisfy the needs of parents and children around three fundamental issues: nurturance, security, and intimacy. Notice, first, the absence of the word "love." This is particularly interesting if one considers the warning offered by Alexander Garcia-Duettmann involving the usage of words.[36] Employing the philosophy of Friedrich Nietzsche, Garcia-Duettmann alleges that the "commonness" of the words "I love you" may lead to a sense of loneliness and isolation, the very isolation, perhaps, to which Erikson alluded when he spoke of the dangers of recoiling from a particular stage of psychosocial development.[37] Said differently, there is a contingency to words that is somehow overcome by the affirming nature of a friendship in which one feels that the present moment will be extended. So, telling me that you love me tonight is fine, but what is the guarantee that you will, as they say, love me in the morning?

Notice next in the Earls and Carlson position the important postulate that children must learn to nurture their parents as well as their siblings and themselves. I must learn to affirm my self, meet the moral requirements of my own gazing upon my self. The gaze goes outward (and inward) in all directions; the summons extends to all in the family. As part of the work of affirmation, children do comfort their parents, nurture and reassure them; children do affirm their siblings and parents. "It's all right, Mommy," they say. "Mommy is a flower." "No, Mommy is a golden tree." "Don't cry, Mommy."

Recall that reciprocal familial affirmations can only be considered authentic if they arrive naturally. To perform the affirmation from the stance of intentionality means, for Levinas, that the person is not compelled but is only acting out of a learned sense of responsibility. I affirm, pure and simple; I do not affirm as a response to your affirmation of me—a defining element in Kegan's interpersonal relationship. The disaffirmed child is neither taking responsibility for the parent nor putting himself in the place of the parent. He is actively (rather than passively) answering what he has learned to be a moral requirement imposed on him by the parent. I do this because my parents tell me I am supposed to. "It's your duty as my child to respect me!" the parents proclaim. Affirmations, after all, should be felt not only as natural actions but also as actions that a person does not recognize having taken until after they have been completed; ironically, the action feels permanently passive. We live, as it were, only with the traces of the "just happened"; this is the essence of what we have called a past participle or after-the-fact experience. We do not choose to fall in love; we find ourselves having (already) fallen in love. It is precisely for this reason that we typically find ourselves unable to come up with explanations for certain behavior, such as the phenomenology of the affirmation, other than that it is "instinctive"; it just seems to have always been there. We simply do not know how certain things "got there" and became part of our self. We do not even know how our self "got there." We never knew we had "it" in us.

How ridiculous it is, we argue, to ask a mother, How is it you feel so strongly about your child that you would sacrifice your own life for her? But that is precisely what being a mother is, she responds. You don't think about these things; they just are; you just do them. Levinas's words return to us: affirmation precedes reason. There is something vital of truly ethical proportions existing in the child's mind even before he or she properly could be said to engage in what Piaget called "preconventional" reasoning.[38] Best we not underestimate the ethical powers and sense of being captured in Piaget's most primitive stage of moral development, the sensorimotor stage. There may be far more in the word "sensory" than ever we imagined. Some behavior, like the act of affirmation, comes not from mere response; as noted, it is not founded on a quid pro quo arrangement. Even without the capacity to reason, developed during what Piaget called the "conventional" and "postconventional" stages of moral development, the baby does not merely respond but offers something because he or she is compelled to.[39] Call it an instinct, if you will, that is either nurtured (affirmed) or extinguished (disaffirmed) by the parents, but it is not simply a learned or even imitated response. The baby can become, not merely substitute for, the parent: "It's all right, Mommy. Mommy is a golden tree. Don't cry, Mommy."

Like the self, the family too dies without nurturance; food comes in all variety of packages. The family, like the individual organism that is forever more than the accumulation of selves comprising it, requires a protective armor: it takes the form of security. I am secure; you are secure; he, she, or it is secure. All forms of security systems are installed in homes, usually by affirming parents and, if Earls and Carlson are correct, by their children as well. Nurturance, security, and intimacy are part of family just as they are part of the constellations of affirmations (and disaffirmations) constituting family systems.

The significant variable for our discussion, however, may be that which Earls and Carlson refer to as intimacy. Without belaboring the point, intimacy is the felt sense of mutual selves conjoining. It is what Pablo Neruda must have had in mind when he wrote "that when I fall asleep it is your eyes that close."[40] The word "otherness" is particularly unattractive in this context, but surely when we are intimate we somehow are experiencing that segment of our selves with which we choose to part as well as that segment of our selves we choose to retain. At least this is how it feels to us, for we never truly part with any pieces of our selves (although some allegedly psychotic people describe exactly this sensation). It is the psychological activity captured in the phrase "giving somebody my heart." Intimacy is the sense of breaking off a piece of my inner world and offering it to another. It is a sort of soulful breaking of bread together. Surely trust, security, and nurturance are part of the "transaction," but the root of it seems to reside in the original affirmation.

More precisely, intimacy is a product of the work of affirmation inasmuch as your taking responsibility for me allows me to feel (be) comfortable in offering you these bits of my self, these peeks at my self. In seeing and recognizing me, as I do in becoming intimate with you, I grow not only more comfortable with *your* self but more comfortable with *my* self as well. I allow you in, as it were, and let those bits of my self out, because I feel the safety created by your presence and your invitation to my self to make an appearance. I am free, in other words, to come out. Held in your gaze, I am outed. In genuine intimacy, moreover, I could not possibly draw the boundary of where your otherness begins and my own commences. In this realm, however limited it may be in the story of the emerging self, we are meshed, undelineated. We do not lose our individual identities precisely because at some level we recognize that only our mutual otherness is meshed. There is more to each of our selves that exists apart from each other.

When we feel all of our selves to be meshed, we call the sensation "enmeshment."[41] Enmeshment implies that I have lost sight of a self existing apart from you. Seemingly, we have become the same person, and although this sounds to be a most romantic ideal, the obliteration of the self can never be the coveted conclusion of intimacy, even though it may seem to be in adolescent love. Intimacy, in other words, is not the act of my becoming you, for always I understand the unity of your self that forever excludes me. No matter what the nature of our attachment and intimacy, you are your own person, and knowing this I offer you genuine fidelity. It is the act of my offering to you my self, once private and internal, that now I dare risk having you see and examine. In intimacy, I only increase the feast for your eyes, only add to the contents of the gaze, and thereby up the ante of the responsibility each of us pledges to the other.

These ideas ought to surprise no one. The attraction to the eyes so important in Levinas's formulation of taking responsibility for the other is fundamentally an attraction to what we imagine is not only the living part of the face, of the entire body; it is, as the proverbial expression has it, the look into the soul. Through the eyes we imagine we see the inner being, and to some extent we are correct. "You look sad, today," we say. "Is something wrong?" "Oh, I recognize that special twinkle of yours. Something good has happened, right?" The so-called healthy look penetrates the inside of the other and lodges in the self. The so-called unhealthy look sees through the other, missing its target altogether. Families too can operate as faceless cocktail parties, the guests constantly looking elsewhere in the hope of discovering a more significant face. (Or is it a more significant fate?)

The original responsibility captured first in the gaze of the other was never limited to this action or that action, this period of life or that one. The realm of responsibility is the total being; I am taking responsibility for your life, which includes your inner world; I shall not kill. "The face of the other," Steiner writes, "is already the prohibition on murder."[42] In our most intimate presence, we are each other, although we never become each other, if this makes sense. We feel ourselves, again, through intimacy made possible by affirmation, to be as close as two people can ever be, but the experience requires motivated activity on both our parts, just as Earls and Carlson alleged. The argument that blood is thicker than water is specious because neither fluid ultimately determines the nature of intimacy or its progenitor, affirmation.

Intimacy allows us to reflect again and again on our sense of being. In fact, along with affirmation, it actually demands that we do. To aver that I am relationships rather than have relationships suggests that in intimacy, in encountering these pieces of your interior, I may determine that parts of my own interior require alteration. Professional interior designers, after all, are not the only ones moving furniture around and selecting new patterns to put on display. Thus genuine affirmation—and the intimacy that follows thereupon—allows me to change or, more directly, become the self I feel in that instant I need or wish to become.[43] I find my self having outed itself, and I am relieved, uplifted, restored even. As Jack Nicholson's character in the movie *As Good as It Gets* says to Helen Hunt's character, "You make me want to be a better man."

Disaffirmation, in contrast, holds me back, tethers my self, prevents it from experimenting with other forms, other realms of consciousness, other definitions of possibility, other people. Just as the expression describes it, I remain in the closet. The healthy family, we conclude, allows each of its members to become that which they feel driven to become by dint of both their relationships in the family and a host of genetic, characterological, and other phenomena as well. The family therapist Murray Bowen might have said it best when he alleged that one of the criteria of the healthy family is that each member allows all other members their own emptiness, the interior space, in other words, to sense and identify their being, their self, as they must.[44] We all require our own space, which in effect is our consciousness. Not only must we be free to emerge from the closet, but we must first feel free to design the closet. So we say to people, "You can't lead my life for me. I have to make my own mistakes." This particular battle, what we call the battle of the wills as observed both in childhood—during the "terrible twos," for example—and in adolescence is actually incorrectly labeled, because in genuine affirmation there is no escaping our mutual responsibility for each other. To affirm you is to affirm your self, is to affirm your freedom, is to affirm your will. Independence and autonomy—the latter word having as its roots "self" and "law"—neither obliterate nor abrogate the original commandment, the law, really, of responsibility.

In affirming the other, I am eternally here. In disaffirming the other, I am absent, invisible, just as you are invisible to me. I am absent even to my self. There is no significant body that others see because I am unable to perceive not only a viable self within me but also a world that would notice me, accompany me, embody me, as it were. When someone says to me that he cannot conceive of my saying or doing something, I respond (to my self) with the words, I cannot even conceive of my self. In the end, I am completely disembodied, a person floating in space without anchor, well aware there is no port in this storm. I am away; nothing about the exterior or interior worlds is felt to be real or true. Indeed, we often speak of the disaffirmed (or disenfranchised) as if they were not here, as if they did not even exist; we call their actions "unreal"; they are immigrants turned away at the border. It is the disaffirmed who, fearing the eye of the other, stranger or not,[45] believe, perhaps, that by disappearing they would make life better for everyone thereby consummating not merely a (perverse) wish but their fundamental sense of self as already being disembodied, invisible, hollow, absent.

Affirmation necessarily becomes a cornerstone of adolescence as the young squirm out of the shells of childhood and seek to become independent and autonomous (as if these two ideals could ever literally be achieved).[46] Still, the courage to undertake these original squirmings, the courage to explore the mind fields of being, rests in great measure on the affirmations of self proffered by others. Affirmations, in the words of Paul Tillich, provide one the courage merely to be and to become, the part of adolescence, ironically, some parents find especially draining.[47]

Affirmation also represents (the felt sense of) beauty, yet another facet of the life force, the singular antidote, moreover, to (the felt sense of) ugliness and disgust of self. If I present my face to you and you fail to return the look thereby rejecting me, it must mean that you find me unacceptable, distasteful. My putting forth my face, my looking at you, which, as I have noted, is a summons to you to take responsibility for me, has been rebuked. You fail to return my look, you fail to respond to my "appeal"—the word literally meaning "to accuse"—and hence, I must conclude that you find me unappealing, disgusting. Literally speaking, you renounce my accusation. Again, my look signifies an invitation to be embraced and sanctified by you, become one with you. But you scorn me and therefore communicate your rejection of my being. "Mommy, am I pretty?" the child asks. "You are the most beautiful child in all the world," the mother answers, responding with alacrity to an utterly sacred summons, even as she tapes the child's most recent drawings to the refrigerator.

Our baby is born, and we see her in the nursery lying in her crib alongside all the babies born that same day. We notice something unusual: our long-standing preconception that newborns appear rather ugly and grotesque seems borne out in the faces of all the newborns in the nursery save one: our own. She is the most glorious being under the sun; we even describe her as "perfect"! Then we realize that the couple standing next to us perceives the exact same scene. For these people too, presumably, all the babies appear unattractive, all except their own.

It has commenced in the look. It happened the instant we first saw them, recognized them, perceived their beauty. We have been taken off guard—Levinas chooses the word "vulnerability." We are totally surprised by what occurs in us merely through the look. As Kegan rightly asserts, vulnerability opens us to hurt, but it also opens us to being recruited by another.[48] The child's mere look causes us to feel an indebtedness. We cannot be absent, we cannot turn away; we are utterly vulnerable to the summoning eyes. "Since your pupils dilate when you see something you like," Brian Hall observed, "and since we all love to be liked, this is probably the genes' way of seducing the parents, of preventing them from abandoning this alarming burden somewhere in the forest."[49] A failure to respond to the summons, the idea that one is invulnerable to the self of the other as well as one's own self, leads to disaffirmation and, in some cases, the destruction of the baby. A person's very survival rests on one's vulnerability, the capacity to appeal to the stranger, to be appealing to the stranger, to hold the stranger in his or her grasp. And note here that the word "grasp"—derived from the word "grope"—implying comprehension as well as "holding on," tends to support the assertions of both Levinas and Kegan that a grasping of the stranger is a grasping of the sense of being. In this moment, the child *is* the life force. In the connection with the stranger, I lose my sense of stranger (maybe strangeness too) to my self.

And if, as Levinas argues, we feel compelled to answer the summons inherent in the look of the stranger, because the appeal is also an accusation of sorts, might we then suggest that the original stranger in our mind is our newborn baby, the original miraculous stranger? We have not seen her before; this is our first look at her, just as when reading the narratives of other people, anonymous ones even, we are encountering their words for the first time.[50] Like the stranger's face, the words of others invade us, breaking through the boundaries of our selves, the boundaries defining our solitude, Levinas observes, and most assuredly our egoistic enjoyments. Faces, like words, constitute an epiphany; their mere appearance in the nursery or on the printed page calls to me, calls me out of me toward them. It had seemed as though I was perfectly content (in my aloneness) until I first encountered your face, your look, your words.

The baby is born, and I behold the face of the stranger. It is the face that holds me. Now something happens, Levinas tell us, that amplifies our appreciation for the concept of affirmation. To begin, the stranger's eyes constitute an intrusion. I do not recall that I have chosen to affirm this newborn; I am obligated, compelled to affirm her. I do not stand before my newborn and say, "Well, I guess this makes me a parent; I better start thinking 'parent thoughts' and doing 'parent things.'" I am stunned by the appearance of the child, stunned, that is, by the sensations called up in me at the initial encountering of the baby. I feel in this instant a sense of having been compelled to assume responsibility for the baby, for I imagine, that is, it feels as though I have always been parent to this child. Moreover, it feels as though she were my destiny. It just seems utterly natural, as do all acts of human affirmation; disaffirmation remains the unnatural act. Do we not within days of our baby's birth claim that we almost cannot recall *not* being parents? My very being suddenly arises from the affirmation, the standing in contrast to the baby—Levinas says "in opposition" to the other in the sense of distinction from the other.[51]

In this manner, Levinas concludes, we are "held hostage" by the other, even our newborn. We are, in a sense, standing in place of the other, sacrificing for the other—Levinas calls this "substitution"—and while these terms may seem somewhat pejorative, they mean something quite fundamental, something the parent of the birth child or the adopted child feels the moment of the first encounter with the child: in the original affirmation, I am responding to the other even before I know that I am. The appeal, the accusation, and most assuredly the summons occur before I sense what has hit me. As we have repeatedly observed, it is a passive experience; everything happens without my knowledge or any power to cease my actions; I am being carried along on an invisible wave. When I become aware of it, it exists in my mind, once again, as an after-the-fact experience. Ironically, as attached as I am to this newborn, not only is my identity becoming concrete, Levinas theorizes, but in the act of substitution I am learning that I am not another but merely me. More to the point, how can I possibly harm the other who holds me hostage! Only through the constant acts of disaffirmation can I ever conceive of harming the child or have it happen even without any preconception, without premeditation. For in disaffirmation, it is *I* who hold *you* hostage.

If we are to believe the foundational work proffered by Levinas, affirmations function almost independently of reason; even as we are "held hostage" by the other, we are in effect set free. In the act of affirmation, the sacrifice I make for the other liberates both of us. In disaffirmation, my failure to sacrifice imprisons both of us. A man I met recently said it this way: "I don't resent one cent or one second I spent with my children." Sadly, however, too many people feel themselves literally held hostage by their children, but our argument here would suggest that this is what they *reason* their condition to be, a form of reasoning derived from disaffirmation. For in affirmation we are not aware of this compelling act, this commandment to take the place of the other and therefore assume responsibility for him or her. To repeat, I underscore Levinas's insistence that affirmations precede reason, in the same manner in which he insisted that ethics precede ontology.[52] We feel our actions of responsibility to be utterly natural, as though we were obeying the laws of some invisible instinct or higher power to whom we frequently appeal, if only because we cannot find adequate explanations for our sensations through the act of reasoning.

What is it like having a baby or falling in love? Who can possibly describe these sensations, these affirmations? We can only live them. The question is, beyond birth, beyond the initial encountering by the adoptive parents of their newborn, how much longer will the child be affirmed? How much more of the relationship will be merely lived, merely experienced? How much of parenting, in other words, becomes not a natural order to take responsibility for the child but an unnatural and contrived means to some end, an action rendering the child himself, perhaps, a means to some end? How many children will report that encounters with their parents had to be a moral lesson rather than an authentic affirmation carrying, as it necessarily does, the seeds of ethical conduct? How many children will report that encounters with their parents denied them, somehow, their unique being and blurred the distinction between themselves and their parents?

We recall that in the authentic affirmation, I stand "in opposition" to you, but this hardly means that I oppose you, resist you, or even stand in contrast to you. To oppose may mean "in balance with you." It may mean that in standing in place of you, in taking responsibility for you, I make possible your ability to define your own being and render that being concrete, not to mention distinct from me. You, in other words, can stand in balance to the exterior world, the world beyond your self; it may be the best that I can offer you. Moreover, it is the best psychoanalytic identification can be, for it provides you the basis of differentiation from me, from everyone. It allows you your (felt sense of) uniqueness. Nothing is more antithetical to genuine affirmation than the control of one being by another, the sort of control we regularly observe in cases of disaffirmation where the allegedly affirming parent refuses to permit the child a sense of being all to itself. Control, after all, is the ultimate expression of power, but the only power of the affirmation is the felt sense of it experienced by the affirmed one: the power to be responsible and take responsibility for another. Said differently, disaffirmation precludes the self from becoming powerful, autonomous, fulfilled. Psychologists allege that the controlling parent infantilizes his or her child, which is to say prevents the child from ever encountering, much less knowing, her or his own maturing self.

Ultimately, the significant message is neither "Say as I say" nor "Do as I do." Rather, it is to be as you must be. As *I* am what *I* am, so must *you* be what *you* must be. As we are distinct beings, your happiness cannot be my happiness, your sadness my sadness. In affirming you, I can be disappointed in something you have said or done but I must not allow my self to be disappointed in your being, your self. In my affirmation of you, moreover, I trust that you will also affirm the stranger, which means that you will affirm me as well. For at one point, I too was a stranger to you. In disaffirmation, however, we live estranged from each other; we even use this rarely heard word to describe the unsuccessful relationships with those we imagine we love but with whom we cannot gain intimacy. "Sadly," we report, "she and I are now *estranged*." Note here that the word "estranged" means "removed"; we are no longer together, we are removed from each other, the period of being held hostage terminated.

To repeat, the mere presence of the other, not simply the proximity of the other, but the look of the other, summons me into the act of taking responsibility for the other; it represents the essence of the connection of two selves, the essence, in other words, of the work of affirmation. When the baby's eyes first opened and she beheld us and we beheld her, strangers still to one another, the connection was established, primordial, sophisticated, mystical, palpable. Her looking at us was all we required to commit ourselves to her: thus, in the first moments of the baby's life (in our life), we find our private selves joyously invaded as we also affirm this newborn child. Thus we celebrate her arrival. Most amazing, the baby's looking at us—and no one will convince us that she does not at once recognize us as her parents—has mysteriously affirmed us as well. Her presence has ratified us (our presence) as parents, and an entirely new history of affirmations has been inaugurated; we are all held wondrously hostage, each by the other.

If Levinas is correct, the locking together of parent and child, the quintessential antithesis of removal, abandonment, or estrangement, occurs well before the child's capacity to reason develops. Indeed, Levinas theorizes, reason does not enter this one realm of human connection. Only after the connection of the gaze is formed will pure reason be established. The more I choose to affirm the newborn, the more I feel summoned by her gaze, the more I feel my self locked to her (self), the more I feel my self. Rightly, one hopes, we use the words "locked" and "feel" to describe the sensation, for it appears that reason has played little if any role in the transaction. The word "lock," moreover, meaning "hole," suggests that in responding to the gaze we feel our selves falling into the hole that is the other and, in taking responsibility for him or her, residing there as well. In this same context, recall that the word "hostage" derives from the words "lodging" and "pledge."

As I have said, affirmation of the (self of the) other invariably becomes affirmation of the self. Affirmation has nothing to do with the other "knowing" me, no matter how much we wish to believe this to be the case. We report that the instant our baby looked at us she "knew" we were her parents, but this is sheer mental construction. All that is true is that in our affirmation of her she is "known" to us, and we to her. I choose to imagine that most parents would agree with these observations. I suspect as well that in the past, parents who gave birth to children so disabled that their physicians, perhaps unwisely, recommended that parents not only leave the child behind in the hospital but also never see the child, know that had they looked but once at their child, even with all his or her neurological or physical disabilities, they would never have abandoned the child; the affirmation of the stranger would have occurred without their having had any conscious control over it. Somehow they intuited the sensation of being held hostage by the gaze, and they knew they would never have released the stranger. (Or is it that they would never have been released by the stranger?) They would have found themselves making the pledge and offering the lodging.

It was the conception of the child with a disability perpetuated by the medical profession that led men and women to believe they could not adequately parent their child. As our knowledge of disabilities increases and, with it, our thinking about children with disabilities, few of these children are left behind in hospitals and relatively few, therefore, disaffirmed by their parents.[53] Still, walking among us are people who, upon the advice of their physician, left their unseen child behind and will go to their graves forever grieving for their own miraculous stranger. Only they know the form of affirmation they offered, not by reason or legal agreement but seemingly by a miraculous compulsion of the sort they had heretofore never experienced. Given all these matters, how does one explain the original attachment of parent and baby? Call it instinct, if you will, but this one phenomenon may not be accessible to *reasonable* explication.

Which raises for us a vexing question: what of those who are blind? Levinas has stressed so strongly the notion of the summons of the gaze, the power of the look, the coupling made between two people through the eyes, that we wonder now what happens if literally I cannot meet your gaze, if I cannot see your eyes. Was the poet Christopher Marlowe correct? Is there really only love at first sight? Or is all this mere metaphorical conjecture?

My answer to this begins in the recounting of a telephone call from a woman, a stranger actually. She tells me, not without sadness in her voice, that she is a member of a group of childless women who meet regularly. They all have conceived children but are the mothers, in her words, of no living children. She herself has had several miscarriages and one birth, a child who died seven days after being delivered. Does the hurt of these tragedies ever end, she wonders? And why is it that such pain persists for so long?

I am thrown by her expressions and questions. Who, but the Divine, knows the answers to such queries? Will my response to her be sufficiently sensitive? How does one even engage in this sort of conversation over the phone? I begin with the words of my own mother who spoke often of heartache of the sort that never wholly dissipates. We all live with holes in our hearts, I tell the stranger, whose name I shall never learn. How possibly can this sort of sadness ever disappear? Of course it makes no difference whether the child is born and one actually sees her or his face or experiences a spontaneous abortion and has the "remains," the traces, surgically removed; a connection with the child has been made. There can be no substitute for any of these "lost" children. We would on some occasions dare give the child born to us the name we had selected for a child that died or aborted, at least this is the practice among some religions,[54] although the successful birth of a healthy child cannot ever supplant the literal existence of these no-more strangers.

Having listened to me, the woman on the other end of the phone states that she has gone over these very same notions again and again with her fellow group members, but still their pain lingers. Suddenly, I find myself speaking to the stranger about the work of affirmation, Emmanuel Levinas, meeting the gaze of the other, finding one's self being held hostage, and most especially the purest form of ethical behavior found in taking responsibility of the other and, with it, the pledge to love and love again. I had not planned to tell her any of this, and even as I speak with her I see the lights flashing on the phone indicating other calls to which I now must respond. But I go on, and when I conclude my wholly superficial and truncated explanation, my synopsis, really, of all that I am attempting to write in these pages, she tells me that for the first time she understands something.

Through the act of the pregnancy, she has been called to take responsibility for a stranger, an act that by definition does not cease upon the death of the stranger or because the stranger, like the subjects of a narrative, will forever remain anonymous. Better than most, she comprehends the idea of the trace of the other, the trace of the Divine in the other, for literally she has been left with little more than traces. Yet her feelings, her sensibilities really, are as intense and vibrant as those of any parent. The oceanic feeling of connection and the "morality of responsibility," as Carol Gilligan has observed, are as vital for this mother as they are for any other mother.[55] She *is* a parent, I assure her, if my remark does not sound patronizing. She says she understands this matter of taking responsibility for an unseen stranger, no less miraculous than any other stranger one may encounter, any other child of any other parent. It is clear, somehow, that from the moment not of conception but of learning that she carries life within her, she has answered the summons. Only imagined perhaps, only fabricated in some mystical manner, she nonetheless has met the gaze of the other and will not, cannot release it or, more precisely, be released by it. Her very biology speaks to her "being in balance" with the anonymous stranger.

Accordingly, I remind her that the gaze holds us, that we are held hostage by it, and hence any counsel to release these saddening experiences that contribute to our sense of being in balance is by definition impossible. We can attempt to release or, as psychologists say, "work through" these emotions all we wish, but given the construction of the affirmation, it is doubtful that we (our selves) will ever be released. One simply does not work through these forms of affirmation inasmuch as they become part of our very being. Thus, I tell her that I feel she is not neurotically "clinging" to what is no longer there, for these children are still "in her life," in that other self holding her hostage. Quite to the contrary, she is like all of us, attached to the traces of otherness, seen and unseen, touched and untouched, heard and unheard. Like her, we all live with the traces of the summons, traces that open in us the felt sense of a life force as well as a death force. We are all, in a manner, identical to her with the one exception being that she has encountered the very tragedy we dread, the tragedy born in the original response to the gaze. For the possibility always exists that we may lose the other.

She thanks me profusely, but it is I who have received the gift. It is evident to me now that a woman experiences the gaze upon the discovery of the existence of the albeit anonymous stranger, not merely upon the literal perceptual sensation of it. As she carries life, so too does she "perceive" life within herself at the same time apart from her self and not apart from her self. An inner eye, the eye of the self, perhaps, perceives the gaze, is recruited by it, and takes eternal responsibility for it. That unforeseeable misfortune like a miscarriage occurs, becomes for the moment secondary to what she is experiencing. She has encountered, not merely imagined, the miraculous stranger. She has not called it up out of thin air; it was most definitely there. Of this she is certain. Granted, all the ruminations of which we have been speaking may be properly placed in the province of the imagined, but this woman has had a baby; all the rest follows thereupon. She lives with a hollowness caused by the exterior childless emptiness, the very space once filled by the fetus, but she has met the gaze and for the first time, perhaps, recognizes that she has answered the summons. She has done all this, moreover, save the experience of the one child who was born, while blind.

All the mothers of miscarriages are blind, as are those parents expecting to adopt a child who suddenly is not forthcoming. It is the single feature that distinguishes them from the mothers of born children. They all have encountered the miraculous stranger, as have I with a woman whose name and face I shall never know. For I too can meet the gaze of the stranger without meeting her eyes. I too meet my self once again by answering the summons of the stranger and feel the sadness, once again, stirred in me by the undistracted "sight" of the tragic.

IF WHAT I have purported about affirmations and disaffirmations holds any truth, then any narrative provides us evidence of a trace of what we live with in our daily decisions to assume responsibility for a stranger or, instead, to look away from the stranger *as if* he or she did not truly exist. The claim of the "moral ought," the claim of beneficence, is that I *should* do good,[56] I should assume responsibility for the stranger, the homeless one, the injured one on the side of the road where I feel my self compelled to engage in what is called "rubbernecking," the faceless one in the newspaper account. But I do not wish to, I am not ready to do so; I don't need any more burdens in my life; I cannot tolerate this scene. Besides, I could get hurt stepping out of my car on a busy highway. Better to glance quickly, fear I may catch a glimpse of the body but hope not to meet the gaze of the injured ones, and drive on. Better to imagine, perhaps, that they have died, better to acknowledge that police officers and paramedics are the ones who should rightly be in attendance. They will get here soon; they always do.

Unlike the childless woman or the woman having given birth to the child with a severe disability, I choose not to meet the eyes, attend to the words, or acknowledge the presence of the unseen precisely because they are unseen. I choose blindness, which in this instance means that I refuse to wonder about where my thoughts and feelings might lead me and, hence, what I might become. I choose, in other words, as Levinas writes in a discussion about God, that much of life is not about what I have to learn but about what is "already-known that has to be uncovered or freely invented in oneself, and in which everything unknown is comprised."[57] I must commit my self to understanding those after-the-fact experiences living within me.

The internal stirring I cannot deny, therefore, represents the traces of my decision to assume or abdicate responsibility and thus (self) knowing. It represents the traces of the other within me. It represents my willingness or unwillingness to make the history of another *my* history as well, which is to say allow any encounter to call up in me that which is not yet known to me, the stranger constantly lurking in my own being. To reject the gaze or the words of another is an attempt on my part to preserve the nature of the (perception and knowledge I have of the) world and my self. It is an attempt to solidify my identity and keep my self from ever changing, ever becoming.[58] "The active identification of beings," Levinas wrote, "by which the ego posits itself as world center constitutes its very selfhood."[59]

To reject any offer to engage my self in conversation becomes, perhaps, an effort to remain precisely as I am forever, a perfectly lovely mental conceit that would in effect render me immortal. My sense of my own uniqueness, as Erikson observed, ought to render me immortal. But now I discover that no amount of pretending wholly absolves me of the feelings associated with turning away; I cannot merely rubberneck and drive off. It is perhaps the guilt and the shame that linger. Already I feel my own personal fable to be crumbling. The voyage itself has been permanently transformed; I am already held hostage by the other, which means that I cannot keep my self constant, unchangeable. I will become, which in turn means that I will not achieve immortality; I will be part of the ever expanding tragedy. The mere look of the other, the mere words of the other, the mere sight of the crumpled car on the side of the road have brought me news of the inevitable tragedy. This, too, I lay at the feet of the miraculous stranger.

In sum, I look on the single human narrative carrying, as it does, the perceptions, history, the self-knowing, the humanness of another, a stranger, as just another form of personal encounter. But since every personal encounter, even the story of another told to me by a third party, by definition carries the possibility of inciting in me a consideration of or reflection on my solitude, my humanness, my finitude, I necessarily act in response manifestly to the account and latently to my response (of humanness) to it. Even third-hand, another's narrative demands that my self confront itself over questions of being and becoming, assuming responsibility for another or rejecting the summons to take responsibility, and choosing to act morally or not. I do not want to be devoured by another; I do not wish to experience the discomfort of (my self) being altered by another. I resent the injured stranger or the person with a physical disability for making herself visible to me and thereby altering my journey. Patients just should not telephone their physicians on the weekend. Do they not understand that this is a healer's private time? And why must the television networks keep showing me video of starving children in the Sudan? At dinnertime no less!

In simplest terms, as yet another common expression has it, encounters of this sort, especially ones of affirmation, become a "test of character." They serve as a provocation to examine the character of my self, the engraved mark of my self that I wear on my self. Clearly the affirmation is a cornerstone of what we call character. Any narrative, in other words, literally calls attention to our selves; it moves us to wonder about the sort of being we are. As I have said repeatedly, this is one of the gifts (and responsibilities) of affirmation. Once again we are moved to wonder about how it is that we came to recognize or understand the mere notion of our being human in the first place and being no more in the last place. The narrative, the unborn child, the child with the disability, and most assuredly the stranger who throws his or her gaze upon us cause us to "know" that we have a being, that we *are* a being, and that this being constantly evolves. But evolves into what, we wonder, as we contemplate the idea of (our) becoming and our becoming no-more.

Once again, the ideas here are not at all esoteric; they are what we think about every day. We hear a woman tell us, for example, that she has recently had a miscarriage, and unthinkingly we seek to comfort her with the words, "As bad as it seems now, you can always have another child." We pass the homeless person on the street and we think, "I really should be doing something to help him." Or, "How could he possibly have gotten into this position?" Or, "If I were a good person, I'd stop and speak with him." Or, "Hey, his life's not my business." We read the account of a child and think, "I should really work with underprivileged children, perhaps become a teacher or social worker." Or, "This child's words are touching and all that, but I don't know him so I don't have to do anything about it. I'm not the one who caused his parents to divorce. Besides, for all I know this one account may be pure fiction!" as A. S. Byatt and others often allege all of history has become.[60]

Given that no individual is ever a means to any end but inevitably the end to itself (its self), any character of any novel, play, or narrative may stir in me the sensations associated with confronting any miraculous stranger. Even when I know the play, *Hamlet* let's say, the stranger is the new performance, the new Hamlet. I do not know but that even an encounter with the words of a person through a brief narrative does not put me in touch with the "fact" that there is another human being "out there" I cannot completely know, just as there is another human being "in here" I cannot completely know.[61] Our responses to the narrative, in other words, come not only from us but from the other as well; that the other is "there" means that I am "here." In the encounter, I have noted, Levinas discovers the source of the ultimately ethical response. Ethical behavior, for Levinas, does not derive from logical reasoning. Nor does it sit somewhere in space ready, somehow, to be activated. Rather, it appears to be born in the encounter with the stranger; this is, perhaps, what makes the stranger miraculous—namely, that we would move toward or have called up in us (a call, as it were, to our humanness) such a series of ethical considerations merely by meeting the stranger's gaze, hearing the stranger's words, feeling the stranger as a stirring (being) inside us. "I probably should have stopped on the highway. I probably should have done the Good Samaritan routine. The worse that would happen is that I could do nothing for the person and I would be delayed ten minutes. What's ten minutes out of a lifetime?"

If Levinas's assertions are correct, does it follow that I am fated to live with the sentiment that if I do not respond to the words and gaze of the other, if I do not stay with my child, if I do not stop by the roadside, I am, somehow, neither a good nor a just person and, even worse, not completely human? In a sense, the answers to these questions are the questions turned inside out. That I even ask them bespeaks my awareness at some level that I have begun to question my ethical posture and with it the nature of my being a good person. That I even ask the question, that I even drive on with a freshly born discomfort, means that my character, my humanness, has come into question; I have called it into question. No, that's not it: it has been *called* into question.

In a word, any narrative, like any artistic product, evokes the matter of our humanness along with those vexing questions involving our definitions of self at the very deepest levels of our capacity to reason and feel. They have the potential to push us inward to those places which feel to us to be the furthest limits of our self-knowing; it feels as if we cannot go any further within ourself. And as painful and difficult as it may seem, this inward return to our selves may represent the best that we can do as sensate beings. For it may represent our feeble attempts to make sense of the (traces of) meanings and sensations of our humanness or merely to see the (traces of the) face of our humanness, our own internal miraculous stranger, just as it represents the best we can do in our encounters with the traces of others, even strangers. Especially strangers.

ANYONE WHO has ever been in a hospital speaks of nurses and their capacity to comfort and reassure us and, hence, affirm that even in illness our being is still intact and noble; no matter the circumstances, we are never humiliated by affirming agents. We speak of the bedside manner of a physician being almost as essential if not more essential for our recovery, in the relief of our suffering—the word "patient" means "to suffer"—than the medicine he or she dispenses. Lying in our bed we feel vulnerable, weak, childlike, helpless (and no one is about to read to us). At last the nurse or doctor arrives, looks down at us, and smiles and touches our hand. In that instant we feel affirmed, our healthy self, really our mental representations of our healthy self, returns to us, and for the moment we consider our self in healthy terms, ignoring all signals from the hospital, every architectural detail and social arrangement that conspire to cause us to consider our self a patient, ill, deformed, unattractive, defective, imperfect.

In the end, a fundamental essence of the work of affirmation is that of the life force itself. This means that in affirming another, I am sanctioning their right to feel a life force, which in turn means that they can feel or sense something that we experience and define as transcendent. The felt sense of transcendence, of surpassing one's self, in other words, is predicated on the ability to feel comfortable with that which is metaphysical, that which is nonmaterial, bodiless. Through affirmation (of the self) we now can "see" the unseeable. Now hold on, we argue, how can I know what is not there to be known? How do I develop a sense of comfort with sensations that derive from a place that would seem to exist beyond my exterior or even my interior? How could I be moved by something beautiful or define something as beautiful or come to the conclusion that something exists beyond me, beyond even that which my senses tell me constitutes my exterior? What does it mean to experience through affirmation the sensation of rising above and beyond my self? And what might Robert Kegan have meant when he wrote that "what the eye sees better the heart feels more deeply"?[62]

I suggest that rising above my self or developing an appreciation of the transcendent is an enhanced appreciation of the connection of the self and otherness through affirmation. It rises above the concrete and the physical characteristics typical of popular culture and pure entertainment for it finds no home in acts of distraction. More precisely, the transcendent suggests an appreciation for the (traces of the) authentic self of another, not just their otherness. To be affected by what we experience as art is to be moved not merely by the otherness of the artist but to be affected by something that comes as close as possible to their self.[63] This notion is captured in the following words of Lee Siegel: "Demanding art addresses that part of us that lives outside the collective 'we,' that follows its own music and destiny, that lives and dies amidst its *own unspeakable experience, in its own indescribable solitude.*"[64] Quite often we refer to that something, that demanding art, as the "soul" of the artist, probably because we append something sacred such as the act of creativity to it and because the product of the soul transports us to what we feel to be the realm of the transcendent, the realm, as it were, of the immortal. We may also call it the soul because we do not directly encounter the artist, yet another miraculous stranger, only his or her product awakening, calling up something from within us. And perhaps we call it the soul precisely because the artistic product has put us in touch with those vessels safeguarding our ultimate knowledge of ourselves. Oscar Wilde captured the spirit of this notion in these words from *The Picture of Dorian Gray*: "He would be able to follow his mind into secret places. This portrait would be to him the most magical of mirrors. As it had revealed to him his own body, so it would reveal to him his own soul."[65] In recognizing the impact the product has had on our sense of our self and that which we now imagine is beyond our self, we assume that the product in this case must be the self. Art is the child of the self, the self as it is created by itself and proffered to others, which suggests that in our mind some of us believe that our self and our soul are one.

When I am "touched" or "moved" by a piece of art—the two words implying something more profoundly affecting than mere physical sensation—I am experiencing a oneness with the self of another. Borrowing from Heidegger and May, I do not *own* art as much as I *am* art. I have been touched, in other words, by a nonphysical force, something that is there but not there as part of a life force. The picture hangs motionless on the wall, protected by glass. It does not literally reach out to me, although that is precisely what I feel; the true artist, as Stephanie Dudek observed, does not take a stand.[66] The artistic product itself becomes the affirmation. I comment, "This picture speaks to me." I do not literally touch it, although I suppress the desire to do just that. It does something more than merely strike my senses. It stirs a part of my self, something perhaps even beyond my (sense of) self that I cannot put into words. Perhaps Foucault was wrong; perhaps not all life is built around language.[67] Knowing at the same time that I am not physically aligned with the picture or the artist (the other), I have entered into the realm of the transcendent, a realm human beings "naturally" appear to covet. I am in touch with the mystery of the life force whose location I now imagine goes beyond the parameters of my (sense of) self but whose presence in my imagination has been made possible (called up) in the first place through the work of human affirmations.

Some psychologists, Erich Fromm among them, believed that the need for the transcendent was inborn. If it is, I would suggest that it is developed through constant acts of affirmation and destroyed by constant acts of shame, a psychological state Erikson designated as rage turned toward the self.[68] Is not rage the seemingly natural response to disaffirmation? Would I not rage against my self if others choose never to meet my gaze or detest the sight of me? I might also wonder whether the need for the transcendent is inborn. Might it be activated by that first encounter, that first observation, that first gaze? Might it be activated, in other words, by the parents' original affirmation of the newborn? Is not birth itself a transcendent experience?

But now let us turn this whole argument on its head and suggest that art itself may be affirming. We might well imagine that in the absence of interpersonal affirmations, a self may be affirmed by some metaphysical connections to art and, hence, artists, truly a different form of selfobject. From authors, painters, dancers, actors, and musicians, some of us discover our first tastes of both the metaphysical and the power of affirmation itself. A painting, play, or musical composition may put me in touch with my aliveness, my life force, and with it the realm of the transcendent as much, perhaps, as the direct affirmations of my parents and teachers. Could this be why so many young people need their music? At least one issue, one component of the equation, is called into question—namely, there is no return of the gaze in art, if literally we mean by this term sharing a glance, having eyes connect. Art does not literally return the look as much as it prompts the self to return its own look at itself. I am reflected in the book, in the painting, in the drama. I not only see my self seeing but I also see my self reflected back from the object of art. I see its beauty, its temperament, its emotions, and, ideally, my own as well. But art, because it fails to see and recognize me, does not pledge to take responsibility for me. It only prompts the idea of responsibility by revealing the ideal good or sense of beauty of my self. It prompts, in other words, the felt sense of affirmation and with it the corresponding life force.

As an inevitable and ironic correlate of the transcendent experience, the affirmation also ratifies a right to feel a death force, a life-no-more. The comedy and tragedy live within one another, and both reside within the self. Of course we laugh at the tragic and cry at the comedic. But how can this be so? If the parent deeply and authentically affirms the child (and the child, through her or his gaze, affirms the parent), then surely the child begins to discern the simple beauty of "merely" being alive. Affirmation, we have argued, is not merely biological drive or that energy (Freud's libido or life instinct)[69] connecting us to all animals, as much as it is the essence of the (felt sense of a) life force. At the very least, the child has encountered the outlines of what arises in him or her as the idea of being alive, an idea that well may be born in the moments Margaret Mahler calls "hatching," the period when the baby, now four to nine months old, begins to differentiate itself from its mother.[70] So where might the idea of death enter this idyllic scene?

The idea of death enters it, I believe, by raising up in the child the fundamental truth of existence, namely, that we all die. Much to a parent's chagrin, finitude is known to the child, even the most manifestly solipsistic, grandiose, or narcissistic child. We hardly need Freud's seminal studies to remind us of the sheer terror aroused in the child by the thought, not even the action, the anticipation, not even the reality, of separation. These experiences represent the earliest encounters with tragic demise. The mother

leaves the room for the barest instant and the child completely falls apart—
an apt expression, as the integrity of the self unravels. The self feels as if it
were disappearing (with the mother). It decompensates or feels itself to be
disintegrating. But the mother returns and in the bat of an eye—another
provocative expression—the child's self, as it were, or sense of self is reassem-
bled; it resumes its integrity. It feels safe and sound once again, all (sense
of) defectiveness having vanished as if nothing had just happened. Which
further implies that the integrity of the self is founded in human connection
as both Bowlby and Basch earlier suggested or, more literally, in the ability
of the self to locate another in its own presence and thereby feel life emanating from the association with another with which it feels eternally connected. My mother is not only always "out there," she is always "in here" as
well. That's point number 1. Point number 2 takes the form of a question:
Might it be that "in here" and "out there" are the same? Perhaps "it" is
always "in here."

From this time on in the child's life, one probably marked by the mere
capacity to remember mother and those earliest moments of separation, the
child knows more than the anxiety of separation; the child knows the terror
of ending, of something being no more, of mother being no more, of self
being no more.[71] Merely to satisfy any one of our sensations, thirst, for example, is to call up in us the memory of the thirst. Without this memory
there is no satisfaction of the original need. An old joke tells it all. A man is
noisily groaning in a train car and disturbing his fellow passengers: "Boy,
am I thirsty. Boy, am I thirsty." To quiet the gentleman and relieve the tension in the car, the conductor eventually brings him a glass of water. All is
at last quiet until the gentleman is once again heard groaning: "Boy, was I
thirsty. Boy, was I thirsty."

Extending this argument, we allege that in genuine affirmation you truly
are led to believe, if only by looking at me face to face and "experiencing"
or *recalling* the form of affirmation I provide you, the richness of the life
force. But just as this felt sense of living is called up in you, so, too, is its
twin, "lifelessness," the reality of disconnection leading ultimately to (the
felt sense of) finitude. To affirm you means at once that in my gaze you are
safe—I will keep an eye on you. But the safety I provide also makes it possible for you to confront the existence (in your self) of your own demise.
My gaze and from it my affirmation of you now make it possible for you
(and me) to reminisce on the subject of separation and tragedy (we both remember our thirsts or our longings). For me to be present in your eyes is
also for me to be no longer physically present, for you can imagine my

absence even as we touch one another, just as you can imagine my presence long after I have died. Said differently, my mere presence, you will eventually learn, cannot guarantee you immortality, and hence, even as we celebrate our connection, our intimacy, the conjoining of our selves, we mourn its (and our own anticipated) ending.

What we both have learned is that as wondrous as the existence of your otherness in me and my otherness in you may be—that truly we *are* each other rather than *have* each other—as wondrous as our mutual affirmations may be, and as essential as these affirmations are for the perpetuation of the life force that both of us comprehend and represent to our selves, they will not keep us away from death's door. The self is not only about being affirmed or disaffirmed, made to feel proud or humiliated, as Basch theorized. It is also about beginnings and endings that are always in sight; our minds would have it no other way. Like it or not, this remains one of the ineluctable dividends of affirmation: birth and rebirth sitting right alongside demise and death. Not pure metaphor, the notion bespeaks the reality that cells die even as they reproduce, wither away even as they grow in complexity.

The instant of my arrival necessarily evokes the impending instant of my departure. We both cherish most the moment of connection, the instant marking the beginning of the longest stretch of time we will enjoy together; it is the rebirth of our coupling (and, hence, the revered selfobject). By tomorrow, by tonight even, we are aware of our time together running out, the coupling not weakening exactly but its tenure, on this occasion anyway, diminishing, which serves as a reminder that our personal time is also lessening; no amount of affirmation can alter this reality. It is the history and destiny of our mutual affirmations that cause this to be the case. Arrivals and departures are shown on separate screens in every airport, but the screens are always mounted side by side. Passengers come and go. Who can say in the busy airport who is arriving, who is about to depart. Who, in a quick glance, can determine who is moving on, who is being left behind. Inevitably we wonder, might this be the last time for us? We know only that lovers cry at reunions as well as departures, just as they weep in encountering narratives of reunions and departures.

5 The Construction of Affirmation

We are approaching in this discussion several intriguing psychological ironies. In one respect, the act of affirmation brings forth two simultaneous needs: the need in affirmation for devotion to the other and the need in disaffirmation to repudiate the other. Said differently, an individual strives, Fromm postulated, for freedom and security if only to escape loneliness, perhaps that of disaffirmation. For Erikson, the competing urges of devotion and repudiation lay at the heart of the so-called adolescent identity crisis.[1] I need (the affirmation of) my parents, what Elizabeth Young-Bruehl and Faith Bethelard call "cherishment," but at the same time I must turn away from them (and their gaze) to establish my own personal sense of being.[2] Let us consider the Fromm argument first, in the context of affirmations.

It was Fromm's contention that as people become freer—and most theories of justice assume the individual's desire for freedom,[3] or is it, as Sartre wrote, that humans are condemned to be free?[4]—they become, ironically, more insecure, lonely, insignificant, alienated. They may even begin to feel more kindly toward a rigid social system laying out for them all the conventions, styles, norms, and customs they will ever require. One thing can be said about disaffirmation: at least our position in life vis-à-vis the other is clear and unambiguous. So we strive, Fromm argues, for more power, more wealth, more status, only to discover that our just dessert comes in the form of a felt sense of alienation.

How, then, do we reestablish our self and regain the sense of security we lost in seeking fame and fortune? We turn in one of two directions: either we become reunited with others, or we live the life of altruistic pursuits. If Fromm is correct, we renounce our freedom and surrender our individual integrity, which leads him in his observations in a direction that amplifies the thinking about affirmations and disaffirmations I present here.

As the individual seeks to regain some precious state of original security, a series of psychic mechanisms are put in motion. He turns to authoritarian rule; he reveals sadistic or masochistic strivings as well as a need for a larger group identification; he desires to see others suffer and enjoys destructiveness in all its forms; and finally, he seeks to eliminate people and objects.

These actions, some of them nihilistic as Basch also observed and born in what might be called disaffirmations of the self, can be justified in the name of duty, patriotism, conscience, and even love. Before meting out punishment, some of us still proclaim, "This is going to hurt me more than it will you."

We do something else, Fromm argued, to relieve the anxiety generated by our felt sense of insecurity: we tend to erase all differences between our self and others' selves. Said differently, imagining that we can become identical to the other, we conform to all social rules and customs. In this manner of being members of clusters we dare not call gangs or cells, we appear to abjure our very personalities. For R. E. H. Muuss, because there can be no identity without social interaction, it is not surprising that adolescents would go through what he labeled a compulsive period of conformity.[5] Children, especially, look to form symbiotic relationships in which they imagine living off another person. Through the process of identification presumably, children seek to become another, or they imagine they can swallow up or be swallowed up by another, a common theme in children's stories and myths.[6] In response to these precarious efforts, parents may do one of three things: give in totally to the child's emerging will; become destructive, in which case, Fromm alleges, children tend to withdraw; or withdraw from their children, in which case children tend to become destructive, not an atypical response to experiences of disaffirmation, as I suggested earlier.

Given our prior discussion, we recognize the face of the disaffirmed self, the self held hostage by no one, the self that has never met the (Levinas) gaze of eternal debt. This lacking self, this self of insecurity possibly advocating violent action, has been summoned by no one and thus cannot know anything resembling freedom because it knows little or nothing of its own being. Without a sense of self, there can be no sense of constraint on the self and therefore no sense of freedom. Of course the self feels insecure in its sense of freedom made inauthentic by its lack of constraint; it barely recognizes the boundaries delineating itself from others. The disaffirmed self, the little or belittled self—the "nehil" of "nihilism," meaning "little thing"—is a self taking responsibility for no one, a self affirming nothing. Its destructive orientations necessarily connote its preoccupation with its own demise.

Not so incidentally, Fromm turns to the power of love to rectify this felt sense of lack, advocating that parents offer respect to their children and help their children develop a balance between security and responsibility. His thoughts in this regard are akin to my own, as I would argue that in the act of affirmation a balance between security and responsibility cannot be adequately struck because the affirmation of being (security) augers the affirmation of nonbeing (insecurity). It is the inevitable irony, the inevitable tragedy, really, inherent in the life force. In the end, however, the affirmation wins out if only in the sense that the affirmed child feels neither the need to swallow the other nor the need to be swallowed up by the other. In responding to the commandment not to kill, the affirmed child eschews any form of violence or destructiveness at the same time recognizing at some level both the distinction between himself or herself and the other as well as the impossibility of his or her ever fully knowing, much less becoming, the other. How possibly could one forfeit one's personality! Inevitably one chooses attachment and devotion to family and life over separation from and repudiation of family and life.

One final aspect of Fromm's theory may prove helpful to this discussion of affirmation. Fromm outlined six fundamental needs, universal drives really, that he claimed were essential for establishing security and escaping loneliness. Interestingly, all six needs can be said to conform to the powers of authentic affirmation. First, in *relatedness*, an individual, Fromm alleged, finds connection with others through love, an act typically yielding an ability to know people as they really are, what we normally call empathy. Failure to accomplish this leads to the familiar patterns constituting the narcissistic personality.

We express these same thoughts when we speak of taking responsibility for the other, an act involving needs for nurturance, security, and the expression of intimacy. Relatedness involves knowing people for what they truly are, Fromm continues; they are that they are. One would argue, alas, that this is not entirely possible. We live only with the felt sense of the other or, put more precisely, the traces of otherness, but tend to feel content in the action of being held hostage by the other (the selfobject). Nonetheless, as affirmed human beings, we do know that as incomplete as our knowledge of the other may be, there genuinely is something called otherness; we acknowledge, in other words, that there is another person out there, apart from us, who is not merely the product of our own idiosyncratic constructions. They are people, importantly, with their own lives, their own selves. In contrast, I suspect that the disaffirmed one tends to imagine that others are but objects of her beliefs and personal constructions, mere characters in the drama she writes for herself, as well as for the world of others. In a sense, the disaffirmed is a potential terrorist. This notion may explain these ruminations of novelist Chester Himes: "My mind had rejected all reality as I had known it and I had begun to see the world as a cesspool of buffoonery. Even the violence was funny."[7]

Fromm's second universal need is *transcendence*, about which I have already spoken, the need to rise above our animal instincts and find purpose in our life, our genuinely creative stance, our unique voice, a sentiment echoed a half century later by Diane Ackerman.[8] Failure to satisfy this creative need, Fromm suggested, leads to destructive behavior. We would express these notions by saying that the purpose is to respond to the summons of the other and thereby proffer an affirmation of the other. It is the most creative act, perhaps, and surely the most ethical act a human being can undertake in that it literally re-creates the life force in another, or at least allows the other a felt sense of his or her own life force while warding off nihilistic tendencies.

Third on Fromm's universal drive list is the need for *rootedness*. Starting with a connection to nature, we move to a series of connections through which we eventually form a system of kinship or identification with something we call our community.[9] As Rebecca Walker writes in a memoir, "I stand with those who stand with me."[10] Fromm believed that we actually replace our earlier roots in nature through our connections with people. We would allege that the fundamental connection to life, be it in the state of nature or in the form of another human being, is found not simply in the respect we show the other but also in the requirement to take responsibility for the other; we have no choice in the matter. We are seen by the other, we naturally respond to (affirm) the other, and in this process of discovering our being and the being of the other and having our respective beings ratified we find precisely what Fromm calls our rootedness.

The *identity* need is Fromm's fourth universal drive, through which we develop our individual talents and in part set the stage for the work Erikson later would develop in several volumes on identity formation.[11] Significantly, Fromm advances the notion that we must develop our talents, intelligence, and potentials if we are to be fulfilled, something Rollo May postulated as well, as did John Dewey in a discussion in which he attempts to clarify the classical Roman concept of justice as being rooted in granting to another that which is rightly his or hers: "Or is what is owed to a person anything less than opportunity to become all which he is capable of becoming?"[12] Fromm is quick to point out that a genuine identity cannot be a borrowed one; it cannot derive completely from our identifications with others as we so often witness happening among adolescents, some of whom tend to identify with popular culture icons. True enough, but we would say that genuine identity finds its date of birth in the moment of the summons when we commence a journey ultimately leading to the recognition of our distinct being. Careers, marriages, and bearing children surely matter in our self-definitions, but genuine identity is located in the internal actions of the self following upon the original affirmation.

The baby whose parents answer the summons of her earliest look is born into an identity. There is nothing magical about this; we even claim to have observed it. A few days old and the newborn is already proclaimed to be her own little person possessing her own personality. Talents, competencies, what Howard Gardner aptly calls "human intelligences," do not an identity make. The fundamental answer to the question Who am I? is, I am that I am. But I cannot reach this conclusion until another makes me aware of the legitimacy of my own being through the act of affirmation. I desire to present my self as fixed. In disaffirmation I am not aware of the legitimacy of my own being; I am not that I am; I present my self as broken. Part of this awareness, furthermore, is the recognition that my being also involves non-being, being no more. More to the point, however, affirmation breeds the desire to know one's self along with the belief that knowledge of self is possible. The antithesis of nihilism, affirmation fundamentally underwrites a willingness to see one's self as it is, free of lenses, if this is ever truly possible. It is precisely what we often label a "generosity of spirit." It would seem to be the foundation, moreover, of the search for one's identity, a search requiring courage and diligence, an open mind, as they say, as well as an open heart, exactly as Kegan intoned.[13]

Although the search for identity may for some moments feel exhilarating, in the end I suspect it leads us all to tragedy. Thus we turn instead to more satisfying, rational constructs such as our gender, our career, and our educational and relational histories to shape that which we call our identity, our own personal story. A sense of my own genuine identity cannot go much further than some bare recognition, first, of being and nonbeing and, second, and equally significant, the fact that another (the other) has made it possible (through the work of affirmation) for me even to contemplate the mystery of identifying my self. The other has thereby given to me the felt sense of possibility that now sits at the heart of any reflection I undertake on my own identity. It is not that I may become a doctor, lawyer, school-teacher, or father that ultimately constitutes the identity conundrum. More precisely, it is that I am able to contemplate moving beyond mere being into a realm I imagine actually involves becoming me, my self.

The fifth of Fromm's psychological needs is that for a *frame of reference* and *object of devotion*. Through our powers of reason and imagination, Fromm suggests, and from our interest in history and our anticipations of the future, we seek to develop coherent views of our social and physical environments. This view or framework allegedly provides us an objective, rational perspective of that which we call "shared reality." Whatever else the framework offers, it ought to provide us some object to which we become devoted and through which we discover or construct meaning.[14] In this context one thinks of devotion to a figure called God.

I find myself drawn to Fromm's words but cannot fully embrace them. I cannot be certain, for example, of the distinction between objective and subjective frameworks, for I continue to wonder whether even the most affirmed among us is able to transcend subjective impressions of self and other, personal worlds and social worlds. I am not really sure how my sense of devotion and the meaning derived from it comes from labeling something objectively this or that. Following on the lines of the argument, moreover, I am not certain that we ever truly discover the objects—or are they selfobjects?—of our devotion but merely, as Levinas might say, the traces of what they are, might have been, or someday may become. The object seems to have vanished even as I discover it. I (subjectively) sense only that it has been here, near me.

Of course I am devoted to family and friends, but somehow they must be distinguished from those who have answered my original summons, those who not only inspired my sense of being but also gave birth in me, through the response to the summons, of a lingering presence of devotion. More to the point, in responding to the summons of the other, I am not necessarily expressing devotion, although in retrospect I may feel it as devotion. The word "devotion," meaning "to dedicate by vow," may just be as close as I can come to describing the sensation of the encounter with otherness. It is the act of answering the summons that causes me to "know" that I am devoted or the object of another's devotion. Once again, all I am left with is the trace of devotion. If I respond to the summons, as Levinas suggests, having reasoned out beforehand that I must do this to reveal my devotedness publicly, as in a vow, then it is not truly an act of devotion. It is reasoned rather than spontaneous, willful rather than automatic, obligatory rather than ethical; some of us, after all, feel married well before we take any public vow of devotion.

I pledge to be a great father throughout the nine months of my wife's pregnancy, but nothing prepares me for the instant of the birth and the first appearance of the miraculous stranger. Spontaneously, and seemingly without any rational action on my part, for I am unaware of thinking about any of this, I am pulled in, drawn to the child for life. As Erikson wrote, there is at work here something resembling a "life principle of trust" wherein persons simply commit themselves to others. But this principle represents a balance between an almost instinctive approach to another and a reasoned one. For as Erikson also observes, it is "prone to perversion by destructive forms of conscientiousness."[15] Thus, as we have repeatedly noted, I will love again and again. There can be no contract for parenting in this light because the sensation is purely subjective; once again, it appears to precede reason.[16] Nothing of it can be codified as the search for meaning or the legal or even moral obligations of the parent. Put it into contractual, rational, objective terms and we are describing a wholly different experience yielding a wholly different set of meanings about wholly different phenomena. Like ethics, meaning and devotion arrive together in the initial summons of the gaze calling us to take responsibility for the other. Referred to as after-the-fact experiences, we do not summon them; we discover they have arrived, one might say, when we were looking. And most of us lack the language to describe them.

The ultimate sense that meaning derives from the act of devotion makes sense to me only if I understand meaning as the appreciation of my own being and the power to create for my self the being in others as a function of the original devotion shown me by my affirmers. I do not really know the *meaning* of education. I do not really know the *meaning* of being married or fathering children. I create meaning partly out of my devotion but not directly because I have located the objects of my devotion. I find, that is, I call up (recall) and create meanings in what I read, but I find something or some sensation having to do with meaning, or so it seems to me, when I look for the first time in the face of my newborn. Here, too, is a template of meaning, a dawning of meaning, but again it is made possible not by some prior attachment or commitment to an object of devotion but in and through the act of devoting, which inevitably is found in the response to the summons.

Fromm's sixth and final need is for *excitation* and *stimulation*. Life, quite simply, is boring, Fromm wrote, without constant stimulation, activity, and the consequent sense of alertness, or what Ellen Langer calls "mindfulness."[17] As is true with the other five needs, the satisfaction of this need also, requires the availability of social and cultural opportunities. Locating the precise role of affirmation in the need for excitement offers a bit of a challenge. Nonetheless, I offer this argument.

Inherent in affirmation is a form of alertness (to the other and to one's self) that remains unparalleled; in contrast, the nihilism derived from disaffirmation yields an alertness essentially to nothing. In the act of affirming I am alert to my own life force, my own being, just as the affirmed one is made alert to his or her own life force, his or her being. To be stimulated by a movie is an action most of us know, but ultimately it may be an action of distraction. Entertainment always has the potential of pulling us away from our self. The stimulating movie or television program can take our mind off of things, can take our mind off of itself; so, too, can a posture of nihilism. The affirmation of another, either directly, person to person, or through the encountering of the artistic product, is stimulating essentially because it necessarily focuses one's mind on itself, allegedly the most stimulating of all mental activities.

If we think of that night with a special friend years ago, we may admit that we experienced a stimulation of a sort we never knew possible. Erotic surely, the experience is magnified because in addition to encountering the presence of another, we have encountered our own self, our own being. What has been aroused in us is not necessarily the sexual urge but the inciting of the mind to concentrate on itself and to affirm itself. For an instant we feel our self to be properly grandiose. Unfortunately, this action also often goes under the name of self-esteem.[18] Our entire culture, seemingly, rests on the need to feel good about oneself. Parents, teachers, and ministers are being taught in every quarter of the country to help people feel good about themselves (as opposed to making people understand the nature of the good life). The efforts are presumably noble, but in thinking about the work of authentic affirmation and, more particularly, affirmation formulated along the lines of taking responsibility for the other, as Levinas has intoned, feeling good about the self remains a purely sensational action, inferior in significance to the action of feeling about oneself or simply feeling one's self, of which the repudiated self appears incapable.

Feeling good about oneself may turn out to be yet another trick the mind plays on itself; how can I feel good about something that I logically call my self when I have never truly encountered my self? One wonders, in other words, whether self-esteem can be considered authentic if it has not been preceded by authentic self-reflection, which itself, if my argument is valid, has to be preceded by some fundamental recognition of the self (as somebody), which in turn derives from the original affirmation, all of them together yielding genuine humility. In this context recall that E. D. Hirsch has said that to praise students merely to raise their self-esteem regardless of their accomplishments ultimately causes a decline in self-esteem. Also consider John Santrock's definition of self-esteem as being "the global evaluative dimension of the self, also referred to as self-worth or self-image."[19] More generally, the actions one takes to make oneself feel good about one's self—"highs" in contrast to the "lows" (and "smalls") inherent in the definition of humility—can be as disingenuous as the actions the ego takes to becalm the throbbing, demanding, distraction-seeking id. Granted, the actions seem to work inasmuch as we imagine we feel a bit better, but genuine confrontation of the self has been cleverly avoided. The danger is to become preoccupied with the celebration of a nonjudging self, the self derived too often from disaffirmations.

Not so incidentally, the word "esteem" means to appraise or estimate, the very acts not engaged in as we affirm another. Affirmation hardly requires that we first make a rational appraisal of the other. Ironically, self-esteem, in the context of the self celebrating itself, too often implies a lack of appraisal or estimation of self and little or no consideration, significantly, of the other.[20] To believe that the celebration of one's self is tantamount to taking responsibility for another is pure whimsy. The affirmed of the culture offer respect to the other; they are not preoccupied with reducing the pain of others, thereby believing they are making them happy. (Some of them even dispense "happy" pills.) In this regard those people who seek merely to raise self-esteem run the risk of acting not unlike politicians speaking out of both sides of their mouth in their effort to gain support from everyone. Even more, the behavior of these dispensers of happiness appears to match the descriptions we find of the children of alcoholics, the classic "people pleasers."

Genuine self-esteem can come forth only in the form of meeting the gaze of the eyes of the other, not one's own inner eye. Which brings up the matter of ethical behavior, an issue prompted in part by these words from C. Eric Lincoln: "Today we are invited to believe that the only real responsibility man has is to himself and his own gratifications, and that all moral alternatives are equally valid since they have no meaningful reference beyond the self."[21]

Just as I can make you feel (that you feel) good about your self simply by helping you take your mind off whatever seems to be troubling you—a classic conceit of distraction—so can I raise your self-esteem even as I lead you down a dangerous and unethical path. Two better examples of disaffirmation, distraction, and immoral conduct, or what Paul R. Gross and Norman Levitt call "moral blankness," could not be drawn.[22] They perfectly reveal retreat from responsibility, the retreat that lies at the heart of disaffirmation. The problem is that the self-regard or self-reverence we seek to establish in the other through the action of building self-esteem can be accomplished only in the experiencing of genuine affirmation in which the reverence captured in ethical conduct is made possible by the act of taking responsibility for the other. Self-regard, in other words, is the act made possible by the affirmation of the self regarding itself. Having a wonderful time with someone or developing one's talents and competencies, as noted earlier, ultimately do not sufficiently increase self-reverence, which would seem to form only as a function of the self confronting itself as it does in the development of what Fromm and Erikson alike call identity.

Put differently, by definition every act of stimulation must pass through an internal judging or experiencing self. You and I go to a production of *Hamlet*. You are enthralled, made ecstatic by what you see and hear. I am bored, as the well-suited expression goes, "out of my mind." Whatever has occurred on the stage before us passed through your mental filters and came out causing you to feel various sensations. My filters, in contrast, appeared to block everything; even poor Hamlet's madness and demise proved to incite nothing in me. In both of us, however, our filters are nothing less than our minds confronting themselves upon the incorporation of external stimuli. It is the work accomplished in these mind fields that determines our reactions to the performance. It is self-work, not mere self-esteem, that makes it possible for us to experience the otherness named Shakespeare. It is exhilaration of self, not merely the celebration of the self or self-esteem, that remains behind in the form of traces of this mind work.

Now the inevitable question: Is this receptivity to *Hamlet* a function of you having been to the theater hundreds of times and my never having even heard of *Hamlet* before this evening? Surely this factor of prior experience must matter. But what also matters is the receptivity to human stimuli made possible by the acts of affirmation, not just by prior experience with great literature. My self must be "open," vulnerable, not just to the stimuli to which I think Fromm refers but also to the reverberations in itself that it experiences as a function of encountering *Hamlet*. In genuine affirmation and in what Levinas called "sensibility"—recall Aristotle's term "insensibility," meaning a form of feelinglessness—made possible through the summons of the other, I find my self able to respond to *Hamlet*; I can feel the stimulation and sense of being roused by *Hamlet* even without ever having read a word of the play. I am responding to the summons of another, Hamlet in this instance, and I am stirred; it is self-esteem writ large because it is the self writ large. I have done the work, literally defined as calling on (or calling up) the traces of affirmations living within me that make me (internally) susceptible to this (external) stimulation. *You* don't do it for me completely, *Hamlet* doesn't do it for me completely; *I* must do it for me completely by my willingness to reflect on my own being, my own self, which I do in part through the confrontation with the Danish stranger. Come to think of it, is not the encountering of a miraculous stranger a moment of stimulation and excitation? Are not the arrivals of our children the most exciting events of our lives?

I understand the social foundation of Fromm's thinking when he insists that none of the six fundamental human needs he advances may be satisfied without the person being supported by his or her society and culture. Poverty clearly dehumanizes and disaffirms people. Its mere existence proves that too many in the society have systematically refused to answer the summons of others in the society. Too many people, in other words, are willing to allow the widow, the widower, the orphan, and those who are homeless go without recognition and shelter. Too many choose to sequester the poor, if only, perhaps, to avoid their gaze. By definition, poverty is a living form of the unethical.[23]

Yet the conditions of poverty hardly confer disaffirmed status on all citizens. Sensibility and poverty are not mutually exclusive; the so-called good life hardly is built on material possessions. Moral poverty, philosophers have taught us, is far more egregious than material poverty. Although most of us rightly cringe at the mere mention of the concept of the "noble savage," it may have merit if only because to one degree or another we are all noble savages; each of us lives with the potential for nobility and savagery. Shakespeare knew this well. He wrote in Romeo and Juliet: "The times and my intents are savage-wild; / More fierce and more inexorable / Than empty tigers or the roaring sea."[24] What causes the nobility and inoculates us from savagery is not social class or social standing, formal education or self-esteem, but the experience of affirmation. And this just might be the result of nothing more than good fortune. Had I had those parents rather than these, my sense of self may have been profoundly different. More precisely, had I had the parents my parents were at the time they gave birth to my other siblings, my sense of self may have been profoundly different.

If ever John Rawls's notion about the individual not truly *deserving* anything is valid, it is in this realm of those chosen for affirmation—literally the "chosen people."[25] Some of us are blessed; we just happened to be in the right womb at the right time. Some of us cannot get a nibble in response to our gazing at others; we are the orphans and the homeless ones others stare at before they choose to walk on. In Kegan's terms, we are able to recruit very little in the way of support and affirmation.[26] People, it would seem, have turned a blind eye toward us, the same blind eye we eventually will turn toward our own self. In the end, there will be no self-regard precisely because the self appears unable to regard itself.

In the same light, the disaffirmed appear unable to regard the exterior world morally, much less confer honor on any of its inhabitants. It is not exactly that the disaffirmed exhibit an inability to call up (or recall) the moral way, what Aristotle called "rectitude" or "righteousness." Rather, it is that the external world, in a manner of speaking, has already been renounced, dishonored, repudiated, and broken through acts of disaffirmation. The disaffirmed, in other words, find no life value, nothing honorable in the exterior world. In their personal nihilistic algebra, there is no worthwhile variable to be discovered outside their own self; they find nothing in it to trust, no source of personal ratification. Which means that cultural dictates, social norms, values determining desirable behavior to which others in their community consent, mean little if anything to them. The same goes for people, even children, especially children, who too often represent convenient objects of exploitation and abuse. Children by nature bruise easily.

Fromm himself has written just this. Self-fulfillment, defined by us as the ability to encounter one's self and contemplate the notion not exactly of potential but of possibility, is the authentic action properly defined as self-esteem. Arthur Jersild described the action as the ability to approach "the reaches of [one's] own strength and ability."[27] To experience possibility may be the greatest rush of all for it represents the rush of freedom born truly in the cradle of justice; it goes by the name of liberty. But again, this liberty connotes a (healthy) reverence of self derived from having been affirmed while comprehending that its perpetuation depends entirely on answering the summons of the other. My child has self-esteem if she has "witnessed" the act of taking responsibility and thereby feels herself to have been born into a genuinely ethical condition ultimately predisposing her to respond to the gaze of the other. Longing to be taken hostage, she will turn outward; she already has.

This brings us to a dilemma offered by Erik Erikson, one understood better after reviewing Erikson's famous eight stages of psychosocial development.[28] Erikson theorized eight developmental eras spanning the life cycle in which the genetic predispositions of the individual—predispositions defined by Heidegger as belonging to the realm of the Umwelt—encounter the constraints and realities of the society and culture. During each of these eight monumental periods, a person confronts a very rudimentary dilemma: Will one's psychological needs (Umwelt, or the world of our biological inheritance) characteristic of the stage be met (in the realm of the Mitwelt) with affirmation or disaffirmation? Will one present himself or herself to the world, in other words, as fixed or broken? And what, moreover, is the ramification for the development of consciousness and identity (the realm of the Eigenwelt) of either outcome?

Erikson argued that at each stage a successful psychosocial resolution of the dilemma remains forever within the individual in the form of a basic strength or virtue. These virtues included hope, will, purpose, competence, fidelity (the strength, incidentally, of the adolescent stage of development, which Erikson labeled "Identity Cohesion versus Role Confusion"), love, care, and wisdom. Employing the language of affirmation, I suggest that these eight strengths make up the felt sense of affirmation in a person living in the final stage of the life cycle. The act of affirmation, however, remains unchanged at each stage. No matter what the child's psychosocial needs may be, the parents' essential role as affirmer remains immutable: regardless of one's age or the nature of the dilemma characteristic of a particular stage, affirmation endures as the sense of being held hostage by the other and thereby forever taking responsibility for the other. Of course we feed and clean the child and hope in this way the child develops a sense of trust (in his or her self and the world) and some measure of autonomy. But the foundation of our optimal response to the child's needs remains the affirmation.

But the self is not totally dependent on social affirmations. As Arnold Modell persuasively argues, the self is also capable of generating itself from within.[29] It does this, Modell suggests, by choosing values endowed with particularistic meanings that we (our selves) impute, although there is often conflict among the dynamics of self-affirmation, self-actualization, and social affirmation.[30] Still, one wonders whether even the self-generating self can do its work (Eigenwelt) totally free of the protective skin of externally based affirmations (Mitwelt). Where, after all, does the self-generating self derive the original meanings it imputes to the values it finds desirable?

Disaffirmation, in contrast, could be said to be comprised of what Erikson called the resulting maldevelopments, weaknesses, we might consider them, occurring at each of the eight critical stages. These included such phenomena as withdrawal, compulsion, ruthlessness, fanaticism, repudiation, rejectivity, and disdain, a collection of psychological variables that well could define the felt sense of nihilism as Basch also asserted. Either way, with strengths or weakness in hand (or really in head) at every stage consciousness is reborn and develops, and with it, the (sense of) self and identity emerge.

Once again, the dialectic formed between devotion and repudiation, grasping and letting go, seemingly an insupportable mental exercise, is made possible in part by the original affirmation. In the first place, the affirmation supplies the hidden lexicon making possible the deliberations called for by the dialectic. The sense of being created by the affirmation—truly the subtext of the period of the life cycle Erikson labeled the "identity moratorium"—allows me to feel the sensation of devotion, which really is the devotion that the other has "placed in me." It is a devotion that I have discovered, that I can recall (call up), not something that I imagine, although I am not conscious of it being placed within me. It, too, emerges as an after-the-fact experience.

At the same time, the affirmation affords me the courage to act as if I did not require that devotion. And somewhere in all this mix lies (the felt sense of) genuine freedom. Wittingly or not, the adolescent relies on the (traces of) affirmation and with it the sense of devotion to break away temporarily from the gaze of responsibility during that stretch of time Erikson designated as the identity moratorium, a period of maximal consideration of self, minimal responsibility to others. Granted, in seeking autonomy, some adolescents focus on the "self" aspect of the concept but not the "law" aspect that allegedly pertains to responsibility. Erikson, too, was concerned that adolescent freedom bring with it appropriate demonstrations of responsibility. He might well have concurred with C. Eric Lincoln's sentiment that "unconventional self-expression is a legitimate and valued aspect of learning, of growing up, even when it is of doubtful immediate practicality. It is one of the more critical rites of passage."[31]

The very concept of an adolescent moratorium, after all, connotes suspension and cessation, in this case of an affirming self. It signifies an interim during which time the gaze of others will not prompt a response; for the moment, all personal recruitment offices are temporarily closed. For the interim, a self-reflective lifestyle has been chosen, not necessarily an affirming lifestyle.[32] One can only assume that upon the completion of these particular self-reflections, sensibilities (directed toward the other) return and the person is prepared to resume a life of ethical responsibility, the days of self-indulgence, as necessary as they may be for the development of identity and, yes, adolescent self-esteem, completed. It is time now for the eyes to once again turn outward as well as inward. The self in self-regard must now include the self of the other as well.

Eventually, the identity crisis and often attending moratorium run the risk of becoming an act, a conceit, the self deceiving itself. There is no pure autonomy, after all; as the ancient Greek philosophers taught us, no one is self-sufficient. We merely pretend to be self-sufficient in order to satisfy the need of the ego to be its own man or woman. As Carol Gilligan and her associates note, "To see self-sufficiency as the hallmark of maturity conveys a view of adult life that is at odds with the human condition."[33] Autonomy may be what we experience at night in bed, in the darkness, in our aloneness, when we feel safe, or at least imagine that we are safe. It is the affirmation, recognized or not, that holds us aloft during those extended moments of the identity moratorium and offers us the language to undertake the sort of ruminations required during our adolescent identity crisis. As Hegel observed, it is recognition or acknowledgment, what we are calling affirmation, that makes self-consciousness possible in the first place.[34] Now, for the first time possibly, we explore not merely what we might become in our careers but reflect as well on our finitude, our sense of debt, our sense of solitude and aloneness, and our recognition of being held hostage by our parents precisely through the original affirmations, the affirmation of them by us and of us by them.[35] Indeed, the act of the self reflecting on itself, speaking about itself to itself and therein discovering its voice, is also born in the original affirmation. How possibly would I deliberate on something whose existence I do not comprehend, whose barest outline I cannot decipher? How do I possibly begin to think about my self? the adolescent wonders. How do I possibly begin to think about being and nonbeing, death and dying, and not terrify my self?

To an extent, the answer lies in the statement that merely asking the questions, merely wondering, commences the reflection of the moratorium. Through the original affirmation, the self already accepts itself to the degree that it can consider being no more, which means that the original affirmations have successfully done their job. At very least, affirmations offer a counterforce to the problem suggested by Ernest Schachtel, who observed that too regularly adults fail to provide children the language in which they can describe (to themselves as well as others) experiences of delight, either during the experiences or afterward. Affirmations supply this language, as well as a foundation for memory. For in establishing a sense of one's being, they at least put one in regular contact with (the felt sense of) sensations.

The affirmed child, in other words, can recall his self, for his self is fixed. He can sense himself, sense his feelings, feel his feelings. The disaffirmed child, in contrast, particularly the abused child, appears impervious to these sensations. There is nothing of value about self to be recalled; life itself comes to be debunked. Many psychologists point to what they call "psychological numbing" as a prominent symptom of abuse.[36] The numbed child may even go to the length of slicing open his skin—the act is called "cutting"—to feel any sensation (of the self) whatsoever.[37]

Taking the argument one step further, we allege that the satisfaction derived from the gaze of affirmation relieves one of the terror although hardly the knowledge of finitude. The heard child, the seen child, the affirmed child, the genuinely recognized child, is reminded (by which we mean lives with the traces) of the experience of living (partly with others), the self revealing itself to itself along with the meanings of being alive (with itself and with others). As Erikson wrote, "In the social jungle of human existence, there is no feeling of being alive without a sense of identity."[38] In addition, the affirmed child is reminded that although death lurks at all hours, it need not destroy the beauty and integrity of the self. Thus is born, perhaps, an answer to the question of what's the point of living when in the end you are only going to die?

In one respect, living and dying, or our mental representations and constructions of living and dying, are captured and made possible by the affirmation. The affirmation forms what might be called the "quality of emotion" attending the felt sense of being alive, the sense of presenting our self to life. Optimism and pessimism, if they do not simply spill out of the physiological chemistry of moods, represent the results of the forms of affirmations or the lack of affirmations. So, too, is resilience, the ability to rebound from defeat or setback. The ability to cope, an often used word in the psychological vocabulary, is really an ability to meet or encounter a particular issue or circumstance. If it is not a component of the person's inborn character, coping, in this regard, is itself a product of the work of (self) affirmation in that the self is taking responsibility for itself. Coping, after all, means meeting, encountering, the self encountering that with which it must cope. "Don't worry," we say. "I'll handle it; I'll cope with it."

Granted, much of human resilience, a concept suggesting a sort of psychological elasticity, is probably a characterological trait; it appears that some children emerge from the womb with greater resiliency than others. It makes sense, furthermore, that the self that has been affirmed would not be made to feel deflated, inferior, or illegitimate merely because of some rejection; it stays strong, realistically grandiose, all the while differentiating itself from the actor or circumstance that has rejected it. No matter the circumstances, the affirmed self can always call up good memories of itself. The affirmed self tends not to personalize the rebuke as much as the disaffirmed self, which concludes that external rebuke, no matter how seemingly insignificant, represents confirmation of the original disaffirmation. That I did not get into the college of my choice *proves* that I am no good. But affirmations do something else as well, as subtle (and postmodern) as this next point in the discussion may at first appear.

How do I ever know whether the life I am leading is something genuinely "out there" or merely my felt sense, my construction, of what is out there? Can I ever know or convince my self that what I feel life to be is what it truly is? Could anybody else ever wholly validate my constructions? Whatever we believe or feel something to be—and many insist that life is but an illusion, the product of one's own mental perceptions and constructions rather than the result of a preordained developmental order—we can always offer up the question, How do I know this to be true? Well, we respond, it sure *feels* that way to me; it sure *appears* that way to me. "You think that way too, don't you?"

Said differently, our answer comes forth in the form of our personal narrative at this point in time, the story we tell, the story we hear ourselves telling, the story that seems always to have been there, for the story is our presentation of self. Essentially this is the felt sense of being and of being alive, the felt sense of the way things seem to be, not to mention the way I feel my self to be. But, in fact, I don't know any of this to be the case. Quite often, actually, my feelings of the way things are and the way I am turn out not to be true, or at least turn out not to be confirmed by anything in the exterior world. I always felt that you did not like me, and I am surprised now to learn that you do, which means that there is something called reality "out there" exempt from my own personal constructions; my periodic discoveries and surprises confirm this.

Putting this point in a slightly different context, affirmation plays a critical role in shaping personality, especially if we conceive of personality partly as the discussions I have with my self and you about the way the world works, the way I work, and how I feel about the way the world works and I work. If I am affirmed, that is, if I feel my self has been affirmed and believe, furthermore, in some deep recess of my self that I must take responsibility for (the lives of) others or for (my sense of) the conditions in which others survive—and affirmations shape these perceptions of the lives and conditions of others—then it is likely that I will not perseverate on the idea of the badness or brokenness of the world. My sight is set on the good (ethical) work I must undertake or, more likely, on the traces of the good I detect and am able to recall from having acted ethically. My sight is set on the eyes (and the I) of the others. The affirmed person, therefore, affirms the exterior of his or her own being, the reality that he or she shares and creates with others.

If, on the other hand, I am preoccupied with how dreadful the world is— and dread is an appropriate sensation for the disaffirmed soul—how terribly I am constantly being treated, then aware of it or not, I am presenting a shamed self, one consumed by a death force. I am left feeling there is no place in the world for my self, a self that has been repudiated, left stranded. In the absence of my being held hostage by anyone, I am sentenced to live the unfulfilled life alone. I have become the widow, the widower, the orphan, the homeless one. I may also have become the shooter in the high school or the batterer in the home.[39]

The affirmed child is startled by acts of violence. He or she finds destruction not appalling, really, but surprising, literally incredible. I reflected on this notion in hearing an account of my grandson, the little puddle jumper, who was bitten by a child in another Seattle park. Obviously hurt, one could have predicted that Luke would have burst into tears and run to his mother seeking comfort. In point of fact, he walked to his mother revealing the hurt not of physical pain but of incredulity. Utterly bewildered, he had never in his affirming home experienced such a thing. The biting, therefore, confirmed nothing at all about him; it reinforced nothing about his reflections on his self. Its sheer unlikelihood left him in disbelief; it did not leave him disbelieving either in himself or in his mother. In a word, his self had not been dislodged from its (sense of) home as is the self, one imagines, of the disaffirmed child, the biting child perhaps.

The violent act of another toward oneself or another becomes an anathema in the affirmed child's felt sense of the life force. It denotes the complete and total violation of the commandment to take responsibility for the other. Thou hast in fact killed! In the act of violence, really in the actor of violence, something has gone terribly wrong to bring him or her to the point of personifying or acting out the death force, thereby making death palpable. The violent person necessarily believes himself or herself to be defined in terms of the death force. An obvious consequence of violence is that it disrupts the life force, ending life altogether. Violence breaks life; that is its sole purpose.

Merely to witness violence or learn of it as we do when the media bombard us with stories of a murder in a school causes us to imagine that our own life force has momentarily been wounded or disrupted. For a while we may even feel traumatized, we imagine that we cannot cope, we cannot go on. Sensing the emergence of a death force within our selves, we say we are broken, destroyed by the news of the violence, and in a sense this pronouncement is valid. All the while, the violent one lives with his memories of the traces of violence he himself has ignited. For the violent one, blinded by rage, has looked into the eyes of another and killed him. He has permanently ended the encounter of the gaze, permanently destroyed any hope of taking responsibility for another. As he has literally witnessed the force of death (his own death force), so does he witness himself as the object of disaffirmation. Others, perhaps, have observed him commit violence; they have witnessed him destroy life. The commandment not to kill has exploded in the faces of the witnesses, as the expression goes, right before their eyes.

Or perhaps only the violent one himself, along with the victim, of course, has witnessed his act of violence; perhaps the act has gone unseen by others, just as the violent one himself feels unseen by others, although, interestingly enough, many of us insist there is always a witness, always someone who gazes down on us, especially so when we believe we are no longer able to gaze on ourselves as being moral. Either way, we have encountered disaffirmation writ large, and no amount of television reportage can bring us anything other than traces of the violence and thus traces of the violent one. No matter how much prime time he receives—and in our culture the more violent and degrading the act, the more prime time he will receive—the more invisible to himself he becomes. For the disaffirmed are typically mere caricatures, people doing their best to model themself (really their self) after someone, something, anything. In this regard, as R. E. H. Muuss observed, "The peer group, the clique, and the gang do help the individual in finding his own identity in a social context, since they provide the individual with both a role model and direct feedback about himself."[40] The disaffirmed live their life with what psychologists call a "false self," a self derived from self-ignorance. Be it willful or natural, ultimately theirs is a self unaware of itself. They may even wish to believe they are doing the right thing, conducting themselves in the right manner, but the right thing for them often turns out to be a caricature of morality and decency.

Ultimately, they are reckless sorts, foolish even, and thus prone to vice and evil rather than virtue. Most likely they remain unable to fashion a proper morality that honors the goodness of people, a notion they would find to be an anathema. As Aristotle observed, it is not so much our abilities that determine our lives as much as it is our choices, the very choices, the

Stoics taught, that lead us toward happiness or unhappiness, a message, as millions of readers know well, that young Harry Potter learned early on.[41] For in disaffirming another, we make it unlikely that he or she will know genuine courage, the moments when, in behalf of another and unseen, one is willing to risk one's own well-being, one's own self. In their lack of confidence, the disaffirmed surely will know cowardice, just as in their excessive, ill-founded, and false sense of confidence they will know recklessness. What makes their sense of confidence ill-founded is that they must forge it in the absence of affirmation. Thus it too often becomes a caricature of genuine self-assuredness or self-reliance, traits often absent in foster children.[42] We know this character as the schoolyard bully, a character known in the psychological literature for his or her inability to make appropriate social psychological adjustments.[43]

In this regard consider Aristotle's categories of courage, each one of which seems to fit the ostensibly (inauthentically) courageous actions of the disaffirmed.[44] The persons who act out of a fear of punishment; the persons who act because their passion boils over and thereby destroys any sense of moral judgment; those who appear so mellow, the so-called cool ones—Aristotle spoke of them as sanguine—they seem almost immune to emotion; and finally the ignorant ones, who presumably either do not appreciate or openly disregard the precarious and outright terrifying circumstances of their lives. As the saying goes, "I may be gutsy, but I'm not stupid."

All the notoriety, celebrity, and fame granted the disaffirmed one by dint of his violent action in a distracted, sensation-driven culture, along with his outright rejection of another, can never compensate for the (traces of) disaffirmation alive within him that he is able to sense.[45] They are, perhaps, the only living pieces of being alive within him. As perverse as it may sound, he himself often reports that he has never been "more alive" than when committing his violent act. He has never been "more in touch" with himself or someone else, never "seen them more clearly" as when he has been involved in the rape or stabbing or murder of that someone. The violent act is even felt to be erotic, a (perverse) life force experience. "The liberating thrill and joy of hate and violence," Stein wrote, "come to be understood as radical affective-emotional-defense against total self-doubt, self-contempt, and utter despair. The banishment to nobodiness is replaced by the self-experience of ecstatic all-ness. If only for a time, 'they,' not 'we,' are nothing."[46] Similarly, in writing about the murders committed at Columbine High School in Colorado, M. Bai observed, "For a few horrific hours the school outcasts finally had all the power—and they wielded it without mercy or reason."[47] As I write these words, a notorious murderer has demanded that his execution be made open to the public. How ironic that to his last breath he seeks a response to his gaze. "Look at me!" he cries out. "At least watch me die." Will we, in response, accept his invitation? And will we demand that at the moment of his death he appear hooded, his eyes hidden from us?

Violent action, a perversion of the life force born, most likely, from the lack of affirmation, rids the other being of possibility, the very sentiment dominating the definition of the violent actor. "What's the point of it?" the disaffirmed one reasons. "It will only come to ruin. I'll never get into college. I'll never pass the test or get the job." "Careful," we reply. "You run the risk of the self-fulfilling prophecy: if you believe things will happen, you will unwittingly cause them to occur." True enough. But the disaffirmed one's nihilistic sentiment, his literally shameful (unaffirmed) outlook, bespeaking as it does a death force, represents his sense of the destructive forces of the world, his meager opportunities in it, his damaged presentation of self, his minimal sense of possibility, his minimal sense of self as possibility. As another expression has it, "We are always our own worst enemies." Often true, but now we recognize that without affirmation, without others accepting our gaze, accepting our being, we never learn to take responsibility for others or for our self. We remain permanently unable to call up this most noble of commitments. In Kegan's words, we can neither solicit aid nor offer it.[48]

Consider in this regard the common act of the father who abandons his family, an act one may well label violent. He literally turns his back on them, refuses to show his face to them. It is an act of the most profound form of disaffirmation. Affirmation, after all, often turns out to be little more than looking at the child. But this implies being there in the presence of (and for) the child. In abandoning his child, the father has announced that he will take no responsibility for the child. In essence, the child is on her own, even if this makes her feel helpless, which of course is the inevitable dividend of disaffirmation.

The result, publicly exhibited or not by the child, is terror and grief. With the life force withdrawn or denied, only the death force, the force of destruction of self and others, remains available to the child. As the father disappears, so does the sense of the life force, not to mention the sense of possibility. If you abandon me, then I abandon my self as well, although to the outside world I act as if I have reciprocated your rejection by abandoning *you*. In his autobiography, Jean-Paul Sartre remarked that if he had had a father, he would have had a future.[49] His words make perfect sense. Others' lives affect our felt sense of our destinies and, again, our possibilities. What is it we are saying when we announce to our children, "I believe you can become anything you wish; I believe that all your dreams can come true"? Are we not affirming the child and articulating the words and (primitive) felt sense of possibility? Are we not telling them they possess an imagination and a free will that can take them almost anywhere? In affirming another, are we not saying that you may now roar your presence in the world? As the expression has it, you may now discover your voice and then broadcast it. "Rest not till you rivet and publish yourself of your own personality," Walt Whitman wrote in "To a Pupil," words, incidentally, that might actually have ruffled Ralph Waldo Emerson, who warned, "My life is for itself, and not for a spectacle."[50]

In abandonment, rejection, and disaffirmation, however, inevitably acts of violence, we communicate just the opposite. Your dreams, your sense of possibility, are now shattered. Your will is no longer free; it is owned, in a sense, by me because of my refusal to accept responsibility for you and thereby provide the foundation of security you require as you develop a sense of life and being. The mere act of the parent who stays, the mere act of the child observing the parent committing to stay—Joseph Goldstein, Anna Freud, and Albert Solnit, we are reminded, called it the need of children for an average predictable environment[51]—serves as an act of genuine affirmation. "Don't worry," we tell our lover. "I'm not going anywhere." We telephone, email, fax those we love. We leave messages, they hear our voice; our presence is still with them: I am here. We need them to be here, we need them to hear us. What could be further from violence! "Mommy and Daddy are going to work now, but we will see you later."

Mister Rogers, the beloved figure of the long-standing television program for children (and adults too) *Mr. Rogers' Neighborhood*, knows all about affirmation. We notice how he concludes every broadcast with affirmations. First, he assures the children that he will return, then he assures them that he likes them "just the way they are." If his affirmations do not begin to creep into the souls of his television audience, children who believe with all their hearts that he is speaking directly to them, he has at least calmed them, temporarily quieted a degree of their unrest and anxiety as if he were reading to them before they fall asleep. As I say, children watching his program know that Mr. Rogers is looking at them! And adults, I suspect, wish the messages were meant for them as well. And so they are.

Affirmation comes to be internalized as (the felt sense of) the reality of possibility. Take affirmations out of our lives, which is done when a caretaker walks off the job (of taking responsibility for us), and we have no prospects, no future, no foundation for hope. We have memory, of course (of the abandonment), as well as the capacity to anticipate (a reunion or reconciliation). But again, without affirmation of the self, all the self can do is conjure a future that resembles or reenacts the past in the manner that Freud called a "repetition compulsion."[52] It may not be a compulsion, however, as much as it is the sole piece of behavior a person finds in his or her personal repertoire. Affirm the child and, as they say, hope springs eternal; the child has made a life of grace, a life of goodwill and gratefulness. He or she is fixed for life. Shame the child, which in a sense is the essential act of disaffirmation, and the child lives a life of (imposed) disgrace.[53] The child has been humiliated and thus perceives itself undeserving of affirmation, which in turn means undeserving of being, which in turn means living a life dominated by flirtations with tragedy and the forces of death. Like broken buildings, certain people require rehabilitation as well.

What is the sign that one has been disgraced, humiliated, shamed, disaffirmed? It is, purely and simply, the inability to reveal one's eyes to another. It is the refusal to return the look, the renunciation of the gaze. Without affirmation, there is nothing resembling recognition, the very recognition that commences in the child when the parents lean down merely to look at him or her. Metaphorically looking away, the self refuses to recognize itself; it *cannot* recognize itself. There is no self-regard because the self can neither regard itself nor reflect upon itself. "Don't look at me!" the shamed child cries out, if in fact we have not already symbolically cloaked him in a veil. In return, we, the shamers, eschewing any communication that might even slightly resemble an affirmation, blurt out: "Leave the room at once! I can't stand the sight of you! How dare you show your face to me!" This is what the child means when he says he has been "dissed." Thus the self riddled by shame, the self lacking affirmation, literally or figuratively disappears. It may force itself to become invisible in the form of self-destructive acts or at least render itself unrecognizable even to itself. As others pledge not to look on the shamed one, so does he or she pledge not to look upon himself or herself.[54]

Societies have always had those they designate as undesirable, intolerable, those not meant for public viewing, the lepers and pariahs. But who has taken the time to investigate the self-perceptions of these disenfranchised ones, these unwelcome strangers? Who lingers a while considering the effect on a person of feeling their self to be ugly, impure, dishonest, unacceptable, stigmatized?[55] We tend to respond only to their faces, their symptoms, their outbursts, their expressions of (narcissistic) rage in which their self-hatred approaches unbearable levels, their utterly inhuman acts toward self and others, their violence. Their mere presence is construed by us to be a public act of violence. How dare they enter our life and cause us to look upon them!

We once imagined that children, along with animals and those who are mentally ill, were incapable of killing themselves. We now know this not to be true.[56] Shamed children "understand" the "value" and "purpose" of self-destruction and act accordingly; this material they can recall. Suicide is not only the hostile message sent to those meant to be one's lifelong affirming figures but may also be the ultimate act in which the self is obliged to engage as a response to (personally imposed) shame or social renunciation. Not surprisingly, a recent investigation reveals that family connectedness seems to be a protection against suicide in adolescents.[57] If affirmation represents the life force (Eros) to the self, then shame necessarily represents the death force (Thanatos). Shaming, the antithesis of affirming, necessarily destroys. It is an act of murder, not only of the soul of the other but also of the self of the other. It is intended to reject or annihilate every last piece of otherness, causing the self psychologically to resuscitate or reconfigure itself. Shaming makes clear my intention to make you disappear, to have you die. The shamed one, Erikson wrote, "would like to force the world not to look at him, not to notice his exposure." Levinas is correct, I believe, when he theorizes that born in the mutual gaze is the summoning of our moral obligation to take responsibility for the other and thereby create the genuinely just relationship.[58] The good (moral) person always has his or her eyes on us; he or she is looking out for us. In shame, however, we enact the very edict Levinas postulated resides within the summoning, the commandment born in the gaze: "Thou shalt not kill," or in the words of St. Thomas, "Harm should not be given to another."

As I write these words, two people, a beloved couple, have been murdered in a quiet New England college town. In mourning, their friends seek to reconnect with them in the only way possible: they remember, they tell stories of the couple to themselves and to one another. "And if you crossed their path and entered into their orbit, even remotely," a friend recalled days after the tragedy, "they would make sure to keep their eye out for you."[59]

In the act of shaming, I kill, you die. I refuse to look at you; you dare not look at me. "All my father had to do was look at me," we say, "and I felt myself dying inside. I wanted to go someplace and disappear." In the act of shaming, I cause you to redefine yourself and thus your right to be; I demand that you hide, or at least hide your face. I cannot look upon you, but it is not because you are the object of shame or, more likely, my shaming of you. Rather, it is because I cannot face you when I realize that I have violated the commandment inherent in the gaze, in the meeting of the eyes, just as Levinas asserts. It is not exactly that you do not deserve to be seen or heard; it is that I dare not look upon you when I violate the ultimate commandment, Thou shalt not kill. I execute no one, be it by shaming, hanging, gas, or injection, without first covering their eyes. First the possibility for the gaze is destroyed, then the self is destroyed. I ask again: if the demands of the aforementioned murderer are met and his execution is televised, will we watch, or will we turn away? Jeff Jacoby may speak for more people than ever we imagined: "Justice will be done on May 16 [2001] when the man who butchered those children is himself put to death. It is wrong that he die in secret, behind closed doors, *as though his execution is something shameful.* It isn't. The death penalty is how a just and decent society responds to murder. Society should be allowed to *bear witness*" (emphasis added).[60]

Do we not justify the murderer's act with our own act through the expression, "An eye for an eye"? Does not the courageous one, the pure and innocent one, demand that he be allowed to look us in the eye, wearing neither mask nor veil, when we commit the act of murder which we justify as the concluding chapter of justice? Does he not look upon us, his eyes revealing forgiveness, for he may never stray from the obligation to take responsibility for us—"Forgive them for they know not what they do." Or does he look upon us with shame in his eyes, rejecting any form of affirmation, thereby wishing to induce in us, in our otherness, the very shame we have hurled at him? At the moment of another's death even, we seek affirmation of our acts, of our being. Treat each day as if it were the last day of your life, we are counseled. Tell people now what you think of them; affirm them now, do not wait until they are gone and then wax rhapsodic in your eulogy when they are no longer there to be seen. Open caskets be damned; their eyes are dead; they have departed, so we imagine, and it may not be sufficient merely to extol their spirit, the trace of them left, perhaps, untouched by our disaffirmations, the trace immune to our intimate appraisals of them.

At every moment life and death hang in the balance. Thus at every moment the living cell, the living being, is either shamed or affirmed, destroyed or rescued. At every moment we answer the summons articulated by Levinas to take responsibility for the other or choose instead to reject it. We choose, in other words, the moral way of seeing the other and affirmation or the immoral way of turning away from the other, the path of shame and disaffirmation. We choose to attend to the story of the other as free as possible of our own stories, or we meet the stories of the other with stories of our own, interpretations, ideologies, attributions of others' motives, outlooks that tend to disaffirm the other's narrative and account. We choose, actually, to affirm or disaffirm the very memories of the other. Are there not those among us, still, who genuinely believe the Holocaust did not occur!

As we undertake these actions, moreover, they are repeated, internalized by the other, who then redefines his or her being, his or her personal narrative, as a function of these choices. For the individual narratives we offer each other, our personal life studies or self-portraits,[61] as I have noted, represent the traces of our being intentionally meant for the other. At least they are the bits (of our self) we are willing to put out there for public consideration, appraisal, and consumption, an act of some courage. They are the pieces of our self that others are free to devour. We even say that, "when I told them my story, they 'ate it up.'" The actor acts, the critics extol and devour. Apparently we also affirm and disaffirm through our stories, at bedtime and all times.

The child leading the moral life has known affirmation, not merely affirmation of the so-called right way of being.[62] Through the affirmation, he or she has been taught to seek the truth, what Susan Reynolds calls "that ghost in the house of fiction,"[63] and eschew the lie, something made difficult for the disaffirmed one whose lies to himself or herself necessarily are experienced as insult or outright assault. A lie, after all, is more than an evasion of the truth; it remains an evasion of the self in both the external and internal worlds and ultimately an affront to or repudiation of affirmation; it lives as confirmation of disaffirmation. The lie, Stephen Tigner has remarked, causes promises to be broken; it undermines any sense of fidelity of the self to itself or to another.[64] That I lie to preserve the perceived (by me) reputation of my (false) self or establish some image of it for others is undeniable. Constantly relying on the lie, however, leaves me utterly alone; everything I encounter disconfirms my fundamental vision of the world, my fundamental sense of self being in the world. Thus, I insult my self and the other, drawing little from my self but dishonest conceptions as well as disingenuous perceptions and presentations of my self and the other. Somewhere in the past, the liar has been assaulted. Somewhere in the future, he may well assault himself, and others.

In stark contrast, the work of affirmation implies truth telling, ethical character, moral behavior, and honest inquiry; we employ the words "authentic" and "genuine" again and again to describe the affirmed ones. When the child learns anything about self or other, he or she necessarily draws on, calls up, his or her personal resources, which, in the case of the affirmed child, are forged from honesty and ethicality, the by-products, we recall, of the original response to the summons. Affirmation brings forth from the child's disposition or personal resources (what one might well label the "self") a repertoire of moral behavior in which dishonesty and violence would seem to be literally unthinkable options.

Affirmation means to the self that its presentation is fixed, its being is ratified, its being is moral, which is to say that it is good that the self is alive; it is good, this self that is alive. We celebrate this self by singing, "Happy Birthday to you . . ." Conversely, shame introduces the face of the immoral, the blind eye not of justice, ironically, but of injustice. For the unjust fail to see, fail to meet the obligation of the gaze; the shamed person's being has not been ratified; no birthday cake for him or her! Now it is not good that the self is alive; it is not good, this self that is alive. The unjust are willing to commit murder, even of a child, and some of the unjust, alas, are but children themselves, blinded not by the brilliance of affirmation but by the darkness of disaffirmation, the absence of affirmation, the absence of the eyes of the other.

Today, the whole world seems to be about Harry Potter. But when I was young there was another hero. Mask, Indian companion, white stallion and all, the Lone Ranger was clever indeed as he traveled the country seeking truth and justice. Obviously steeped in the classics, young Dan Reed (who would become the Lone Ranger) recognized that the good life is one of virtue guided by intelligence.[65] His true identity might have remained unknown, but his eyes were constantly there to be seen, his look constantly there to be returned by the just, spurned by the unjust; one look from him and cowards would scurry away. He, too, offered an invitation to others, as do we all if we are willing to look and offer, first, our narrative, our self, then our willingness to hear the narrative of the self of others, our lenses now removed. We are back where we started: listening to a bedtime story.

Truth be told, genuine seeing is believing, in the other and the self, believing in otherness and selfness, but only if one is willing to risk responding to the summons, take responsibility for the other, and, in looking back, meet the gaze, underwrite human possibility, and affirm the miraculous stranger.

PART

III

6 Average, Expectable Environments

SATURDAY, and a bas mitzvah ceremony in Connecticut. The shul is filled as it is every Saturday morning, although today the ceremony is led by two celebrants, twins girls who read from the holy scroll, the Torah, chanting, reciting the words of Hebrew at breathtaking speed but with clarity and assuredness all the same. As one invariably wonders in these moments, have these children any idea what they are saying, much less a feeling for the philosophical debates and interpretations underlying the mystical stories? It is impressive to learn that these girls understand full well the meanings and impact of the words they speak. Indeed, highest praise comes from the director of their school, who calls them "the best arguers in the class." From a conservative Jewish ceremony thousands of years old, in the lives of two young celebrants, who in their recitation and chanting contribute to this thoughtful and moral ritual, one begins to discern the outlines of what the work of human affirmation is all about.

To memorize prayers or be able to read words that were wholly foreign to one for the first several years of life is a significant achievement, one to be honored, but one not necessarily having all that much to do with reasoning. Reciting, memorizing, and praying, as sacrilegious as this may sound, are not automatically acts of thoughtfulness. When the leader of the ceremony instructs everyone to open their book to page 47 and read together at the top, Christians turn their pages toward the left, Jews toward the right, but the act of the mind is somewhat the same for both groups: recitation, but not necessarily reasoning.

When, however, a man stands up in the Connecticut shul and proclaims that these two girls are the best "arguers" in the class, he is saying that his school allows for thinking, reflection, argument, reasoning, and the interpretation of historical events, as well as the causal connections. Apparently, the school invites its students to become intrigued and enticed by the very structure of a so-called logical argument. At the same time he is offering up personal and powerful affirmations of the two young women. Logic, deduction, induction, mental activities of the highest abstract order are taking place in their school. Of course, these actions require words and language, rules of speaking, grammar, syntax, and logic. Students of the mind know that without the words and the rules there cannot be much reasoning taking place. But there is something else going on. Children are making assessments of themselves, rational, irrational, who really can say. But they are appraisals, and as such they represent or at least awaken in us the idea of affirmations of self or, in some instances, the absence of affirmations. Deeply personal matters have come into view, most all of them requiring some final deliberation, some final judgment.

Driving home, one thought kept coming back to me: these two girls were perfectly exemplary, not only as celebrants in an ancient rite but also as young women. To all of us in that temple, they could properly be called role models, and as such, there is a connection to be made between their performance and the concept of affirmation I have been exploring in this volume, especially as it exists in the minds of children. It is precisely this matter of role models, one of the more complex psychological constructs, made even more so by the type of discourse one regularly hears in the popular media where anyone, apparently, of any degree of recognition, though rarely children becoming *bas mitzvah*, has the potential to emerge as a role model, a model, literally, of and for the self by an other.

In a distracted culture of high-powered media and public relations industries, a culture in which false selves preoccupied with reputation and to a great extent ignorant of motivation seek the status of celebrity, it hardly surprises one that people become "hot property."[1] Children rarely do, unless they are in some trouble or become a cause célèbre, like the young Cuban Elian Gonzales, and his celebrity lasted only a few months. It hardly surprises one that even when celebrities become ill they become hot property. What troubles me is that our culture can become so obsessed with the lives of celebrities that it often looks away from everyday truths and everyday people. It would appear that we have invented a class of individuals whose mere celebrity provides them, at least in our eyes, a false status of immortality. Investment in them would seem to yield a (false) sense of infinite life. Perhaps one does well taking a clue from the character Solanka in Salman Rushdie's novel *Fury*, who at one point proclaims, "The more he became a Personality, the less like a person he felt."[2]

The notion of celebrity, athlete, or movie or rock star as role model has been discussed until it has become cliché.[3] Every other minute, America's stars pledge their loyalty to fans and promise proper, even ideal demeanor. Events are staged to promote this (imagined) role model power and to address the matter of children and teenagers aping the behavior of their beloved idols, literally becoming their ideals and, hence, incorporating the ideal behavior of others into themselves. How these people are affirmed! Only logically, even the ones making horrific errors of judgment or behavior and pledging never to make the same mistakes again are raised to the level of demigods and thus representatives of the infinite.[4]

Affirming this or that, promising this or that, teaching this or that, celebrated role models continue their media road shows despite the trend data which indicate that all this adulation of stars, all these benefits, award shows, pledges, and products, and all this stuff about role modeling have made only the tiniest of dents in improving the lives of America's most susceptible population, its young people, if any dents can be detected at all. But why should we be surprised that only the merest of dents in a child's being may be detected when popular culture role modeling could not possibly become part of the genuine cognitive structure of any person, even a child manifestly disinterested in knowing his or her self. Popular culture role models are merely external objects (that well may become selfobjects), like rocks, trees, and books, part of what philosophers call "exteriority," that may or may not become part of the self. More about this later. For the moment, consider some "evidence" supporting the notion that only the smallest of beneficial dents are being made in the lives of children and adolescents by faux role models.

Alcohol is now consumed by teenagers at a rate far greater than ever before. Teenagers are being sexual, getting pregnant, having babies and abortions at rates far greater than ever before. Teenagers run away from home, drop out of school, and commit suicide at rates far greater than ever before. More young people carry more guns to more schools in more cities than ever before, popular role models and their urgings notwithstanding.[5]

The lyrics of some of the songs and raps may teach nonviolence and the omnipresent award winners may flash their familiar peace signs and appeal to heaven itself, but children are killing one another at rates far greater than ever before, and most projections show these rates to be increasing. Children may dance to the sounds of hip-hop, they may listen to the tapes and discs again and again, most assuredly they can lip-sync every lyric, but quite frankly, not all that much is better. And more significant for our concerns here, children fail to be authentically affirmed by these popular cultural role models. Let no one believe this popular diet is genuinely improving the health of America's children, unless, of course, distraction is the country's number one goal. Surely now distraction has become one of the country's prominent industries.[6]

Popular culture joyously, albeit momentarily, distracts us from ugliness, sadness, tragedy, and a sense of hopelessness. But all the entertainment in the world, all the teenybopper magazines, music videos, star interviews, celebrity autobiographies, authorized and unauthorized, rap songs, and compact discs (CDs) apparently have had only the slightest effect on affirming the fundamental ingredients of the human personality. Ultimately, it is the noncelebrity doing his or her affirming work with children during this era of compulsive entertainment that will make life better for children and their families.

Celebrities sizzle; celebrity events dazzle and delight. In this manner they contribute to the pile of stuff meant to be accumulated by the child; certain people and events are capable of momentous distraction. But agents of a needed affirmation, not to mention social change, they are not; they never were meant to be. More precisely, these certain people reveal how the culture has moved, often in not the most salubrious direction as far as young people are concerned. Assuredly no cadre of celebrities can be blamed for creating the contemporary human condition, at least not celebrities who play professional sports, record CDs, or perform in movies or television sitcoms. The trouble still lies in the reality that 20 percent of America's children grow up in poverty, which means that they live in untenantable homes and usually attend substandard schools and that countless millions have been abused. The trouble lies, in other words, in the reality of injustice, the nature of it, the face of it, really, and the ways children first encounter in the world as well as in their own minds the nature of justice and injustice, although this notion clearly raises complex matters regarding the self and that which is exterior to it. Recall, moreover, that children in countries many of us still label "underdeveloped" have a better chance of surviving their first year of life than do children growing up in the United States.[7]

The trouble lies as well in Americans, rich and poor alike, who have lost touch with the truths of their own personal existence or, at very least, with the work that must be attempted as people seek to find the truth, for as I have noted, even children are in part philosophers. Merely to wonder about dying or the idea that life goes on forever renders the child a philosopher, if only because it is the mind that has constructed these ideas. If American voters are alienated from their government, individuals continue every day to lose touch with the tone and content of their inner voice, that which they may wish to understand as their self, and the form and direction of their own impulses and desires. We even claim we are not always certain of the sorts of human affirmation children require or that we, their elders, require.

So the conditions persist on personal and social scales; they will persist, moreover, in the same way that the proverbial beat goes on and America perpetuates its ambivalent involvement with celebrities (and celebrity) and listens to the West Coast disc jockey count down this week's top forty.

As the media driven expression of the day goes, a certain piece of behavior "sends a message." Again, thoughtlessness, not to mention the power of television, generates this rather questionable notion: performance models yes; role models—well, that's another discussion altogether. For the moment, to stimulate thinking about thoughtlessness, a concept key to understanding the nature of personal and public affirmation, hold in mind that earlier observation that never in the history of America have so many alleged role models from sports and entertainment—which really are the same thing—visited so many schools and classrooms, and never in the history of America have children from these classrooms committed more crimes, gotten pregnant more often, tried more drugs, contracted more sexually transmitted diseases, and died. In 1997 the human immunodeficiency virus (HIV) was the seventh leading cause of death among people aged fifteen to twenty-four, the same age group, incidentally, showing increasing numbers of suicide attempts and completions. It is evident that the number of adolescents infected with HIV has been rapidly increasing, this from the Centers for Disease Control and Prevention. The rate of HIV cases for young people of color, moreover, continues to be higher than that for the general population. In other words, messages surely are being sent; they are, however, not necessarily being heard or internalized. Let me offer some further evidence on this matter.

Given the extraordinary performance of the American economy over the last years, it seems almost sacrilegious to remind ourselves of the state in which so many American children continue to live. Yet with all the wealth that abounds and the growing number of people living lives they may never have imagined, vast numbers of American children confront circumstances that can only be described as perilous and disaffirming.

In surveys conducted by the National Council of Alcohol and Drug Dependence, 82 percent of high school seniors reported having used alcohol. This in comparison with 65 percent who have smoked cigarettes, 50 percent who report having smoked marijuana, and 9 percent who admit to trying cocaine. In research published in the *Boston Globe*, 76 percent of high school students and 46 percent of middle school students reported that illegal drugs are kept, used, or sold on school grounds. Not so incidentally, more than

one-third of the students surveyed claimed that drugs were the most press-
ing problem facing today's young people, and one cannot be certain whether
these students classified alcohol as a drug.[8]

If merely consuming drugs were not sufficiently serious, how young persons behave while under the influence of drugs may be even more significant. Alcohol, for example, is correlated with the leading causes of death and
injury among young people, namely, motor vehicle accidents, homicides,
and suicides. In addition, a National Center on Addiction and Substance
Abuse survey found that almost 32 percent of young people in state-operated
juvenile institutions were under the influence of alcohol at the time of their
arrest.

Now, a few words about violence. According to a report in the *Carnegie
Quarterly*, nearly 1 million adolescents between the ages of twelve and nine-
teen are victims of violent crime each year, with many of these crimes occurring on school grounds. A 1993 North Carolina Youth Risk Behavior
survey indicated that a significant percentage of students did not feel safe at
school, going to school, or returning home from school. Ten percent of the
high school students surveyed reported being threatened or injured by a
weapon on school property, and 40 percent were involved in some form of
physical fight at school.

Despite laws preventing people under the age of eighteen from possessing
firearms, 11,500 young people are killed or kill themselves each year with
firearms. Almost 30 percent of the students in the North Carolina study
reported carrying a weapon within the month prior to the survey. Predictably, almost every student reported that the weapon was meant for self-
protection.

Interestingly, while a plethora of research indicates that teaching sexual
abstinence significantly reduces sexual activity and, hence, unwanted pregnancies, a 1999 study conducted by Family Planning Perspectives revealed
that only one-third of 825 American school districts surveyed teach abstinence outside marriage as their sole educational message to students in sixth
grade and above. In a similar vein, while some critics claim that dispensing
contraception to high school students only encourages sexual activity, a National Adolescent Health Information Center study estimated that as many
as 2.1 million pregnancies may have been averted through publicly funded
reproductive health programs. Not so incidentally, family planning care
remains the sole source of contraceptive care for two-thirds of all teenagers.

For some reason, I keep thinking of those twins in the New Haven shul—
the chanters, the arguers. At thirteen, their minds have formed to the point

where they now can hold several competing abstract notions simultaneously. Quite a feat, especially if they can play and work with these notions and truly tease out meanings and implications of every word that is uttered or every idea that pops into their rich and wondrous heads. To ask for reasons is to practice the fundamentals of reasoning that ultimately will lead to genuine thoughtfulness and, quite likely, authentic affirmations of self and others. "There is a dark side of every mirror," Burton Blatt wrote, "a side beyond inspection because it is without thoughtfulness."[9] And note that this same thoughtfulness leads in the direction of manners, politeness, and civility, for don't we compliment the polite person using that same word: "How *thoughtful* of you!"

Will their schools push this exercise, one wonders? Will their schools help them to investigate thinking, reasoning, and morality such that logical connections, the philosophical connective tissue, becomes a palpable texture for them? Will they learn other languages that will afford them entrance into other cultures, histories, and communities and, for all I know, other parts of their mind? Will they, in other words, learn to read again and then in college learn to read yet again, with each new learning advancing their capacity to reason and become increasingly more respectful of words and thus thoughtful and moral humans? Furthermore, how will these experiences shape the core of their affirmations, the very definition of affirmation that will live forever in their minds?

The presence of so-called role models and the abiding belief in the ability of these models to alter the lives of young people not only flies in the face of the work of genuine affirmation but also reveals the degree to which our culture is often caught in the web of personal distractions, social events, and phenomena intended to take our mind off of, well, our self. In genuine affirmation of the sort required by each of us in the leading of our life, the whole point is to face our self and one another in the most direct way possible, free of distraction. Yet again and again, the culture seems to spew distractive forces at us in mightier and still mightier intensities.

The search for truth, the search for a reality that exists beyond our mere beliefs, becomes part of the self's search for affirmation, or is it the other way around? Truthful accounts represent that one is properly respected, properly appraised, properly honored. To be lied to, to be diverted or distracted from some external or internal reality, is the quintessential opposite (and enemy) of genuine affirmation. "Don't beat around the bush," we say. "Tell me the truth no matter how painful it may be." Affirmation assumes truth, not artificial self-enhancement. We never affirm children by allowing them to graduate when they cannot read or manipulate numbers. We never affirm children in our families when we overlook lapses in character or outright immoral behavior. Without authentic affirmation, there can be no moral conduct. What could ever come from imagining that people, even young ones, cannot handle the truth?

Granted, there are times when people seem unable to take in more accounts of painful events such as scenes of war, famine, or terrorist attacks; they need respite, a break from the game, a moment on the sidelines. Toward the end of the first war in the Persian Gulf, in almost religious rituals, Americans sat for long moments before the altars of television sets, making time for the "truths" of the war as they were fed to us by the communications industry. In these moments, I would argue, a form of disaffirmation ceremony was taking place: people were becoming aware of how, through its public relations/entertainment machinery, the culture was ushering them away from truth, as well as from the cognitive and psychological modes that lead one to it; many of us literally felt distracted. Suddenly, people everywhere seemed ready to join those strong enough to ask the questions, collect the accounts, and take the pictures associated with probing the barbed realities of war. In those moments, as in the moments of children's and adults' personal accounts of their individual self and their experiences, people sense a lack of affirmation of their very being. They feel, somehow, as though they are being lifted out of time, out of a world where they genuinely confront the realities of others and thereby sense a lack of personal affirmation that only palpable untruths can yield.

Most of us acknowledge that powerful American industries such as the government, public relations organizations, the communications media, and various entertainment businesses depend in part on satisfying our need to be distracted, even if it means we feel disaffirmed. Companies urge us to buy products we hardly need by employing slogans and wording meant to urge us to think in certain ways. We need only look to presidential elections to see how politicians, campaign managers, and so-called spin doctors work to distract us from the realities that ought to be the substance of our political ruminations and debates. The entertainment industry, moreover, offers diversions and distractions practically every minute of our life, along with the liquor business, while the media and especially television offer us still more distractions, along with informational and educational programming.

Distractive thinking is part and parcel of the way we speak, learn, reason, intuit, analyze, and feel about others and our self. It is an essential feature of the development of our conscious life, our very consciousness. It affects our family involvements, all friendships really. It is at work in our schools and places of employment. It lives in our definitions of career, our worshiping of achievement, even though we know full well what Erikson meant when he spoke of the "special weaknesses" of some achievements,[10] our turning people into celebrities, even (false) heroes, and our reading of political events as well as the most intimate events of our lives. Probably, too, distractions generate much of what happens psychologically as we sit in front of our television sets believing we are watching the "truth" or clicking our remote control mechanisms—what Boston television commentator Chuck Kraemer calls the "hovering thumb"—in the hope of feeding a consciousness demanding constant satisfaction of appetite. Distraction, moreover, is a fundamental ingredient in America's preoccupation with a narcissistically driven "me generation," a generation seeking affirmation and recognition frequently in the most distracted ways.[11] We are a culture, moreover, that despises the idea of someone being "nobody," "a nothing." Yet those (affirmed ones) with self-assurance, those who exhibit a self-effacing manner, seem unneeding of celebrity and constant recognition. The affirmed appear content with modest status and anonymity; the disaffirmed, distracted to the end, compensate for their hollowness of self in rapaciously self-aggrandizing gestures.

One definition of "distraction" is familiar to all of us: "to divert or draw the mind away" from something. We also recognize in distraction the feeling of wishing to draw our mind away from something that troubles or bores us. Distraction also means to cause conflict and confusion. These aspects of distraction we probably notice only when someone calls our attention to them. A person suggests to us that we look distracted, and we are forced to focus on what we are feeling or, more precisely, the feeling we are left with when we are unable or unwilling to focus on what we are feeling. One might argue that in genuine affirmation, we are seeking to reduce the distractive elements in our appraisals of self and others. We are essentially focusing on the event or experience or, most likely, the face before us, or the gaze of the other. Thus, in these moments of true affirmation, we seek to provide honest reporting, honest assessing. We provide, one might suggest, the words meant to convey our reasoned thoughts, our deliberate intentions, our most intimate feelings. Conversely, we are proffering what we know or suspect others wish to hear, acts most likely of disaffirmation.

Granted, most everything affects the shape and content of our consciousness; life affirming or not, every stimulus with which we come into contact, every word or sign, every image on television, every sound of every song fills our consciousness, or at least looks to find a bit of room for itself. When examined closely, American society reveals a host of forces seeking to capture our attention, our fancy, our consciousness. Predictably, we focus on Madison Avenue as well as the media and especially television, because they represent the obvious examples of industries committed to getting their messages and products into our consciousness; they make no bones about it. They want us to buy their products and watch their programs. Irrespective of whether they want to teach us something or merely entertain us, they demand our conscious attention. Most important, these messages and products find their way into our own self-appraisals. They begin to shape the ways we assess and feel about our self, the nature of our critical thinking, as well as our sense of moral responsibility. And one thing more: they have begun to play a prominent role in the very nature of the construction of the personal affirmations that in part define us, and contribute to that which we call our esteem or, in some cases, the personal affirmations we long for.

To think that a decade ago millions of us sat transfixed before our television screens looking at famous news anchors and retired generals actually "explaining" a war says something about the molecular activity, the sheer noise and impact of visual stimuli—what the writer Don Delillo calls the "hum of human existence"—competing for space in and eventually constituting our consciousness. It says something about the way we learn about and make sense of nature and our self, as well as the ways we explain our self and the world to our self. It says something, too, about the way our consciousness works (and plays) to keep us from losing and finding our self and our mind.

At first blush, one hates to admit that in "watching the war" on television, one was wishing for the sight of blood. One hates to admit that antiseptically transmitted and censored communications did not suffice for many of us when real war could have been on the stage. Like children terrified of swimming pools but nonetheless daring to dangle their feet in the shallow end, the war drew us a mite closer to battle and to death, which is the point. Requiring truthful affirmations of our life means at all times requiring recognition of human finitude. The fantasies and distractions (appear to) nourish us only so long. After a while, we hunger for the genuine nutrients, authentic accounts, authentic encounters, authentic affirmations.

How intriguing the notion, therefore, that whereas people seek distraction, literally desiring to have their attention drawn or moved away from some object or focus, physical change and major fluctuations often take a significant toll on children. The arrival of a baby in the home can set a child into a tailspin, although children are rather adept at revealing their despair and disapproval in clever ways, such as hitting the newborn or torturing a pet. Moving a child from one room to another or even rearranging her furniture may prove seriously upsetting. Parents altering job schedules, not even changing jobs, and certainly a family moving from one city to another have profound effects on the child.

Children are not alone in this need for the average expectable environment. Research has shown, for example, that moving one's place of residence is one of the greatest stress inducers for adults as well. It literally causes people to feel that they not only are being separated (drawn away) from significant objects and people but also are coming apart, internally unraveling. (A prize, therefore, to the moving company that hit on the name Allied, but what does one say about a Massachusetts moving company calling itself Mom's Moving?) In simplest terms—and frequently children only deal in the simplest terms—"average" to the child means the way it usually is. Expectable means that I can await events without fear for I have lived through them before and know (how) they usually come out all right, a sentiment bespeaking affirmation.

Few children ever take this matter of an average and predictable home life for granted, thereby confirming Anna Freud's aforementioned observation of children's need for such an environment. Irrespective of their protestations, even teenagers are rattled by seemingly insignificant shifts in others' moods or behavior. Children surely know when Dad or Mom is perturbed—most probably, they were able to sense at two weeks old when something was amiss—and when these upsets were not being caused by work and career setbacks. In their way, when children are not doing their "own thing" (a common expression that derives from the drug culture), they often act as miniature social workers on perpetual home care visitation.

All too often in my research on families I will hear a child bemoan the "boring" quality of his or her home life. "Dad's always the same," a boy grouses. "Every night he comes home from work and puts down his coat in the same place and calls to my mother and says, 'Hi, Honey, how was your day?' She has just come home from work too and is in the kitchen, like always, listening to public radio, *All Things Considered*, of course, and she smiles at him and drops the cucumbers on the counter, and they kiss and hug and she says, 'Fine, darling, and how was *your* day?' And he says 'Not that bad, all things considered,' and they glance at the radio and giggle and he says, 'Well, something in here smells awfully good.' And it goes on like this week after boring week after boring week."

We may smile at this syrupy description, but a serious point lingers: following the fundamental definition of affirmation, parents need to be an ongoing and regular presence in the lives of their children; quality time will never suffice if the child perceives that parents have bigger fish to fry. Many Americans, nonetheless, continue to manipulate child-rearing strategies and philosophies seemingly to excuse themselves from the responsibility (inherent in the affirmation) of child rearing. They continue to dicker with child-rearing realities, strategies, and philosophies as if the lives of their children could be played with or moved around as easily as tossing about characters on a word processor screen. Contrived techniques, we continue to imagine, can win out over simple everyday nurturance, security, and, of course, affirmation. In our distracted ways, we continue to try out every variety of child-rearing practice, when, as Earls and Carlson have reminded us, as if it were even necessary, the needs of children have not changed in centuries.[12] It is the same misguidedness that leads many of us to believe that powerful technologies can win out in competition with natural events and human and physical evolution. The most extraordinary computers, satellite dishes, and radar equipment still cannot guarantee accurate weather predictions, no matter how intensely we imagine that they do.

American businesses seem all too ready to accept and reward our manipulations of child-rearing strategies and feed us still more distracting possibilities. With a child crying for his or her parents, teenagers claiming there is no one in the world for them, homicidal gang boys proclaiming that only gangs teach love and fidelity, students demanding that they be treated as people and not as numbers and claiming that if they died it would be so long before they were discovered their decomposed bodies no longer would be recognizable even to their parents (this sentiment from an interview with a college junior), it begins to seem that the whole world is out of joint. The psychoanalyst John Bowlby apparently felt much the same thing when he wrote, "We have created a topsy turvy world in which the production of material goods counts as a plus in our economic indices whereas men and women power devoted to raising happy, healthy and self reliant children . . . does not count at all."[13]

We note again this physician's unmistakable message and the almost homey wording. Another psychoanalyst, Bruno Bettelheim, wrote that one need not be a great or perfect parent; good enough was, well, good enough, just as David Winnicott suggested in his explorations of the so-called good-enough mother. One need not be a child-rearing expert, researcher, or psychologist, Bettelheim taught. Some evidence indicates that the children of psychotherapists often experience a rather difficult time, precisely because of the nature of their parent's professional perspectives and corresponding behavior.[14]

One may take one's clues from watching other children raise their brothers and sisters or from Fred Rogers. We may scoff at Mr. Rogers, smirk at his gentle manner, but all we are doing is seeking to neutralize the strong feelings we once held for him and his affirming messages as well as the importance he played in our life or the lives of our children.

Ask parents who turn to Mr. Rogers at the miserable hour of five o'clock in the afternoon what they think of him and his neighborhood. Trying to come down from an exhausting day that has hours still remaining in it, caring for a couple of agitated and temporarily inconsolable children (and to think that four or five times each day teachers regularly care for and hope to educate as many as twenty-five children simultaneously), preparing dinner, and sustaining that one last remnant of sanity, many parents would give a Nobel Peace Prize to the man who not only engages their children for thirty uninterrupted minutes but also hit upon the (distracted) generation's one healthy phrase that every child (and adult) needs to hear: "I like you just the way you are." It is the affirmation available every day to us, even in reruns.

Why, exactly, we resonate to the words of Mr. Rogers is difficult to know. We do know that it was the parents of these baby boomers who often invested in careers that took them away from the daily ongoing lives of their children and contributed heavily to the rise in the divorce rate.[15] Mothers leaving home to go off to work, as mothers always have done (the matter only became part of a national debate when affluent women went off to work), like fathers going off to work, hardly constitutes abandonment, disaffirmation, or the devaluing of children. Abandonment is only felt and, hence, the cleavage of bonds experienced when, by dint of the words and deeds of their parents, children recognize their parents' career and social pursuits to be more important than their, the children's, life. Then again, there is this rather chilling observation from Sartre: "There's no good parent. Don't lay the blame on parents but on the bond of paternity, which is rotten."[16]

There is nothing complicated about this. No one has to feel guilty about working outside the home (as well as inside the home) and leaving a child in a good child care situation. Of course one feels conflicted, but genuine guilt emerges in part when there is a realization that one would rather go to work than be with children and knows one is not "supposed" to feel this way. My children knew full well when my mind was on my work and not focused on them. It was painfully obvious to all of us when I was failing to attend to them either by not being around or, worse, by not being around even when I was around—when I was distracted. Often the matter comes down to a simple decision: do you accept a business obligation on the day your child is celebrating a birthday, appearing in a play, participating in a game? ("When duty calls," goes the line in a play I recently saw, "hang up!") And even these are not make-or-break issues. It is when you distract yourself from the truth: namely, that your happiness is far more important than your child's, which is precisely what happens in a great many divorce cases.[17]

Bonds between generations become assaulted when parental ambition and accomplishment are placed before a child's welfare, development, and nurturance. Because economic achievement and personal advancement, generally, are the touchstones of American society and human welfare remains a lower national priority (as attested to by national budgets, the insufficient number of first-class child care centers, and the pittance paid to child care workers and teachers), it does not take much critical thinking on the part of the child to recognize just how insignificant is his or her role and position in the family and the culture generally.[18]

Another clue picked up by children is the parent's intense need for children to accomplish and perform. How well a child does in school may be a clue to the child's happiness, well-being, sense of self, capacity to adjust, as well as inherent brightness (defined here as the ability to do what schools demand, which is not necessarily a test of intelligence). A better clue to how the child is faring may be direct observation of the child's happiness. Does this sound redundant and foolish? Well, it would be difficult to argue that the names of the happiest and most secure children invariably appear on a school's honor roll.

Granted, attaining high grades usually (but not always) makes a student happy. Yet the grades and honor roll entry also may tell us very little about the child's sense of his or her own well-being, his or her sense of self. How many teenage suicide cases bring forth this response: "I can't believe it. He was one of the brightest kids. I mean, he was almost a perfect child." Failing grades may be a signal of a child experiencing some psychological trouble, but this country has millions of children doing perfectly well in school who are profoundly unhappy, if not clinically depressed. So we have grades as potential indications of a child's unhappiness and grades as potential distractions from the real problems facing a family, not just the child.

Not unlike a parent's decision to attend either a board meeting or a child's

birthday party, the decision the child must make looms especially complicated. The child must decide, first, whether achieving high grades, the ultimate sign of accomplishment, brings him or her love and affirmation from
parents or whether the affirmation was there before, during, and after the
marking period; this represents a perfect example of "conditional love." Often parents who themselves experienced conditional love, despite the
pledges they made to themselves years before having children of their own,
tend to offer the same love contract to their children. If children conclude
that their parents are happy only when the children do well, they must decide whether to give good performance to get the love parents usually proffer
in return, or to risk the love, shove the whole family catastrophe in their
parents' faces (thereby bringing the family's problems into the open, something that some anorexic girls, for example, tend to do) as they sabotage
themselves with poor performance. In this way they hope they get the message across to their parents that they require love, nurturance, security, and
affirmation because they are who they are and not because of some entries
on their résumé.[19] I believe this to be true, the following observation of
adolescents by R. E. H. Muuss notwithstanding: "Falling in love . . . is an
attempt to project and test one's own diffused and still undifferentiated ego
through the eyes of a beloved person in order to clarify and reflect one's own
self-concept and one's ego-identity.[20]

This matter of performance being the measure of all judgment works in
the adult world as well, where employment résumés often become more
significant to potential employers than the applicant who actually sits before them. One is better off, it appears, spending money on desktop publishing software and producing a jazzy biography than on palpable self-
improvement. To some, apparently, how a person *appears* on paper is more
revealing and ultimately more significant than how they *perform* in person.
The notion is reminiscent of a television studio audience watching a program in progress. Invariably the audience watches the monitors rather than
the actual participants, as if the monitors alone contained some ultimate
truth of these human beings.[21] A young woman once told me, "I wish my
father had spent the time reading to me as a child he now spends studying
my report cards." And now notice her conclusion: "*He* would have been a
happier person."

One hears variations of this same theme in numerous teenagers' accounts
of their lives. One hears it from college students as well: all I want, goes a
common lament, is for the institution, the school, the church, whatever, to
treat me as a person. Take me for me (take my self for my self), not for some

demographic feature, college board score, or grade point average. If one takes a child for how he or she produces or performs, one has bought into the heart of distraction and possibly disaffirmation. In writing about adolescent development, Erikson pointed to the need for personal industry, initiative, competence, fidelity.[22] Significantly, he did not say much about contingencies related to performance.

The balance struck in a family between achievement values and love or affirmation becomes a delicate one. Someone, after all, made a fortune designing those tiny T-shirts that read "Harvard '20??" And what parents celebrate a child's D and E on a report card! We say, as long as you do your best and, not inappropriately, as long as you give your schoolwork your utmost effort, we're happy. Some of us say this, but our children hear the unsaid words as well: as long as your best effort brings acceptable (to us) results, we're happy. It's all right to fail, we tell children, as long as you give it your best shot. Some of us actually mean this. Others utter these words all the while wishing we could have inquired of our own parents, "Will you still love me if I fail? Or will failure mean that I am indelibly defective and disaffirmed?"

I am reminded in this context of the story of an eighth-grade student who came home with a dreadful report card. Recognizing the enormous pressure he had imposed on the boy, the father chose to say not one word about his son's grades but instead left a simple message on the child's pillow. It read, "I love you."

It is not necessarily the case that parents raise their children according to the way their parents raised them. It is also not necessarily true that parents raise their children to accomplish things and attain levels of success or achievement that they were never able to do or attain; would that the social psychology of family dynamics were so simple. Still, with all the complexity, the power of generational differences remains. What that means is that irrespective of how in touch they may be with the ongoing currents, trends, and values of the contemporary generation, no parents can fully divorce themselves from the generation in which they grew up. Nor can they ever shed the reality that the past was couched in the values of another generation.

To one degree or another, the asymmetry of the relationship between a parent and his or her child is born with this generational strain: the child knows but one generation, his or her own, and the parent two; it often goes under the name of "experience." But if parents have difficulty understanding or appreciating the times in which their children grow up, children often reveal a tendency to explore only minimally the times in which their parents grew up, which means that some children forfeit the opportunity to affirm their parents. Indeed, many children find the scenes of their parent's childhood to be almost titillating, if not illicit and thereby somehow "off-limits" for discourse.

One can look at this same matter from another perspective. As one of its significant by-products, the birth of children creates a set of experiences sociologists call *generational continuity*. For some people, the flow of time, the emergence of history—if one may properly use this phrase—is little more than the flow of family members, one generation to the next. Life itself is affirmed, along with the idea of being alive, when one's children are born. One feels there is now some legacy, some continuity, some psychological antidote to the idea of finitude. We oversimplify this point when we say somewhat derisively that *all* people want out of their children is to perpetuate their own or their family names or even their own personal rituals and traditions.

Granted, some people probably do enjoy the idea that they can achieve immortality—and thereby trick time, as it were—by having their children "carry on" for them. Granted, too, many parents presumably view their children as the means to some ends; children, therefore, become little more than appendages or narcissistic reflections of their parents. But in assuming these perspectives, we tend to overlook a more universal phenomenon cultivated in and through the dynamics of generational strain and intimacy.

One of the most terrifying and dreadful human sensations is the feeling of helplessness. The culture, surely, holds up independence and autonomy as ideals for children just as it shuns the notion that people should ever feel dependent. Dependency in our culture still depicts weakness, the lack of self-sufficiency or industriousness, particularly, as William Pollock points out, in what he calls the "boy code"; it probably even denotes effeminacy in some parents' minds.[23] Ideal or not, the point is that the laws of human nature render everyone dependent on other people. Shunning dependency speaks not to human truths but more likely to that terrifying feeling, the dread of being helpless, not only disaffirmed but *un*affirmed as well.

The sensation of helplessness commences in infancy. Without a parent or some caretaker, we never get to experience a life force; we die. For that matter—and how many adolescents decry this point—if it were not for a couple of parents, we wouldn't even be here. Or anywhere. So our very being in the world (and our attachment to a life force) depends on the existence not only of two other people but also of the dynamic power of generations enduring. The expression of taking over the reins is an apt one. When people are old enough, they take over for their parents, at least they do in agrarian societies where it is expected that children will follow in their parent's footsteps. In industrial cultures, the matter of taking over the reins is greatly diminished if not rendered altogether irrelevant. That a parent may wish to pass on the reins hardly guarantees that the opportunity to do so may eventually arise. But notice that where the reins go free—and the metaphor seems apt—the children, in effect, are asking to lead their own lives no matter how terrifying the absence of their parent's support may appear to them.

Given all the expressions of generational strain and intimacy inherent in the parent-child association, traditionally it is the mother in the family who protects the child from experiencing the pains of helplessness. In the minds of some family members, in other words, the impress of the parent on the child only commences when the parent imagines the child is old enough to "make it" on his or her own, which means not crumble at the first trial at self-sufficiency. In this regard, the parent introduces the child if not exactly to the outside world, then at least to the feelings and belief systems that a child must adopt and honor when dealing with the outside world, essentially the world apart from the mother.

However, both the mother and the father offer to or impose on the child a far more complex message and mission than that described by their individual and unique personality. In fact, the substance and power of generational continuity (yet another facet of the Mitwelt) is constantly being impressed on the child. The living and lived experiences of an entire generation play their role in shaping the child's sense of his or her identity and emerging aspirations. By definition we may be obliged to "study" individually a boy and his parents or a girl and her parents, but if the universal features of which we speak are to be delineated, then we must assume that any parent-child association has been shaped in part by the individual as well as collective evolution of entire human groups. Let me make this argument more concretely.

When a man tells his child of his, the father's, role in the family or even believes that there are special paternal tasks that he must undertake, is he not addressing matters associated with the generic definition of being a father? That is, he does not draw his definition of the role of parent, if he even uses this word, or some inchoate sense of parenting, "parentness" or parenthood, from out of the blue. Nor are they entirely described by the way his own parents raised him. Cultures shape the definition of parent-child associations, as do societies, along with the numerous institutions that speak to the manner in which children and parents relate to one another, or at least define those qualities constituting their relationship.[24] That is to say, cultures shape the definitions of the associations, but ultimately it is up to the individual to determine his or her own idiosyncratic definition and character of parenthood.

Surely parents wish to treasure these idiosyncratic aspects of their relationship with their child; they wish it to be special, unique. Yet the very uniqueness they seek draws its life from universal truths governing these unique bonds; that is what is meant by the capacity to deal not merely with the abstract term "parenthood" but also with the historical emergence within a culture of this delicate union. In practical terms, the notion of "parentness" or parenthood is made understandable in part by the work of affirmation as well as by the evolution of generations and the completeness or felt sense of this evolution that parents experience when their children are born: the sensation of responding to the gaze. The chain is not complete, a parent senses, until the next link arrives. That, in part, is what Earls and Carlson mean by the idea of relationships making it possible for generations to endure.

I do not, of course, suggest that only people who become parents feel this linkage between generations, merely that the parent-child association is in part influenced both by the impact of the individual personalities involved and by the nature of the entire dynamic known as generational continuity. A parent and a child encounter each other, but their encounter encompasses the nature of "parentness" meeting "childness." Thus whole generations are conjoined in this encounter, even though the principals involved feel and define the encounter in wholly different terms. And as time passes, they will continue to rearrange and recontextualize their feelings about and definitions of the encounter. But let me pursue the temporal nature of the encounter one step further.

Certainly, the parent has experienced a form of what the child is experiencing or someday will experience. For that matter, each knows an experience analogous to what the other has experienced or presently is experiencing. In some cases, parents work hard, consciously or unconsciously, to make certain their child goes through experiences analogous to what they, the parents, once experienced. We might even allege that some parents treat the parent-child relationship as if it were a sacred club and therefore choose to initiate their child into the club.

Although this particular metaphor may seem foreign to some, an exami-

nation of various societies, fraternities, and fraternal orders would support
the claim. Any initiation ceremony has its subordinate and superordinate
memberships often opposing one another with the purpose of the initiation
being a test of the initiate's manhood or womanhood. To be allowed entrance into the club, the membership, "the order," as it is often called, constitutes an initiation procedure or ritual carried out in a variety of ways in
various cultures. Nonetheless, note the symbolism: the older one and the
younger one, the former hoping the latter will "make it," which implies
getting through on his or her own. If there is doubt raised about the so-
called initiation ceremony, the parent figures can always announce that they
are asking nothing more of you than we ourselves have already experienced.

Personhood itself seems to be at stake in most of these clublike ceremonies: surviving with grace and competence when put to the test, the infamous "test of character." The ritual reveals parents doing their job of "deliv-
ering" the child out of childhood into adulthood. Besides being a temporal
act in character, the transition reveals its gender overtones as well, for does
not tradition define a boyhood dominated by a mother as feminine? Said
differently, manhood often implies not requiring the mother anymore,
which is further intended to mean not needing *anyone* but oneself. If it were
not a man's job to get his child beyond the (seemingly weakening and cheap-
ening) dependencies of childhood, why else would all these traditional initiation ceremonies into manhood so assiduously exclude women?

Clearly there are just some things and events, often of a secretive nature,
that fathers and sons, on the one hand, and mothers and daughters, on the
other, must do together. These are precisely the times when a mother cannot
be both mother and father to a child, as the common expression goes. In a
few instances, one senses that the foundation of these activities and events
may be the biological alliance that parents "only naturally" form with their
same-sex children. I am like Daddy, not like Mommy, the son decides or is
taught to believe. True enough, the biological (Umwelt) or at least anatomical differences are what keep the boys from the girls or, in psychological
terms, the boys from *becoming* the girls. Traditionally, parents had to make
certain that the anatomical distinction is not the only feature that legitimates
a separation or differentiation of a boy from his sisters or girls generally, or
a girl from her brother and boys generally. For this job to be successfully
completed, it may have been the case that one of the parents had to be
excluded.

Combining these points illustrates another theme: namely, that parents
do far more than live out the unhappy or ungratifying moments of their

own life. Granted, the characterization of parents pushing their child to fill the voids in their own life finds confirmation in numerous life histories. Yet arguing that this is the dominant mode of the parent-child association is to assume the position that parent-child relationships essentially are predicated strictly on the individual parent's psychopathology. One can just as rightly allege that parents struggle with the task of leading their life partly to prepare for the future of their child's life; many parents assume just this responsibility for their children. Nonetheless, the point to be stressed is the distinction between the parent serving as a bridge connecting the generations, on the one hand, and having the world of one's child be compensation for one's own felt sense of inadequacies and disaffirmations, on the other. This is not to say, however, that many parents feel no ambivalence about their role. More than one parent in the course of history has muttered words about the sacrifices he or she has made for a child. Still, as we have seen, sacrifice and compensation are hardly of the same psychological character. They bespeak wholly different sociological orientations to the role of parent and child.

The parent remains the primary teacher for the child if only because it is the parent's role to assist the child in his or her growth toward a self-governing life posture. Not surprisingly, this dynamic of self-governance requires that the child lean heavily, if not feel utterly dependent on, his or her parents. In traditional terms, however, it fell to the father to convince the child that dependency can in no circumstance be considered an acceptable posture. Again, if Earls and Carlson are correct, the dependency aspect of the relationship assumes significance because parents generally face the problem of reconciling their dependencies on each other as well as on their children.[25]

Parents' preoccupation with self-governance or self-rule may stem from the fact that neither of their own parents ever allowed them dependency for too long a period of time. Whatever the explanation, the irony, of course, is that autonomy, or personal self-governance, is an utterly unattainable ideal. The model of the self-governing nation-state is a perfectly lovely one for the individual personality to follow. Perhaps the Greeks, in their conceptions of the polis and of democracy generally, established an even loftier example than Western culture has ever realized. But individual autonomy in this personal self-governing fashion may not be an appropriate ideal.

For one thing, as Fromm pointed out, there is far too much ambivalence associated with both self-governance and dependency.[26] Ultimately, whether or not we wish to acknowledge it, we all rely on a host of other people. Similarly, people come to depend on their parents with far greater intensity than they may wish to acknowledge. We all recognize, surely, the genuine difficulties one faces in becoming what we call the "self-made" man or woman. Typically, "self-made" implies that one has received little or no help from one's parents. But if individual life histories teach us anything, it is that no child honestly believes he or she goes through life untouched, unaided, that is, by his or her parents or teachers. In part, this is what Rawls meant when he claimed that no one *deserves* anything; we all have been influenced in numerous ways.[27] The mere biological fact of one's predecessors, one's progenitors, seems to strike each of us as sufficient evidence for the fact that in some deeply existential sense we are not self-made, a point that takes us into what might be considered a spiritual aspect of the parent-child alliance.

If their encounters can genuinely be called spiritual, parents and children must find in each other or, more precisely, *sense* in each other the notion of the mystery or the mysterious. That they may share the same gender ties them together in some atavistic fashion. That they are of the same flesh and blood—a metaphor the Bible frequently underwrites—further affirms their spiritual attachments. But there is something else: Do we call it destiny, time, the miracle of life perpetuating life? Do we call it generational succession, human inheritance, the flow of one family to the next and, hence, the consummation of enduring attachment?

Whatever it means to us, parents and children are united in spiritual ways, forming yet another aspect of affirmation; they are the living representatives, the closest approximation of one another's past and future. It is within this context that one finds the living power of such words as "ambition," "self-made," "success," and "failure." At some point in all our lives, we must wonder about the more comprehensive schemes we have devised to explain the concept of existence, being alive, to ourself and to others, what we call our being. What truly is the life force of which we speak? What does it mean to be alive? What does it mean to say *I* am alive or to "know" that you are alive? What is the connection of my life to those of others and especially significant others, such as my parents and my children? And is part of this (felt sense of) connection the original affirmation? Quite probably these questions are not addressed until people in biological, spiritual, and philosophical terms are able to appreciate the literal and symbolic association of parent and child or, more precisely, the nature of the affirmation of the parent and child, each by the other.

The attachment to living, the inchoate understanding of merely being for the child, may be the parent. Or perhaps it is this way until the upheavals of adolescence commence. Perhaps the final appreciation occurs when the child becomes a parent. The attachment to the transcendent and the spiritual, again, may be through this association with parents. When we speak about the parent-child association, therefore, it may be that the sacred symbol is the hyphen, the connection of these two units in time and space. When we speak, furthermore, of a parent who lives out his or her own life through his or her child's life (hardly a form of authentic affirmation), we may find ourselves jumping immediately to the notion of psychopathology. But we could jump as easily to the notion that parents and children *are* attached to one another as well as to life itself through affirmations; thus an accomplishment by a child is in spiritual, if not psychological, terms an accomplishment of the parent, if one dares to consider affirmation an accomplishment.

Said less extremely, a parent's deed (affirmation) is automatically a child's reward, just as a parent's loss (disaffirmation) becomes the child's burden. It is true not because they are one and the same people but because they are conjoined spiritually and thus experience in one form or another the burdens and gratifications of each other's successes and failures, each other's affirmations and disaffirmations.[28] Following this line of thought, the concept of guilt takes on a slightly new meaning. Granted, children and parents alike feel guilt about acts committed in the context of their relationship. Parents and children surely feel guilt, moreover, stemming from thoughts never uttered in the context of their relationships. But if one may say so, as pernicious as they may be, these are the profane faces of guilt. The sacred or spiritual faces of guilt may derive from the existential force to feel that one is autonomous when surely one must "know" the unbreakable atavistic attachment to one's successors and progenitors. There is no escape from genuine affirmation; there is no reason to escape, for the life force itself lives within the affirmation.

One is not made to feel guilty by the mere act of being alive but more likely by the notion that autonomy, self-governance, and independence are human transgressions from the just and real nature of the parent-child bond: they represent transgressions from the nature of the authentic affirmation. Both the literal nature and the symbolic nature of the encounter give birth to a sense of guilt, the guilt of (false) freedom; one cannot fully believe in the very notion of independence and self-sufficiency when one is forever dependent on others' lives for giving biological, philosophical, social, and ultimately spiritual meaning and gravity to one's own existence. But let us add one more piece to this mysterious puzzle.

All too regularly we hear of parents wishing they might have had the fortitude to do what their parents or children had done. Perhaps a man hopes his child will dare to confront aspects of the world he was unable to confront. This theme might be labeled the need for a "living or existential courage." Notice, too, the capacity of many parents to speak of the courage required in recognizing how much one's individual life is caught up in the realm of others' lives—primarily through affirmations—shaped in part by these others' lives, such that one life draws its strength although not its identity directly from the other in a manner that need not be labeled pathological.

Said differently, it takes courage "merely" to be, just as it takes courage to be attached to others, associated with persons not strictly by reason of the will.[29] (For that matter, it takes courage to recognize that we live in and among *many* relationships, that we *are* many relationships.) Parents and children do not choose one another; they are given or delivered to one another, reborn as it were—the word "deliver" meaning "to liberate"—potentially through the affirmation. For want of a better phrase, it appears to us to be an act of human nature, biological chance, or the will of God that one is obliged to encounter the (presence of the) other. Whereas adolescence in part is characterized by the expression of a courage to stand alone, make it on one's own, to the extent that this is possible,[30] adulthood in part is characterized by the willingness to accept encounters, attachments, marriages, interdependencies, human associations for the life-affirming bonds and sense of self they necessarily render. Ironically, one may state that an act of courage is expressed in the willingness to love someone other than oneself. The act of courage may well be observed in the experience of devotion.[31]

Common lore (and popular culture) contains the phrase, "One cannot love another until one loves oneself." During our adolescent years we "work" hard at this matter of self-love; we do a bit of playing at it as well. In realistic terms, the capacity to love another derives from the experiences of having been loved, having been affirmed. We love another only after having been loved by another, affirmed by another, or after we have participated in encounters born in moments of utter helplessness. Self-love, therefore, is an intermediate process lying between having been loved (affirmed) by another and finding the courage to love (affirm) another.[32]

In traditional terms—although this presently is changing in the culture— it was the father's fate to encounter his child only after the child had first been the recipient of his mother's love. One might say that the presence of the Victorian father was an "after-the-fact" experience. Traditionally, a father rarely entered the "business" of loving his child but instead chose for himself the role of educating the child in how to deal with the external world. Respect, obedience, and adulation were far more appropriate ideals for the child than love for or intimacy with the father, not to mention affirmation. Thus the encounter was built on agentic rather than communal terms.[33] There were "real" things to be taught, not mere (metaphysical) feelings to be felt, and every moment counted. Still, the feelings were there in fathers, no matter how disguised, no matter how deeply and assiduously repressed, no matter what the culture may have dictated to the man about his role as father. Children experienced guilt about this fact too. So did many of their parents. Even today, one hears men associating the expression of emotions with courage.

Adding to the complexity of the parent-child relationship is that ontogenetic root of the association. One develops in the womb of one's mother. Irrespective of how this gets confused in the child's mind, the father's role in the conception remains deeply mysterious. Quite likely, this complexity, this matter of the father being essential in the conception yet not, seemingly, intimately bound to the child (and, hence, not intimately bound in the original act of affirmation), continues on in a variety of forms as the child matures. One might suggest that it is symbolic of many father-child associations.

The child realizes the essential nature of the father but cannot articulate, perhaps, the basis of this essential character. Similarly, the father appreciates his role in the conception of the child and thus his role in affirming the child—some fathers even see their children as the products of *their* life work—but cannot always live out this felt sense of being essential and needed.[34] Strain results from this "essentialness" conjoined with a peculiar form of distancing inherent in the period of pregnancy and often during the period immediately following childbirth as well. It produces a push for intimacy and attachment, on the one hand, and for separateness or differentiation, on the other. Yet at some level, the father and child imagine they are united. At some level lies the notion that they are one and the same, *identical*, hence the power of psychological identification. This fact, too, contributes to the tension and sense of guilt over one's individuality, individuation, identity, and, for all we know, personality as well.

We have spoken of parents and children alike discovering their connection to be almost clublike, tribalistic. Initiation into this clublike status often revolves around some ritual in which one person's blood is mixed with that of another, something in which even today's adolescents engage. In the case of parents and children, this mixing of the body's fluids has already been accomplished through the act of conception. Inevitably, their encounter is consecrated by biology as well as by the psychological and sociological processes and routines governing their lives and, of course, their affirmations. So the ritual of blood mixing is actually one of repeating an earlier biological happening.

The push for individual accomplishment, therefore, indeed the entire competitive struggle between children and parents, may find its origin in the earliest affirmations, identification dynamics, and the mysteries enshrouding the very existence of both parents.[35] On the one hand, children must work at psychologically differentiating themselves from their mothers. A point is soon reached where they cannot return to the original psychobiological relationship they once shared (and knew) with her. But what exactly are they to do about differentiating themselves from their father when their original "fusion" with him remains so ambiguous? When did he, the father, ever share this same sort of psychobiological relationship with his own father?

The point is that much has been written in psychological and particularly psychoanalytic literature of the relationship between a child and his or her mother. Much has been written, moreover, of the ambivalent manner, perhaps, in which a child beholds his or her father. Studies also exist on the attempt of one sex to differentiate itself from the same or other sex, the fear of androgyny, and any variety of related topics. What we know little about, however, is the association formed by parent and child through the original affirmation established not as a mutual pact meant to assist them as individual selves but as a partnership, albeit an asymmetric one. In being connected they also differentiate themselves from all other parents of the same, former, and future generations. Said differently, it may be the bond, the association in which parents invest, again, the original affirmation, on which they unwittingly rely as they seek to ward off the anxiety of mortality and the uncertainty over their role in the conception and perpetuation of life. Affirmation, after all, makes possible a sense of reliance on the other. Aware of it or not, we do lean on the affirmation; it holds us aloft. It is for these reasons, therefore, that one is compelled to speak of the so-called spiritual nature of the parent-child relationship and the ultimately spiritual nature of the affirmation. Let me make this same point in another way.

What studies of individual parents reveal goes far beyond individual instances of strain, a search for tenderness and intimacy, explications of hurt and frustration, or cases of competitive envy or narcissistic assault. These investigations speak to the fundamental existential nature of the bond of affirmation ineluctably holding together people of different ages and generations.[36] The strains of merely being alive, the dread of helplessness and the unknown, the terror of personal loneliness and failure, the exhilaration of risk and challenge, all of them manifestly individual experiences, on closer examination turn out to be essential constituents of the association constructed through biological as well as social-psychological mechanisms by parents and children. They derive directly, moreover, from the act of affirmation.

One may properly suggest that the parent-child relationship contains elements of the sacred in that it transcends the mundane matters of everyday life, but it is the work of affirmation that makes it sacred. More significant, life itself, its meaning and purpose, as best as one can deduce, are embedded, one imagines, in the fabric defining the parent-child bond, the parent-child affirmation. In a fundamental sense, the affirmation represents a universal bond because it contains elements pertaining to all people as they exist in the world essentially through personal encounters. Here I am speaking not only of two parents or the child and the parent but, as Earls and Carlson as well as Minuchin suggested, parents and children alike. The very words connote not merely another person—the parent as parent to the child, the child as child to the parent—but an association of these two people created by the original affirmation. Although by definition each parent-child relationship is unique, quite likely the universal qualities of parent-child relationships must be captured in each of these unique and singular relationships; at least the felt sense of the affirmation is universal.[37]

The very meaning of being is encountered in the association I have been examining in these last pages. One properly looks at the parent-child bond in terms of life and death forces; it possesses this significance and this dramatic urgency. Parents who prepare for their child's life, compete with their child in some manner or other, or even compensate for their own felt sense of inadequacy by "living through" their child's achievements are not merely playing out the existential givens of the association; they are instead playing out the givens of disaffirmation. The two lives remain intertwined. The ontological givens and mysteries never recede, no matter how unique, individuated, autonomous, self-governing a parent or child *believes* himself or herself to be. Either party may choose not to be concerned with the reality of the association. Either party may choose to ignore the contribution of the other's life (being) to his or her own life (being), but these actions are mere fictions, contrivances meant to assist one in achieving a sense of personal mastery and a temporary respite or freedom from dependency and inter-dependency.[38]

Inevitably, the truths of the association and power of the original affir-mation are felt; they become part of the felt sense of self. It may take the death of the child or the parent for the survivor to appreciate fully the mag-nitude if not the substance of the association, and with it the affirmation. Yet in the end, each of us, parents or not, comes to learn of these realities and truths.[39] To not know them is to be unwilling to face the truths of our own being. Moreover, it is to avoid looking face on at the woman and man who bore you and, because of the nature of the affirmation, were born by you, acts, I have alleged, constituting disaffirmation, or the lack of a felt sense of self. And so it continues.

7   The Affirmation Curriculum

It is evident that Mr. Rogers's caring and insightful senti-
ments have captured the essence not only of much of contemporary American family struggles but of contemporary American culture as well. Nonetheless, although his words constitute lovely messages, the fact is that many
of us continue to find failure unacceptable and an indication, perhaps, of
significant danger to come. Many of us, moreover, deem failure to be inex-
cusable and patently avoidable or we blame it all on so-called external factors. Frankly, some psychologists advance the notion that at some level
much of our personal failure should be perceived as intentional and thereby
a signal for seeking professional help for the child. "There's simply no reason
for this to have happened," we bark at the child, hoping to discover something redemptive in the report card, all the while uttering one of the most
illogical statements the world has ever heard. Of course there is a reason; we
just may not be interested in it or, more likely, do not wish to know it,
fearing perhaps it may portend the unraveling of one's self and possibly our
entire family. In this moment of disapproval and disaffirmation, we are not
interested in the reasons for the child's failure; we are not interested in those
aspects of his or her self that contain failure, resemble failure, initiate failure,
or remind us that failure lives in *us* as well! So please do us a favor, we beg
the child. Don't fail (us) anymore!

What would happen, I wonder, if instead of asking children every day,
"Did you do your best?" we asked, "Did you have fun today at school?"
What would happen if instead of teachers always forcing themselves to slosh
through the prescribed curricula and academic frameworks, they designed
curricula that at times were meant to create joy in their students? What
would happen if, periodically, not necessarily all the time, teachers constructed classwork around topics and activities that they, the teachers, absolutely loved and found to be utterly worthy of study, whether or not national
tests would address these topics?[1] What would happen if five minutes, say,
of every class hour had to be devoted to giggling, laughing, and just plain
silliness, all of it amounting to the students knowing that their teachers
genuinely enjoyed seeing them and, important, teaching them every day?
For that matter, what would happen if we took seriously Rousseau's obser-

vation that "institutional learning stifles the morality, the innate goodness of the child"?[2]

If these notions seem absurd, unreasoned, and irresponsible, which perhaps they are, consider the present state of many American schools.[3] Consider high school graduates' appreciation and knowledge (or lack of them) of ancient and modern history, foreign languages, literature, mathematics, and science, to name just a few subjects. Consider, too, the brutal conditions awaiting children in many communities,[4] and then argue forcefully that present educational curricula, philosophy, and politics truly work, that educators and politicians honestly assume responsibility, as Levinas argued, for students or young people generally.[5] Political effectiveness often requires that people not act as adolescents because the required stereotypic expressions of feelings and thoughts require a lack of spontaneity normally associated with the young, the very spontaneity that made Holden Caulfield such a hero to so many readers of *The Catcher in the Rye*.[6] Sadly, many adolescents simply have no place in our lives; they appear unworthy of our affirmations. What really is it about school that so many of the young dislike? Would the majority of American students agree with one Massachusetts high school senior who told me, "I like school a lot, it's the classes I can't stand"?

Now consider the child who does well in school, the child, recent research suggests, who tends to cheat as much as any other student in school, feels depressed if not suicidal as much as any other student in school, and, according to one study, is as prejudiced toward gay people as any other student in the school.[7] Typically, we interpret his or her performance not only as a sign of proper psychological adjustment, which of course it may well be but as an indication as well that he or she can do even better. When you think of it, grades truly are a wonderful invention. The child gets an A— and we decide, let's push him harder, perhaps the school will reintroduce the A+, which should never have been taken off the books before our own child graduated.[8]

If accomplishment alone drives us, we never will be satisfied with any accomplishment or any level of accomplishment; it may well become yet another dominating distraction. I know of a middle-aged man who, although he cannot remember a single grade he earned in high school, did well enough to earn acceptance to a prestigious university. He was president of his student government, captain of several athletic teams, and the lead in several of the school's dramatic productions. He recalls having had a steady girlfriend who never got pregnant, and not once was he arrested by the police. And do you believe that every one of his report cards contained these exact words, words he remembers *verbatim*: "Henry's not working up to his potential."

Now, either his teachers had high if not outrageously inflated ideals for him, or they maintained utterly absurd and unattainable expectations. Then again, perhaps they bought into some educational or psychological philosophy popular at the time he attended school advocating that one must never go all out and lovingly reward (affirm) the child for fear that it will inhibit his or her drive to achieve. Said simply, praise gives children a swelled head. Just keep raising the bar, went the philosophy, and the child will continue to reach upward, or break his or her pride, and neck, in the process.

I remember once, after winning some insignificant award when I was twelve, walking with a woman I loved very much. With her arm around my shoulder she explicitly admonished me not to develop a swell head because of this one modest achievement, although as an aging man, I know that swell heads derive from lives that have known very little security, competency, love, reward, sense of accomplishment, or affirmation. Heads swell, in other words, as compensatory responses to disaffirmation and shame. Genuine pride and a sense of goodness and self-worth tend to render children's heads perfectly normal in size.

The previous self-congratulatory description notwithstanding, I always have tried to heed her advice. But I do not recall her ever congratulating me on the award or hearing her say that she was proud of me. I know she never told me that it was all right to enjoy the award or let it be a reminder that I was a good person. Hers was clearly an important message, but only half complete; it lacked, for me, the affirmation. Consequently, I still carry a childlike wish that all children would emerge from their homes and schools knowing for certain that their heads, like their very beings, are just swell.

Let us not lose sight of the point. The child wishes to be loved for who she is, not for what she potentially could become or could have become had she studied or practiced harder, or might still become if she learns how to study or practice harder. He or she longs to be loved merely because he or she is. Recall that the original affirmation contains none of these contingencies. Believing that work and accomplishment define the person lingers as a dominant refrain in American culture. It shows that we still reward humans who *do* more than humans who *be*.[9] We still reward the *products* of self more than the self itself. We may resent the ineluctable cocktail party question, "And what, exactly, is it that you do?" Yet when someone politely tries to get to know us, we imagine they are "coming on" to us, are utterly affected, or are somehow compensating for their felt sense of indifference. Still, we know the hit of the evening was the conversation with this one person whose name we know full well, the person who took especial interest in us, the person who fixed their gaze upon us. Ask me about myself, a common sentiment has it, and I shall follow you anywhere.

Parents do not need to elucidate their child's shortcomings. We always do—quite often, actually, to strangers—but we don't need to. The child already knows about the shortcomings we observe in him; he's desperate now to hear the "longcomings." I knew at age seven I could throw a baseball. I also knew I could not draw or do arithmetic. My school teachers encouraged me in art and mathematics classes as best they could, but I was pathetic and we all knew it. The child knows all his or her faults—some even his or her parents have not yet discovered.[10] But elucidating faults is a far cry from proffering love or undertaking the work of affirmation, even when it is performed in what we graciously call a "constructive manner." It has nothing to do with requiring love. I needed love before I fought with my sister, while I fought with her, and especially the night I almost killed her when I threw a marble at her from across the living room.

Children also observe our faults, although never are *they* allowed to grade *us*. (Interesting, isn't it, that the Bible contains no commandment requiring us to honor our children.) Sadly, many people's lives are destroyed by the assessments made of them by their parents that they then never seem able to shed or transcend. The child of the alcoholic is a perfect example of this phenomenon.[11] Simultaneously loving, pitying, and resenting their alcoholic parent, these children may spend their lives trying to please people, no matter how conflicting their perspectives and demands; their assessments of their parents have deeply affected their own contemporary self-images, aspirations, and perspectives on living.[12]

The need for a child to experience parental as well as classroom affirmation and acceptance of idiosyncratic personalities, traits, and talents is captured in a poignant scene recalled by the actor Leonard Nimoy.[13] We have to travel back to Mr. Nimoy's childhood, when his kindergarten teacher instructed her students to draw a tree. Never one to imagine himself the new Matisse, young Leonard set about to do his best when he happened to glance over at the drawing of his friend. The little boy had created a perfectly magnificent tree whose leaves appeared to float freely and majestically among the branches as if the wind were blowing them about on the paper. On closer inspection, Leonard realized the effect had been created by drawing the leaves unconnected to anything. It was with shock that he heard the teacher's comments to his friend: the tree, she proclaimed, was drawn "incorrectly." It went without saying that the leaves had to be connected to something, otherwise they would fall to the ground. Grimacing slightly as he recounted this event of forty years before, Mr. Nimoy noted that in that one instant an almost lifelong distrust of formal education was born.

How foolish the idea, sometimes, of grades. Give young Leonard the A+ since his leaves were attached to the twigs which were attached to the branches which were attached to the trunk which sat on the ground, but give the other boy a D− and tell him to make the proper connections and appreciate the power of gravity or see me after class. We couldn't just abolish grades, I suppose, and affirm both the children?

Some children feel emotionally abandoned when we praise them for their A in mathematics and focus on the B− in history or the C+ in French. It is perfectly understandable that we wish to have them "pick up" all their grades. But many children might wish to linger a bit on their triumphs; who knows, such success, they imagine, may never come again. At the heart of this matter, however, is distraction; what the child craves is nonjudgmental affirmation. The A is sublime; of course it makes us feel good. But judgment of the child, not merely the child's efforts, remains part of the interaction. After a time we tend to lose sight of what the child requires and focus instead on what *we* require from and of them (requirements born, no doubt, in relationships with our parents and teachers, not our children).

Many children are more than able to articulate their needs for approval, security, and affirmation. Not all of them, however, are allowed publicly to proclaim these needs, these pieces of their selves, for fear that the adults in their lives may be offended and take punitive action. An exception to this is a high school sophomore from Atlanta, who, upon the suggestion of his father, wrote ten attributes of a good father. Among these commandments are "2. Accept the fact that every child doesn't have to be 'normal'; 3. Don't always judge by actions; . . . 7. Recognize that I want to be treated like an adult; 8. Emphasize my good points instead of dwelling on the bad; . . . 10. Realize not everyone has the same abilities and the same ideas of what's important." Tom Rusk and Randy Read, two physicians, put it this way: "Gifted children . . . often feel they are strange, and they get hurt easily. They soon develop a false sense of being defective. All children need a great deal of understanding and comfort from adults. But exceptionally gifted children need more than most. Otherwise they misinterpret their tendency to get hurt easily and to see things differently as evidence there's something wrong with them. This understanding and comforting is rarely offered. It is no wonder so many geniuses lead such tortured lives."[14] Then again, many nongeniuses lead tortured lives as well, so perhaps these people also require understanding and affirmation from their parents lest they too feel themselves to be strange and defective.[15]

The futurist Harris Sussman reminds us of the extraordinary power of affirmation by pointing to studies indicating that low birth weight babies—babies living in seriously compromised circumstances—actually exhibit an increase in survivability by being constantly touched.[16] Healers know well what they are talking about when they refer to the laying on of hands or even the approximation of this experience in the art of Reiki. All people require a laying on of hands, regardless of age, birth weight, height, or Dunn and Bradstreet rating. The common expression having to do with something like a child's poetry being "touching" reveals how deeply felt is the laying on of hands and how well we remember the hands laid upon us.

Hold in mind the image of that tiny baby being touched. The child has not asked for this touch, cried for it, or deserved it; it just comes with the territory, the birthright. Most everyone longs to touch a baby, and the more ways the baby is touched, caressed, stroked, and, most important, held, the better it is for the baby, despite the incorrect admonition of those parents who insist on teaching others the singularly "proper" way of holding their baby. Not surprisingly, we learn that early on in their sexual activity, adolescents also, often reveal a craving for little more than touching, good old-fashioned, atavistic skin-to-skin touching. (Remember in this context Erikson's notion regarding an adolescent's need for fidelity, not necessarily sexuality.[17]

This is what children crave too. The grand reward, affirmation, should come to them merely for being them. And while it sounds glib, I suspect that those people who fear the negative effect on a child of affirming them too strongly when the child is not achieving may be the very people looking for justification to withhold love in the first place. Or perhaps this is the message they carry with them from their own childhood: don't give it if you didn't get it! Need we even make the connection between this sentiment and distractive thinking and the role of disaffirmation in a person's life? Remember, too, how Levinas insisted that affirmation cannot be considered a rational action; without rational planning for it, we discover that it has happened; it lives within us as a sense of self.

It saddens me when I hear thoughtful, sensitive young parents ask professional child-rearing experts this sort of question: "My baby is eight months and he screams madly when he loses sight of me. He wants me with him all the time. I can't even go to the bathroom by myself; I understand all this. But if I stay with him like he wants me to, won't that spoil him?"

What lurks beneath this question? Surely these parents are not hunting for a way out of an ongoing contact with the baby. Are we urging parents to separate from their children earlier and earlier in our culture so that they, the parents, can get back to the *important* things of life? Has someone actually convinced parents that constant attention and devotion lead to spoiling babies? Don't we know by now that the so-called spoiled child is the one who gets everything she asks for except the one thing she genuinely wants and requires? Do we not wonder about people who, despite possessing rooms filled with material possessions, constantly feel compelled to shop? Of course children continue to demand as if they were entitled, and parents continue to give and grouse about perpetually sacrificing for their children. But who of us wishes to address the matter of affirmation, nurturance, and attachment to which the child *is* entitled or at least requires? Instead, we focus on telephone and credit card bills, clothes, shoes, body piercing, and generic mall behavior!

On the subject of children's needs and family distractions, consider this totally reasonable question asked every day of psychologists: What should parents do about their child's shyness? The answer, obviously, is to suggest behavioral changes that might render the child less shy. But consider now the assumption underlying the question—namely, that shyness is something needing to be fixed.

Unthinkingly, most of us tend to assume that shyness constitutes a symptom of low self-esteem, shame, or even disaffirmation. For that matter, much of the behavior we do not like in a child, worry about in a child, or cannot believe a child of *ours* would ever exhibit, we view as a sign of pathology. Research, however, indicates that 80 percent of Americans characterize themselves as shy and that the shyness observed in babies of six months will be present in these children years later.[18] All this suggests that, like it or not, shyness may be a perfectly normal character trait analogous to handedness. In the old days, the child fixers "corrected" left-handers, but no longer. Now we leave them alone, while continuing to assess shyness as a psychological disorder that, if left "untreated," will erupt in childhood depression or adolescent suicidal ideation.

More generally, a great deal of children's behavior may be perfectly normal, part of their unique character and temperament. Think, for the moment, of Heidegger's and May's discussion of the Umwelt, the biological realm of being into which we are by definition thrown, containing as it does our entire genetic makeup and with it that which is called our character, the nature of our inimitable brain's development.[19] Why, then, do we rush so quickly to label so much of children's behavior pathological or even assume that it is something *we* have caused? Why do we tend to psychologize infants, toddlers, and teenagers as if they were all patients and we were all psychiatrists?

Are the millions of children who wake at night and want to crawl in bed with their parents automatically exhibiting serious sleep or behavioral disorders or acting out their doomed role in the Oedipal drama? Can't a child be afraid of the dark anymore, of monsters under the bed, or snakes in the hamper? Can't a two-year-old boy crying in a child care center just miss his parents? Does it have to mean he has been, somehow, shamed or disaffirmed? Maybe he just hates child care. Do his actions, therefore, *have* to connote separation anxiety? Maybe his parents were ready for child care but he was not. Maybe the most powerful sign of affirmation at his age is to love his parents and miss them intensely when they are away. Maybe he feels that a part of his (sense of) self leaves when his parents drop him off in the morning. Of course there is a painfully inhibiting behavioral phenomenon properly labeled separation anxiety, but it may be the case that we attribute it too quickly and too often to children who do not deserve the appellation.

Children get angry, they get frightened. They become suspiciously noisy one minute, suspiciously quiet the next. They adore clothes in June, become nudists in July. For months they sleep through the night like angels, then suddenly go through a stretch when they awaken eight times an hour. All I suggest by enumerating these points is that perhaps we do not always have to fix shyness because it is not always a sign that something (in the self) is broken. Fixing shyness, in other words, may not be part of the work of affirmation. Of course if we as parents covet an assertive, aggressive, achievement-oriented, high-performance, Yale undergraduate–Harvard Law School child who, on completing her Rhodes Scholarship, will run for high political office, we are going to despise shyness; we will also probably buy heaps of books on child rearing and prepare lists of outstanding child psychoanalysts, just in case.

Rather than focus on shyness, therefore, we might wait to see if the child appears unhappy or disaffirmed (now *there* are two nonpsychological words!). Perhaps the child's shyness is in part the parents' problem. Perhaps it is the story of the world perpetuated by parents that causes them to determine the nature and ultimate treatment of childhood shyness rather than the unique story of shyness safeguarded by their own child.[20] Somewhere in their narrative, after all, parents learned that shyness is another word for pathology. But the shy child could well be unhappy not because he is shy but because he knows his parents are terribly unhappy about something very natural, he believes, living within him. If, at two months, he felt our irritations (and distractions), then surely he senses our most recent displeasure with him. And when we show concern for or fear of a child's trait, the child feels that we disapprove of *him*, not merely the trait. Granted, affirmation remains a delicate, even magical proposition, but as I noted in earlier chapters, there is no fine line between affirming the child and affirming the child's trait, as some parents fear. Affirmation has more to do with *us*, the affirmers, than with those we affirm, hence we need not fear damaging a child's sense of self when disapproving of a particular deed or trait.

It may be time to stop attributing pathology to children, particularly adolescents, and cease spewing all these popular psychological terms. We might better retrieve the adjectives used by novelists, such words as "rambunctious," "mischievous," "antic," "bumptious," and "inquisitive." It may be less damaging to the child to swear in front of her than pepper her with our scintillating psychological lexicon. Of course, we have to be psychologically sensitive and aware with our children. But being psychologically sensitive often means little more than being thoughtful and self-reflective (or reflective about another's self). Parents need not always rush into believing there is a problem or that a child is "problematic" merely because popular culture has determined that adolescence is another word for undesirable pathology and shyness remains an un-American trait. Parents obsessed with psychological assessments of their children stand as perfect examples of what John Dewey had in mind when he claimed that unself-reflective people who fail to see beyond immediate circumstances, impulses, tastes, and momentary fads tend to lead their lives with enslaved minds.[21]

To claim that shyness is pathological may just be a way of saying that it is personally and socially objectionable without saying that it is personally and socially objectionable. Shyness alone tells us little about the child. Shyness may be a sweet and endearing trait; a shy child may even be sweet. I know for certain that lots of grandmothers without advanced psychology degrees think so. And it never stopped them from affirming their grandchildren and quite a few of the neighborhood children as well.

THE SCENE is a Boston area public high school auditorium where I am taking part in an evening panel discussion on teenagers, drinking, and drugs (even though some would properly question why we continue to make a distinction between alcohol and drugs; others may wonder why panel discussions involving adolescents so often focus on the topic of drinking and drugs). The cavernous room is about one-third full, mostly with women; fewer men typically attend school functions of this sort. Children, apparently, remain the responsibility of women (and a few aging psychologists).

Late in the program as we are about to adjourn, a young woman on the panel suddenly rises to speak. An outstanding senior, I learn later, with a long and impressive list of extracurricular activities, interests, and hobbies and on her way to an Ivy League university, she stuns the audience by announcing that she is about to explain why it is that she loves getting drunk every weekend night! From my seat on the stage, I scan the audience imagining I will be able to detect her mortified parents.

"Every single thing I do," the young woman begins, "is judged by someone or other. Everything! I comb my hair a different way, someone remarks on it. My father questions whether I've done all my homework [something, frankly, I myself did with my children every night of their lives], and this is after I have been admitted to college. My mother looks at me in the morning and says, 'You're not really going to school looking like *that*, are you?' My teachers grade my papers, my classroom participation, my every word, my every syllable, my overall level of cooperation. They even wonder about my mood. My boyfriend rates me on . . . I leave it to you to guess about what. My girlfriends judge me on the way I act with my boyfriend and other girls. Everyone comments on my taste in music, my selection of radio stations, my choice of movies. You better believe I love getting drunk"—and these are her words verbatim—"it's the only time I can be me!"

In reflecting for a moment on this matter of drinking, we might note a dichotomy some young people have created for themselves.[22] Either they can identify so intensely with some celebrity that somewhere in their mind they actually "become" that celebrity, or if this young woman speaks for other alcohol-and drug-using youngsters, they can totally obliterate social and psychological realities and most especially the pain of their existence, killing off entirely any contact with their exterior and interior worlds. They can actually obliterate every sense of self they have ever had. Either way, they have discovered two forms of distraction that lead them away from themselves (their selves), their own thoughts and dreams and boredom, their own voices, their own being.[23]

One of the messages we take from these children is that constant judging precludes their turning to themselves free of outside stimuli or medication.

Constant judging and grading, be it undertaken by peers or the elders who instruct them, tend to turn children away from themselves (their selves) and toward the direction of any distractive element or human being guaranteed to keep them from finding happiness. In their need to develop esteem, not borrow it from the illusory strengths of stars and drugs, children do not wish to stand before judges; they wish to fall into the protective arms of loved ones, affirming ones.

That night in the auditorium was the first time I had heard freedom and the opportunity to live as one's true self advanced as reasons for heavy drinking. For me, drinking was merely another form of distraction, a rather deluded one, but distraction nonetheless. Still, it says something about the power of adults' (and young people's) assessments and expectations (and appetites) and how distracting these can be, whatever our age or status, when we are obliged to react to other people's adverse assessments or unreasonable (and unreasoned) expectations of us, some of which properly may be designated as disaffirmations.[24] The young, we too often forget, also possess a sense of *our* selves.

Ostensibly, the notion of an expectation involves the establishment or assumption of a goal, purpose, or future orientation. It involves, as well, a need to accomplish or do something. As your parent, I *expect* you to get better grades, act politely at the party, and wear appropriate clothes to church. The values we seek to inculcate in our children often live within our expectations; the very act of socialization implies the act of expecting. Indeed, much of social interaction and the concept of civility coalesce around the reality of an expectation.

Yet an expectation may also carry a message about the present and past: I expect you to earn high grades, we admonish our child, but in the silence we all hear the unspoken words, "unlike last semester when you really blew it, young man!" The expectation, in other words, may be intended to direct the ship on a new course, but the child often hears it as yet one more criticism of the old course. Like those faults we need not elucidate for our children, expectations, too, need not always be articulated. The children know them all too well, for we have already screamed them in a variety of ways. Such a family interaction is but one of many in which what is being said and to whom it is addressed remain immaculately ambiguous. Keep in mind the fear that one is defective and unlovable, "unaffirmable." Keep in mind as well that one emotion which may hover about the child or lurk in their sense of self as shame.[25]

Then, too, some of our expectations remain unrealistic; the child cannot possibly meet them. Nor can *we* perhaps meet them, which remains an important matter our own parents never completely understood. Some expectations emerge, moreover, as so outlandish that they quickly become little more than further distractions. This is the variety of expectation we impose on our children which speaks to those inadequacies of our own life. I expect you to get the good grades I never got and therefore give me the gratification (and affirmation) my own parents never received from me, which, had they, would have given me great gratification. But wait, it gets even more complicated: I expect you to get good grades so that I can receive the gratification (and affirmation) from my parents that I should have received just by being me, irrespective of my grades. Besides, I take your bad grades to mean that you are as angry with me as I was with my parents—and feared they might be with me as well—which is precisely the reason I never gave them the gift of good grades in the first place and why I could never take out my anger at my parents and instead took it out on my self (as disaffirmation). Now, who could possibly get any studying done with all that noise going on!

The distracted child who turns to the celebrity or material product—and often there is only a minimal difference between the two—for sustenance, happiness, and basic life foods, as so many children presently do, well may become the child who misses out on happiness, health, and self-reliance.[26] If John Bowlby is correct, then only strong attachments (yielding affirmations), and not merely to Mr. Rogers, can yield these ingredients. The distracted consumer, looking to material goods that economic index purveyors so adore, as well as contrived and unworkable philosophies and outlooks, is left with unhappiness, illness, and total dependence on other people and things, mere stuff, to guide (and distract) him or her along life's inauthentic paths. False gods, these people and products have been called, for the true gods are to be found among those who raise and care for us, affirm us, and who, in their enduring attachments to us and ideally to one another, teach us how to know our self genuinely, love our self and others, and eventually introduce this same affirming curriculum to subsequent generations.

Today, tomorrow, or sometime next week, I will watch some young celebrity being interviewed on television. If history proves me correct, I will hear him or her say in response to some question, "Well, you know, in order to love others, you have to learn to love yourself." Then he or she will go on with this grandiose philosophical tenet that justifies him or her loving only himself or herself for the next several decades. Millions will take from the message, the counsel really, to go home and pamper, worship, and, above all, love yourself. It is not a bad idea to love yourself. But a profound distraction nonetheless hides in this notion and comes at one from two directions, both of them relevant to my discussion here.

First, the culture somehow has determined that self-love, not merely a sense of self, is the highest philosophical and psychological ideal. This determination stems in part, perhaps, from the fact that an entire generation has grown up insufficiently loved, nurtured, parented, or even valued. The means, learning to love yourself, suddenly become the end in itself. Narcissism and self-celebration triumph; the only face and soul we ever need glorify, nourish, and affirm is our own. Simultaneously, we learn that you can teach your self to love itself, which probably is true. But the fundamental truth remains that children come to love and affirm their (sense of) self by having been loved and affirmed by their parents *and* by watching their parents love and affirm each other, not to mention by becoming competent at various activities. In a sense, affirming parents essentially do much of the early affirming work for their child. Children are meant to emerge fullblown, someday, as self-loving, self-approving, and self-affirming adults, capable and desirous of loving others, hopefully forever. They ought to obtain these qualities not because honor grades were achieved in the infamous childhood curriculum, but merely because they were enrolled in the childhood curriculum. In this one curriculum, everyone is accepted and affirmed, or ought to be, without even having to apply. I am that I am. Being affirmed is intended to be a part of the unwritten and laughably lopsided arrangement, but not contract, entered into by parents and children.

All this may sound peculiarly saccharine. One hopes that it does not fall into the growing literature of self-esteem, at least that literature which says all efforts must be made toward developing self-esteem while forgetting that much of self-esteem, like the dividend from a stock, may be the by-product of something far more significant, such as affirmation. The development of good character and competence typically yields a perfectly reasonable self-esteem. No self-esteem can be built on a foundation without character. Love, however, surely plays a role, as Fromm noted a half century ago.[27]

Love and work, Fromm observed, as had Freud before him, represent two activities allowing us to restore meaning to life and providing us a genuine sense of belonging, completeness, and above all self. With love supported by a moral scaffold, we unite with others, become altruistic, do unto others as we would have them do unto us, and, just as Kant taught, hold these actions to be universal moral laws. Love, for Fromm, was the most desirable way to derive meaning from life if only because it is the most desirable form of human interaction. He was perfectly prepared, moreover, to develop entire societies from it. A balance between security and responsibility is afforded by love, he alleged (along with the development of that moral scaffold), and affirmation sits deep in the heart of respect that a parent offers to a child, a respect the parent hopes the child will incorporate as part of his or her sense of self.[28]

The love and affirmation offered by parents also provides the basis of a so-called love for and affirmation of life, nature, all living things. It leads a child, Fromm wrote, to be attracted to human growth and development, constructive life forces, authentic creativity. It causes the child to define influence in terms of reason and example (affirmation), rather than aggressiveness, coercion, and outright force (disaffirmation). As it makes the child look outward toward the world, it tends to focus her or him on the expansiveness of the future rather than on the constricting elements of the past. It allows the child, in other words, to imagine possibility rather than believe in (the continuation of) impossibility, a sense akin to Basch's nihilistic worldview. Notice that Fromm's words suggest the significance of turning the child away from himself or herself in the direction of contributing to others, which in a sense is the basis of moral behavior and a far cry from the more modern version of self-esteem theories which essentially instruct the child to turn inward toward himself or herself.

Some children, however, are not exposed to the love or affirmation curriculum. They know relatively little about love, conditional or otherwise. Some children never even receive their copy of the birthright affirmation contract. Instead, they receive the "How to Survive Childhood" or "Home Alone" contracts. These are the psychological if not literally latchkey children, the ones always home alone, even when others may be around.[29] These are the children constantly asking to know the time and eager for the hours to pass so they can hear Mr. Rogers say directly to them, "There's no one in the world exactly like you. . . . I like you just the way you are."

For the venerable grammarian we recite *amo, amas, amat,* or I love; you love; he, she, or it loves. For the venerable psychologist we recite I am loved, I love myself, I love another. Just as easily, we may substitute the word "affirm" for love. Love and affirmation launch my search for self-reliance and beneath it a sense of self that I value, not begrudge. I can even get angry with my father and not fear that he will hurt, abandon, or disaffirm me; I can rely, in other words, on his presence and my own felt sense of his affirmation. The former cannot endure, but the latter can. This, too, is part of what is meant by the average, predictable, and ultimately affirming environment so beneficial to children.

Wouldn't it be marvelous to hear celebrities speak more about the ways they actively love and affirm other people? Better yet, wouldn't it be wonderful to enjoy people just doing the things they do that earn them celebrity status, while focusing on our own love life and not theirs? Wouldn't it be fun to imagine a time when celebrities buy magazines in which *our* fabulous lives and those of *our* children, in which the lives not of the rich and famous but of the "just getting by and not at all known but properly affirmed," are featured? Sometimes I wish that people could feel comforted in the thought that they will not be famous, for fame may not be such an ideal devoutly to be wished. It may even carry with it all varieties of disaffirmations. After all, for John Updike's famous character Henry Bech, it was "a cherished calamity."[30]

Let us just do the work that permits us to be loving and lovable, affirming and affirmed, the child in me keeps repeating. Fame, yet another precarious distraction, is but a prop meant to fill the emptiness and hollowness. Although fame may afford wealth and momentary power, it may well live as *the* grand compensation, the embodiment of an ego inauthentically affirmed. Children who are genuinely affirmed, loved "merely" on that average and predictable basis, require no stardom for one obvious reason: they have already achieved it, without even cutting their first CD. I often wish Andy Warhol had not uttered that infamous remark having to do with the fifteen future minutes of fame to which we are all "entitled." Most of us in this culture never will experience those fifteen minutes of fame Warhol promised; many of us are unable to remember fifteen minutes of genuine family history. But let me amend this one observation.

Hundreds of millions of people will receive neither public attention nor prominent roles in movies or television shows. In the context of America's public relations/entertainment mentality in which outrageous or unseemly folks at times are paraded out before television cameras, their own life is deemed boring.[31] They are called, simply, ethical parents, affirming people. Produce a television show about them, and most audiences would turn away in droves. They simply appear too usual, too common. People of this sort, parents doing a nice job, raising nice children, continue to be called "the silent majority," Homer's term in *The Iliad*, not so incidentally, for the dead.

I have met many of these parents and their children, some of whom, truthfully, made it tougher for my own children to be admitted to college. I've seen well-mannered, intelligent, moral, pleasant, dare I say affirmed young men and women in high schools and college admissions offices across this country, and besides standing in my children's way, not that I'm at all competitive, they appear nothing short of terrific. I rarely think of them as the children of the silent majority or even the children of average, expectable environments. Before this book, I never even associated them with the word "affirmation."

Rather, I imagine that regularly in these young people's lives, in their homes, schools and communities, they heard and internalized Mr. Rogers's deceptively simple message spoken to them by heaven only knows whom, but I suspect that they *hope* it has been their parents: "There's no one in the world exactly like you. . . . I like you just the way you are."

Notes

Chapter 1. The Act of Affirmation

1. See Howard Gardner, *Frames of Mind: The Theory of Multiple Intelligences* (New York: Basic Books, 1983).

2. See Jerome Kagan, *The First Two Years* (Cambridge: Harvard University Press, 1981), and *The Nature of the Child* (New York: Basic Books, 1984).

3. See Susan R. Walen, Raymond DiGiuseppe, and Richard L. Wessler, *A Practitioner's Guide to Rational-Emotive Therapy*, 2d ed. (New York: Oxford University Press, 1980). See also Albert Willis and Robert A. Harper, *A New Guide to Rational Living* (Englewood Cliffs, N.J.: Prentice-Hall, 1975).

4. Eli H. Newberger, "Treating This Heavy Mid-Life of Men," *American Journal of Orthopsychiatry* 71 (July 2001): 279.

5. Walt Whitman, "Song of Myself," from *Leaves of Grass* (Garden City, N.Y.: Doubleday, 1926).

6. Robert Kegan, *The Evolving Self* (Cambridge: Harvard University Press, 1982).

7. Robert Kegan, *In Over Our Heads: The Mental Demands of Modern Life* (Cambridge: Harvard University Press, 1994).

8. Heinz Kohut, *The Search for the Self*, vol. 2, ed. Paul Ornstein (New York: International Universities Press, 1978), and *The Kohut Seminars: On Self Psychology and Psychotherapy with Adolescents and Young Adults* (New York: Norton, 1987). See also Arnold Goldberg, ed., with summarizing reflections by Heinz Kohut, *Advances in Self Psychology* (New York: International Universities Press, 1980).

9. Peter Marris, "Holding on to Meaning through the Life-Cycle," in *Challenges of the Third Age: Meaning and Purpose in Later Life*, ed. Robert S. Weiss and Scott A. Bass (New York: Oxford University Press, 2001), 15.

10. Thomas J. Cottle, *At Peril: Stories of Injustice*. (Amherst: University of Massachusetts Press, 2001), chap. 1.

11. Ralph Waldo Emerson, *Self-Reliance and Other Essays* (New York: Dover, 1993), 90.

12. See M. Rose, *Industrial Behavior* (London: Allen Lane, 1975).

13. Interestingly, the word "name" in one Native American language means "the place where we are tied together." Cited in Caroline E. Heller, *Until We Are Strong Together: Women Writers in the Tenderloin* (New York: Teachers College Press, 1997), 109.

14. See, for example, Bruce Narramore, "Serving Two Masters? Commentary

on 'Dealing with Religious Resistance in Psychotherapy': Reply," *Journal of Psychology and Theology* 22, 4 (1994): 261–63.

15. John Dewey, *How We Think* (Amherst, N.Y.: Prometheus Press, 1991).

16. On this point see Stephen Kemmis, "Action Research and the Politics of Reflection." In *Reflection: Turning Experience into Learning*, ed. D. Boud, R. Keogh, and D. Walker. (London: Kogan Page, 1985), 139–64. I am grateful to Arthur Beane for this reference.

17. Hazel Markus, "Self-Knowledge: An Expanded View," *Journal of Personality* 51, 3 (1983): 543.

18. Jean Piaget, *Six Psychological Studies* (New York Random House, 1967), 64.

19. At the time I wrote these passages, I had not read pediatrician Barry Zuckerman's prescription that he and his Reach Out and Read program colleagues would be providing their young patients to give to their fathers: "Read to your child every day." See Barry Zuckerman, "Read to Your Child Every Day: An Rx for Dads Everywhere," *Boston Globe*, June 17, 2001, F7.

20. Selma H. Fraiberg, *The Magic Years: Understanding and Handling the Problems of Early Childhood* (New York: Scribner's, 1959).

21. Jerome Bruner, *On Knowing* (Cambridge: Harvard University Press, 1979), 20.

22. See Gerald Michael Erchak, *The Anthropology of Self and Behavior* (New Brunswick, N.J.: Rutgers University Press, 1992).

23. See Bruno Bettelheim, *On Learning to Read: The Child's Fascination with Meaning* (New York: Knopf, 1981).

24. See the National Academies, 2000, "Policies, Programs that Affect Young Children Fail to Keep Pace with Scientific Advances," press release, available at <http://www4.nationalacademies.org/news.nsf/(ByDocID)/56B752E9E7D320858 52569 6D004AAA45?OpenDocument>.

25. Brian Hall, *Madeline's World: A Child's Journey from Birth to Age 3* (Boston: Houghton Mifflin, 1997), 118. I am grateful to Professor Evelyne Ender for this reference.

26. See Peter I. Glauber, "Federn's Annotation of Freud's Theory of Anxiety," *Journal of the American Psychoanalytic Association* 11, 1 (1963): 91.

27. See John Maguire, *The Power of Personal Story Telling: Spinning Tales to Connect with Others* (New York: Jeremy P. Tarcher/Putnam, 1998); M. Mair, "Psychology as Story Telling," *International Journal of Construct Psychology* 1, 2 (1988). 125–37; A. Parry, "Universe of Stories," *Family Process* 30 (1991): 37–54; and Bert O. States, *Dreaming and Story Telling* (Ithaca: Cornell University Press, 1993).

28. See Thomas R. Blakeslee, *Beyond the Conscious Mind: Unlocking the Secrets of the Self* (New York: Plenum Press, 1996).

29. Rollo May, *The Discovery of Being: Writings in Existential Psychology* (New York: Norton, 1983), 10.

30. Joseph C. Hermanowicz and Harriet P. Morgan, "Ritualizing the Routine: Collective Identity Affirmation," *Sociological Forum* 14, 2 (1999): 197–214.

31. Mircea Eliade, *The Sacred and the Profane: The Nature of Religion*, trans. William R. Trask (New York: Harcourt Brace, 1959).

32. Gloria Denise Mays and Carole Holden Lund, "Male Caregivers of Mentally Ill Relatives," *Perspectives in Psychiatric Care* 35, 2 (1999): 19–28.

33. Eliot Turiel, "The Development of Social-Convention and Moral Concepts," in *Fundamental Research in Moral Development: A Compendium*, ed. Bill Puka. (New York: Garland, 1994), 2: 255–92.

34. Erich Fromm, *The Sane Society* (New York: Holt, Rinehart and Winston, 1955), 60.

35. On this point see Gail Melson, *Why the Wild Things Are* (Cambridge: Harvard University Press, 2001).

36. Cited in Parker J. Palmer, *The Courage to Teach: Exploring the Inner Landscape of a Teacher's Life* (San Francisco: Jossey-Bass, 1998), 16.

37. Carroll was refering to Brian Stock's book, *Augustine the Reader*. Cited in James Carroll, "Books Make Us Free and Also Human," *Boston Globe*, June 19, 2001, A15.

38. William James, *Principles of Psychology* (New York: Dover, 1950), cited in Arthur T. Jersild, "Social and Individual Origins of the Self," in *Relevant Readings in Human Development*, ed. John J. Mitchell (Berkeley, Calif.: McCutchan Publishing, 1971), 111.

39. Carl Rogers, *Client-Centered Therapy: Its Current Practice, Implications, and Theory* (Boston: Houghton Mifflin, 1965), and *Counseling and Psychotherapy: New Concepts in Practice* (Boston: Houghton Mifflin, 1942).

40. See William H. Quinn, "The Client Speaks Out: Three Domains of Meaning," *Journal of Family Psychotherapy* 7, 2 (1996): 71–93.

41. Monica Gundrum, Germain Lietaer, and Christiane Matthijssen Van-Hees, "Carl Rogers' Responses in the Seventeenth Session with Miss Mun: Comments from a Process-Experiential and Psychoanalytic Perspective," *British Journal of Guidance and Counseling* 27, 4 (1999): 461–82.

42. Jeff Stone, "What Exactly Have I Done? The Role of Self-Attribute Accessibility in Dissonance," in *Cognitive Dissonance: Progress on a Pivotal Theory in Social Psychology*, ed. Eddie Harmon-Jones and Judson Mills, Science Conference Series (Washington, D.C.: American Psychological Association, 1999), 175–200.

43. Leon Festinger, with Vernon Allen, *Conflict, Decision, and Dissonance* (Stanford: Stanford University Press, 1964).

44. Leslie S. Greenberg and Sandra C. Paivio, "Allowing and Accepting Painful Emotional Experiences," *International Journal of Action Methods* 51, 2 (1998): 47–61.

45. On this point see Judith Guss-Teicholz, "Loewald's 'Positive Neutrality' and the Affirmative Potential of Psychoanalytic Interventions," In *Psychoanalytic Study of the Child* (New York: International Universities Press, 1995), 50:48–75.

46. Hans W. Loewald, "Ego and Reality," *International Journal of Psychoanalysis* 32 (1951), and "Instinct Theory, Object Relations, and Psychic Structure Forma-

tion," *Journal of the American Psychoanalytic Association* 26, 3 (1978): 493–506. The Winnicott citation comes from Fred Weinstein, *Freud, Psychoanalysis, Social Theory: The Unfulfilled Promise* (Albany: State University of New York Press, 2001), 22.

47. See, for example, Byron Killingmo, "Affirmation in Psychoanalysis," *International Journal of Psychoanalysis* 76, 3 (1995): 503–18.

48. Mark Sehl, "Stalemates in Therapy and the Notion of Gratification," *Psychoanalytic Review* 81, 2 (1994): 301–21.

49. Michael Robbins, "Therapeutic Presence in Holistic Psychotherapy," in *Therapeutic Presence: Bridging Expression and Form*, ed. Arthur Robbins (London: Jessica Kingsley Publishers, 1998), 153–81.

50. See, for example, Kohut, *Search for the Self*.

51. On this point see Lucien Stryk, *The Awakened Self: Encounters with Zen* (New York: Kodansha International, 1995).

52. Martin Heidegger, *Being and Time*, trans. Joan Stambaugh (Albany: State University of New York Press, 1966), and May, *Discovery of Being*.

53. John R. Suler and Anthony Molino, eds., *The Couch and the Tree: Dialogues in Psychoanalysis and Buddhism* (New York: North Point Press, 1998), 321–43.

54. Kathleen Hirsch, "Circle of Friends." *Boston Globe Magazine*, March 11, 2001, 15.

55. Sigmund Freud, *A General Introduction to Psychoanalysis*, trans. G. Stanley Hall (New York: Liveright, 1935), and *The Basic Writings of Sigmund Freud*, trans. and ed. A. A. Brill (New York: Modern Library, 1938).

56. James B. Allen and Jennifer L. Ferrand, "Environmental Locus of Control, Sympathy, and Proenvironmental Behavior: A Test of Geller's Actively Caring Hypothesis," *Environment and Behavior* 31, 3 (1999): 338–53.

57. Terence G. Wilson, "Acceptance and Change in the Treatment of Eating Disorders and Obesity," *Behavior Therapy* 27, 3 (1996): 417–39.

58. Markus, "Self-Knowledge."

59. In this context see Joshua Aronson, Hart Blanton, and Joel Cooper, "From Dissonance to Disidentification: Selectivity in the Self-Affirmation Process," *Journal of Personality and Social Psychology* 68, 6 (1995): 986–96.

60. Joanne V. Wood, Maria Giordano Beech, and Mary-Jo Ducharme, "Compensating for Failure through Social Comparison," *Personality and Social Psychology Bulletin* 25, 11 (1999): 1370–86.

61. Martha M. Dore, Lani Nelson Zlupko, and Eda Kaufmann, " 'Friends in Need': Designing and Implementing a Psychoeducational Group for School Children from Drug-Involved Families," *Social Work* 44, 2 (1999): 179–90.

62. On this point see Kathrin Asper, *Being-in-Oneself, Being-in-the-World: Finding a Home and Regaining Self-Worth* (London: Guild of Pastoral Psychology, 1994), and Theodore Isaac Rubin, with Eleanor Rubin, *Compassion and Self-Hate: An Alternative to Despair* (New York: D. McKay, 1975).

63. Dusty Lee Humes and Laura Lynn Humphrey, "A Multimethod Analysis of

Families with a Polydrug-Dependent or Normal Adolescent Daughter," *Journal of Abnormal Psychology* 103, 4 (1994): 676–85.

64. Gloria Denise Mays and Carole Holden Lund, "Male Caregivers of Mentally Ill Relatives," *Perspectives in Psychiatric Care* 35, 2 (1999): 19–28.

65. Nathalie Des-Rosiers, Bruce Feldthusen, and Oleana A. R. Hankivsky, "Legal Compensation for Sexual Violence: Therapeutic Consequences and Consequences for the Judicial System," *Psychology, Public Policy, and Law* 4, 1–2 (1998): 433–51.

66. Joseph Veroff, Elizabeth Douvan, Terri L. Orbuch, and Linda K. Acitelli, "Happiness in Stable Marriages: The Early Years," In *The Developmental Course of Marital Dysfunction*, ed. Thomas N. Bradbury (Cambridge: Cambridge University Press, 1998), 152–79.

67. Gary R. Birchler, Diana M. Doumas, and William S. Fals-Stewart, "The Seven C's: A Behavioral Systems Framework for Evaluating Marital Distress," *Family Journal of Counseling and Therapy for Couples and Families* 7, 3 (1999): 253–64.

68. Sandra L. Murray, John G. Holmes, Geoff MacDonald, and Phoebe C. Ellsworth, "Through the Looking Glass Darkly? When Self-Doubts Turn into Relationship Insecurities," *Journal of Personality and Social Psychology* 75, 6 (1998): 1459–80.

69. Harry R. Moody, "Why Dignity in Old Age Matters," *Journal of Gerontological Social Work* 29, 3 (1997): 13–38.

70. Jane R. Pretat, *Coming to Age: The Croning Years and Late-Life Transformation* (Toronto: Inner City Books, 1994). Work of a similar nature was performed with homeless people as well. See Ann E. Berens, "Search-for-Meaning Groups for the Homeless," *International Forum for Logotherapy* 15, 1 (1992): 46–49.

71. Constance Rooke, "Old Age in Contemporary Fiction: A New Paradigm of Hope," in *Handbook of the Humanities and Aging*, ed. Thomas R. Cole and David Dirck Van Tassel (New York: Springer, 1992), 241–57.

72. See Hilde Bruch, *The Golden Cage: The Enigma of Anorexia Nervosa* (Cambridge: Harvard University Press, 1978), and Joan Jacobs Brumberg, *Fasting Girls: The Emergence of Anorexia Nervosa as a Modern Disease* (Cambridge: Harvard University Press, 1988).

73. David Krueger, "Food as Selfobject in Eating Disorder Patients," *Psychoanalytic Review* 84, 4 (1997): 617–30.

74. Bruch, *Golden Cage*.

75. We do the same thing with our investment in weather forecasters who we imagine are able not only to predict but also to magically control natural occurrences. That these forecasters are frequently wrong matters little to us; our concern remains the fantasy of the predictability and controllability of the unpredictable and the uncontrollable.

76. Bill Thornton and Jason Maurice, "Physique Contrast Effect: Adverse Impact of Idealized Body Images for Women," *Sex Roles* 37, 5–6 (1997): 433–39.

77. Carl G. Jung, *Basic Writings*, ed. and intro. by Violet Staub de Lazlo (New York: Modern Library, 1959). See also David Ray Griffin, ed., *Archetypal Process: Self and Divine in Whitehead, Jung, and Hillman* (Evanston, Ill.: Northwestern University Press, 1989).

78. Marie-Louise von Franz, *Archetypal Dimensions of the Psyche* (Boston: Shambhala Publications, 1994). See also Anthony Stevens, *Archetypes: A Natural History of the Self* (New York: Morrow, 1982).

79. Not ironically, the word "yoga," the various practices of which are intended to yield this sort of conjoining, actually means "union," with Jnana yoga being the practice of self-knowledge.

Chapter 2. The Relational Aspect of Affirmation

1. Stephen M. Drigotas, Caryl E. Rusbult, Jennifer Wieselquist, and Sarah W. Whitton, "Close Partner as Sculptor of the Ideal Self: Behavioral Affirmation and the Michelangelo Phenomenon," *Journal of Personality and Social Psychology* 77, 2 (1999): 293–323.

2. Tanya S. Scheffler and Peter J. Naus, "The Relationship between Fatherly Affirmation and a Woman's Self-Esteem, Fear of Intimacy; Comfort with Womanhood, and Comfort with Sexuality," *Canadian Journal of Human Sexuality* 8, 1 (1999): 39–45.

3. Peter J. Naus and John P. Theis, "The Significance of Fatherly Affirmation for a Man's Psychological Well-Being: A Comparison of Canadian and Dutch University Students," *Canadian Journal of Human Sexuality* 4, 4 (1995): 237–45.

4. Keith S. Beauregard and David Dunning, "Turning Up the Contrast: Self-Enhancement Motives Prompt Egocentric Contrast Effects in Social Judgments," *Journal of Personality and Social Psychology* 74, 3 (1998): 606–21.

5. See Steven Fein and Steven J. Spencer, "Prejudice as Self-Image Maintenance: Affirming the Self through Derogating Others," *Journal of Personality and Social Psychology* 73, 1 (1997): 31–44.

6. Susann R. Hill and Toni R. Tollerud, "Restoring Dignity in At-Risk Students," *School Counselor* 44, 2 (1996): 122–32.

7. Anne Sved-Williams, "A Group for the Adult Daughters of Mentally Ill Mothers: Looking Backwards and Forwards," *British Journal of Medical Psychology* 71, 1 (1998): 73–83.

8. See John C. Gunzburg, " 'What Works?' Therapeutic Experience with Grieving Clients," *Journal of Family Therapy* 16, 2 (1994): 159–71.

9. Martin Heidegger, *Being and Time*, trans. Joan Stambaugh (Albany, State University of New York Press, 1966), and Rollo May, *The Discovery of Being: Writings in Existential Psychology* (New York: Norton, 1983).

10. Lev Vygotsky, *Mind in Society* (Cambridge: Harvard University Press, 1978), 57.

11. Lauren Lawrence, *Dream Keys for Love: Unlocking the Secrets of Your Own Heart* (New York: Dell, 1999).

12. Heinz Kohut, *The Search for the Self*, vol. 2, ed. Paul Ornstein (New York: International Universities Press, 1978), and Donald Palladino Jr., "Poets to Come: Walt Whitman, Self Psychology, and the Readers of the Future," unpublished manuscript, 2000. See also M. Rosenberg, *Conceiving the Self* (New York: Basic Books, 1979).

13. In this same regard, Caleb Gattengo suggested that "to recognize oneself as energy, is to become aware of what is in us outside of objectifications, and his new awareness is precisely what takes place in the revision of the content of his 'soul,' which the adolescent undertakes" (*The Adolescent and His Will* [New York: Outerbridge and Dienstfrey, 1971] 64) Cited in Andrew G. Wright, "American Teenagers Distracted," unpublished manuscript, Boston University, 2001.

14. James L. Fosshage, "Self-Psychology and Its Contributions to Psychoanalysis: An Overview," *Journal of Analytic Social Work* 5, 2 (1998): 1–17.

15. See Jeanne L. Jensma, "Kohut's Tragic Man and Imago Dei: Human Relational Needs in Creation, the Fall, and Redemption," *Journal of Psychology and Theology* 21, 4 (1993): 288–96.

16. John Bowlby, *Loss, Sadness and Depression*, vol. 3 of *Attachment and Loss* (New York: Basic Books, 1980). See also Jeffry A. Simpson and W. Steven Rholes, eds., *Attachment Theory and Close Relationships* (New York: Guilford Press, 1998).

17. Richard I. Evans, *Dialogue with Erik Erikson* (New York: Harper and Row, 1967), 35.

18. Mary Ainsworth, "Deprivation of Maternal Care: A Reassessment of Its Effects," in *Maternal Care and Mental Health*, by John Bowlby (New York. Schocken Books, 1966).

19. Pat Sable, "Attachment, Detachment, and Borderline Personality Disorder," *Psychotherapy* 34, 2 (1997): 171–81.

20. Michael F. Basch, *Doing Psychotherapy* (New York: Basic Books, 1980), and *Understanding Psychotherapy: The Science behind the Art* (New York: Basic Books, 1988); John T. Pardeck, *Social Work Practice: An Ecological Approach* (Westport, Conn.: Auburn House/Greenwood Publishing Group, 1996).

21. Lorna Smith Benjamin, "Good Defenses Make Good Neighbors," in *Ego Defenses: Theory and Measurement*, ed. Hope R. Conte and Robert Plutchik. Publication series of the Department of Psychiatry of Albert Einstein College of Medicine of Yeshiva University, no. 10 (New York: John Wiley, 1995), 53–78.

22. John Dewey, *Theory of the Moral Life* (New York: Irvington Publishers, 1980), 90.

23. Erik Erikson, *Childhood and Society* (New York: Norton, 1950).

24. Anna Ornstein, "A Developmental Perspective on the Sense of Power, Self-Esteem, and Destructive Aggression, *Annual Review of Psychoanalysis* 25 (1997): 145–54. See also William Damon, *The Moral Child* (New York: Free Press, 1988).

25. Gunnar Karlsson, "Beyond the Pleasure Principle: The Affirmation of Existence," *Scandinavian Psychoanalytic Review* 21, 1 (1998): 37–52. See also Sigmund Freud, *Beyond the Pleasure Principle, Group Psychology, and Other Works*, trans. James Strachey (London: Hogarth, 1955).

26. See Fred Weinstein, *Freud, Psychoanalysis, Social Theory: The Unfulfilled Promise* (Albany: State University of New York Press, 2001).

27. William Cooney, "The Death Poetry of Emily Dickinson," *Omega: Journal of Death and Dying* 37, 3 (1998): 241–49.

28. Kohut, *Search for the Self,* 667.

29. Viktor E. Frankl, *Man's Search for Meaning: An Introduction to Logotherapy*, trans. Ilse Lasch (Boston: Beacon, 1963); *Psychotherapy and Existentialism: Selected Papers on Logotherapy* (New York: Washington Square Press, 1967); and *The Will to Meaning: Foundations and Applications of Logotherapy* (New York: New American Library, 1970).

30. William Blair Gould, "Boundaries and Meaning," *International Forum for Logotherapy* 18, 1 (1995): 49–52.

31. Salman Akhtar, "The Distinction between Needs and Wishes: Implications for Psychoanalytic Theory and Technique," *Journal of the American Psychoanalytic Association* 47, 1 (1999): 114–51. See also Don C. Dinkmeyer, *Child Development: The Emerging Self* (Englewood Cliffs, N.J.: Prentice-Hall, 1965).

32. The remaining three needs are, first, the need of the self to know that its physical requirements are legitimate; second, the need for interpersonal and intrapsychic boundaries; and third, a need for understanding the causes of events both external and internal to the self.

33. Joy G. Dryfoos, *Safe Passage: Making It Through Adolescence in a Risky Society* (New York: Oxford University Press, 1998), 39.

34. Richard Stevens, *Erik Erikson* (New York: St. Martin's Press, 1983), 64.

35. Joseph Adelson and Elizabeth Douvan, *The Adolescent Experience* (New York: John Wiley, 1966), 176.

36. See Anthony Storr, *Solitude: A Return to the Self* (New York: Balantine Books, 1988).

37. George Berkeley in Charles J. Rzepka, *The Self as Mind: Visions and Identity in Wordsworth, Coleridge, and Keats* (Cambridge: Harvard University Press, 1986), 11.

38. Ibid., 6. See also Eugene L. Stelzig, *All Shades of Consciousness: Wordsworth's Poetry and the Self in Time* (The Hague: Mouton, 1975).

39. Parker J. Palmer, *The Courage to Teach: Exploring the Inner Landscape of a Teacher's Life* (San Francisco: Jossey-Bass, 1998), 72–73.

40. See, for example, R. D. Laing, *The Divided Self* (Baltimore: Penguin, 1965).

41. Salvador Minuchin, *Families and Family Therapy* (Cambridge: Harvard University Press, 1974).

42. See Arthur T. Jersild, "Social and Individual Origins of the Self," in *Relevant*

Reading in Human Development, ed. John J. Mitchell (Berkeley, Calif.: McCutchan Publishing, 1971), 113.

43. Jean Piaget, *Six Psychological Studies* (New York: Random House, 1967), 66.

44. Patricia A. Cameron, Carol J. Mills, and Thomas E. Heinzen, "The Social Context and Developmental Patterns of Crystallizing Experiences among Academically Talented Youth," *Roeper Review* 17, 3 (1995): 197–200.

45. Basch, *Understanding Psychotherapy*. See also M. Pines, "The Universality of Shame: A Psychoanalytic Approach," *British Journal of Psychotherapy* 11 (1995): 346–57.

46. René Descartes, *Philosophical Works*, trans. Elizabeth S. Haldane and G. R. T. Ross (Cambridge: Cambridge University Press, 1911).

47. Immanuel Kant, *The Critique of Pure Reason*, trans. Norman Kent Smith (New York: St. Martin's Press, 1965).

48. See ibid., and David Hume, *Philosophical Works*, cited in Rzepka, *Self as Mind*, 14.

49. Thomas J. Cottle, *Mind Fields: Adolescent Consciousness in a Culture of Distraction* (New York: Peter Lang, 2001).

50. Mihaly Csikszentmihalyi, *Educating for the Good Society* (New York: HarperCollins, 1993), xv–xvi, 29.

51. Robert Kegan, *The Evolving Self* (Cambridge: Harvard University Press, 1982).

52. See Joseph Goldstein, Anna Freud, and Albert J. Solnit, *Before the Best Interests of the Child* (New York: Free Press, 1979).

53. Palmer, *Courage to Teach*, 69.

54. Martha B. Straus, *No Talk Therapy* (New York: Norton, 1999).

55. Thomas J. Cottle, *At Peril: Stories of Injustice* (Amherst: University of Massachusetts Press, 2001), esp. 34–49.

56. On this point see A. Blasi, "Identity and the Development of the Self," in *Self, Ego, and Identity: Integrative Approaches*, ed. D. Lapsley and F. C. Power (New York: Springer-Verlag, 1988).

57. John Locke cited in Rzepka, *Self as Mind*, 14.

58. Mark Epstein, *Going on Being: Buddhism and the Way of Change* (New York: Broadway Books, 2001), 85; Robert A. F. Thurman is cited in Epstein on page 97.

59. On this point see Alice Miller, *The Drama of the Gifted Child*, trans. Ruth Ward (New York: Basic Books, 1981).

60. Basch, *Understanding Psychotherapy*, and Erik H. Erikson, *Identity, Youth, and Crisis* (New York: Norton, 1968).

61. Rachel Naomi Remen, *My Grandfather's Blessings: Stories of Strength, Refuge, and Belonging* (New York: Riverhead, 2000), 49.

62. This reference derives from R. D. Laing, *Reason and Violence: A Decade of Sartre's Philosophy, 1950–1960* (New York: Pantheon, 1964). Cited in Rzepka, *Self as Mind*, 15.

63. Dalai Lama cited in Remen, *My Grandfather's Blessings*, 355.

64. Kohut, *Search for the Self*.

65. See M. Stein, *Transformation: Emergence of the Self* (College Station: Texas A&M University Press, 1998).

66. George Herbert Mead, *Mind, Self, and Society from the Standpoint of a Social Behaviorist* (Chicago: University of Chicago Press, 1934). See also Cottle, *Mind Fields*.

67. See Charles H. Cooley, *Sociological Theory and Social Research* (New York: A. M. Kelly, 1969).

68. Henry David Thoreau, "Life without Principle," in *The Norton Anthology of American Literature*, 5th ed., ed. Nina Baym et al. (New York: Norton, 1998), 1: 1987.

69. Sigmund Freud, *A General Introduction to Psychoanalysis*, trans. G. Stanley Hall (New York: Liveright, 1935); and Maurice Merleau-Ponty, "The Child's Relations with Others," trans. W. Cobb, in *The Primacy of Perception*, ed. J. M. Edie (Evanston, Ill.: Northwestern University Press, 1964), 96–155.

70. Kegan, *Evolving Self*.

71. See Erikson, *Childhood and Society*.

72. Paul Ricoeur, *The Conflict of Interpretations* (Evanston, Ill: Northwestern University Press, 1974) 112. Cited in Rzepka, *Self as Mind*, 19.

73. Rzepka, *Self as Mind*.

74. Jacques Lacan, *Language of the Self: The Function of Language in Psychoanalysis*, trans. Anthony Wilden (Baltimore: Johns Hopkins University Press, 1968).

75. Diane Ackerman, *Deep Play* (New York: Vintage Books, 1999), 108.

Chapter 3. The Gaze of Affirmation

1. See Geoffrey Underwood and Robin Stevens, eds., *Aspects of Consciousness* (New York: Academic Press, 1979).

2. V. S. Naipul, *Half a Life* (New York, Knopf, 2001), 210.

3. Thomas J. Cottle, *At Peril: Stories of Injustice* (Amherst: University of Massachusetts Press, 2001), esp. the afterword.

4. John Mack, *Nightmares and Human Conflict* (Boston: Little, Brown, 1970).

5. Richard Cohen, ed., *Face to Face with Levinas* (Albany: State University of New York Press, 1986), 28.

6. Rollo May, *The Discovery of Being: Writings in Existential Psychology* (New York: Norton, 1983), 98; Louis Breger, *From Instinct to Identity* (Englewood Cliffs, N.J.: Prentice-Hall, 1974), 107.

7. On a similar point, see Peggy J. Kleinplatz, "The Erotic Encounter," *Journal of Humanistic Psychology* 36, 3 (1996): 105–23.

8. Friedrich Nietzsche, *The Will to Power*, trans. Walter Kaufman and R. J. Hol-

lingdale (New York: Vintage Books, 1968); Emmanuel Levinas, *Ethics and Identity: Conversations with Philippe Nemo*, trans. Richard A. Cohen (Pittsburgh: Duquesne University Press, 1982).

9. Erik Erikson suggested that an intolerance of people who are "different" represents a defense against a sense of one's identity confusion. Similarly, the act of stereotyping selves is a defense against the discomfort experienced during an identity crisis. See Erikson, *Childhood and Society* (New York: Norton, 1950).

10. Emmanuel Levinas, *Totality and Infinity: An Essay on Exteriority*, trans. Alphonso Lingis (Pittsburgh: Duquesne University Press, 1969); Erik H. Erikson, *Identity, Youth, and Crisis* (New York: Norton, 1968).

11. "A story isn't everything that happened," Ernest Hemingway once observed. "It is every important thing that happened."

12. See Emmanuel Levinas, *The Levinas Reader*, ed. Seán Hand (Cambridge, Mass.: Basil Blackwell, 1989).

13. Cited in ibid.

14. Cottle, *At Peril*, esp. the afterword.

15. Levinas, *Totality and Infinity*.

16. Gary M. Sasso, "The Retreat from Inquiry and Knowledge in Special Education," *Journal of Special Education* 34, 4 (2001): 187.

17. John Rawls, *A Theory of Justice* (Cambridge: Harvard University Press, Belknap Press, 1971).

18. With this in mind, we recall Thoreau's words, "Let us not underrate the value of a fact; it will one day flower into a truth."

19. Material here and in the following paragraph from Levinas, *Totality and Infinity*; Heinz Kohut, *The Search for the Self*, vol. 2, ed. Paul Ornstein (New York: International Universities Press, 1978), and *The Kohut Seminars: On Self Psychology and Psychotherapy with Adolescents and Young Adults* (New York: Norton, 1987). In the novel *You Know Who*, by Nicholas Freeling, a character remarks about empathy: "Not that sappy feeling-with but the genuine feeling-into. The stepping, if need be slipping, into another's skin." Cited in Margo Jefferson, "The Critic in Time of War," *New York Times Book Review*, October 28, 2001, 35. I am grateful to Caroline Heller for this reference.

20. See Michael Novak, *Belief and Unbelief: A Philosophy of Self-Knowledge* (New York: Macmillan, 1965).

21. On this point see Cornel West, *Race Matters* (New York: Vintage Books, 1994).

22. Joel Kovel, *White Racism: A Psychohistory* (New York: Vintage Books, 1979).

23. Sigmund Freud, "The Ego and the Id," in *The Standard Edition of the Complete Works of Sigmund Freud*, trans. James Strachey (New York: Norton, 1962), 19: 58; emphasis added.

24. See D. J. Flannery, M. I. Singer, and K. Wester, "Violence Exposure, Psy-

chological Trauma, and Suicide Risk in a Community Sample of Dangerously Violent Adolescents," *Journal of the American Academy of Child and Adolescent Psychiatry* 40, 4 (2001): 435–42. See also L. Wurmser, *The Mask of Shame* (Baltimore: Johns Hopkins University Press, 1981), and Randall W. Summers, ed., *Teen Violence: A Global View* (Westport, Conn.: Greenwood, 2000).

25. John Dewey, *Theory of the Moral Life* (New York: Irvington Publishers, 1980), 110.

26. See R. F. Valois, K. J. Zullig, E. S. Huebner, and W. Drane, "Relationship between Life Satisfaction and Violent Behaviors among Adolescents, *American Journal of Health Behavior* 25, 4 (2001): 353–66.

27. Michael F. Basch, *Understanding Psychotherapy: The Science behind the Art* (New York: Basic Books, 1988).

28. Robert Kegan, *The Evolving Self* (Cambridge: Harvard University Press, 1982).

29. Adriaan T. Peperzak, *To the Other: An Introduction to the Philosophy of Emmanuel Levinas* (West Lafayette: Purdue University Press, 1993); Jacques Derrida, "The Other Heading," *PMLA* 108 (1990): 92; cited in David Steiner, "Levinas' Ethical Interruption of Reciprocity," *Salmagundi*, nos. 130–31 (2001): 128; emphasis added.

30. Seán Hand, ed., *The Levinas Reader* (Oxford: Basil Blackwell, 1989), 181; cited in Steiner, "Levinas' Ethical Interruption of Reciprocity," 126; Emmanuel Levinas, *Otherwise than Being, or beyond Essense*, trans. Alphonso Lingis (Boston: Martinus Nighoff, 1981).

31. Levinas, *Totality and Infinity*.

32. See Jack Levin and Arnold Arluke, *Gossip: The Inside Scoop* (New York: Plenum Press, 1987).

32. Cohen, *Face to Face with Levinas*, 27.

33. Emmanuel Levinas, *Ethics and Infinity* (Pittsburgh: Duquesne University Press, 1985), 96.

35. <http://home.pacbell.net/atterton/levinas>; cited in Adam Gold, "Affirmation and the Concept of the Gaze in Psychosocial Identity Formation," unpublished manuscript, Boston University, 2001, 9.

36. Hand, *Levinas Reader*, 64.

37. Gold, "Affirmation and the Concept of the Gaze," 4.

38. Martin Buber, *I and Thou*, trans. Ronald Gregor Smith (New York: Scribner, 1958).

39. Denis Donoghue, *Adam's Curse: Reflections on Religion and Literature* (Notre Dame: University of Notre Dame Press, 2001), 56.

40. Cited in ibid., 52.

41. Ibid., 53; emphasis added.

42. Ibid., 56.

Chapter 4. The Miraculous Stranger

1. Robert Kegan, *The Evolving Self* (Cambridge: Harvard University Press, 1982), 19.

2. Roger Scruton, cited in Douglas Sears, "A Message from Douglas Sears," in *Update* (Boston: Boston University, School of Education, September 2001), 1.

3. See Elisabeth Hansot, "Civic Friendship: An Aristotelian Perspective," in *Reconstructing the Common Good in Education*, ed. L. Cuban and D. Shipps (Stanford: Stanford University Press, 2000) 173–85. See also Sibly A. Schwarzenbach, "On Civic Friendship," *Ethics* 107, 1 (1996): 97–128. Trevor Griffiths, *The Comedians* (London: Faber, 1976).

4. Erik H. Erikson, *Childhood and Society* (New York: Norton, 1950). See also B. Warton, "The Hidden Face of Shame: The Shadow, Shame, and Separation," *Journal of Analytical Psychology* 35, 3 (1990): 279–99.

5. Stephen Tigner, "Harry Potter and the Good Life," unpublished manuscript, Center for Character Education, Boston University, 2001.

6. See Eugene J. Wright, *Erikson: Identity and Religion* (New York: Seabury Press, 1982).

7. Sissela Bok, *Lying: Moral Choice in Public and Private Life* (New York: Pantheon, 1978) 31.

8. Lawrence R. Broer, "Images of the Shaman in the Works of Kurt Vonnegut," in *Dionysus in Literature: Essays on Literary Madness*, ed. Branimir R. Rieger (Bowling Green: Bowling Green State University Press, 1994), 197–208.

9. See Judith Herman, *Trauma and Recovery* (New York: Basic Books, 1992).

10. Erving Goffman, *The Presentation of Self in Everyday Life* (Garden City, N.Y.: Anchor Books, 1959).

11. Heinz Kohut, *The Search for the Self*, vol. 2, ed. Paul Ornstein (New York: International Universities Press, 1978). See also Erik H. Erikson, *Identity, Youth, and Crisis* (New York: Norton, 1968).

12. Heinz Kohut, *The Analysis of the Self: A Systematic Approach to the Psychoanalytic Treatment of Narcissistic Personality* (New York: International Universities Press, 1971).

13. Jean Piaget, *Six Psychological Studies* (New York: Random House, 1967); Anna Freud, *The Ego and the Mechanisms of Defense* (New York: International Universities Press, 1946); John Dewey, *How We Think* (Amherst, N.Y.: Prometheus, 1991); William Deresiewicz, "The Radical Imagination," review of *Where the Stress Falls*, by Susan Sontag, *New York Times Book Review*, November 4, 2001, 7.

14. Erikson, *Identity, Youth, and Crisis.*

15. Emmanuel Levinas, *Ethics and Infinity* (Pittsburgh: Duquesne University Press, 1985), 116. On a similar point see his "Philosophy and the Idea of the Infinite," *Revue Philosophique de la France et de l'Etranger* 7, 9. (1957): 241–51.

16. Benjamin DeMott, cited in Diane Ackerman, *Deep Play* (New York: Vintage Books, 1999) 31.

17. See Salvador Minuchin, *Families and Family Therapy* (Cambridge: Harvard University Press, 1974). Martin Heidegger, *Being and Time*, trans. Joan Stambaugh (Albany: State University of New York Press, 1966).

18. Roy F. Baumeister, Arlene M. Stillwell, and Todd F. Heatherton, "Interpersonal Aspects of Guilt: Evidence from Narrative Studies," in *Self-Conscious Emotions: The Psychology of Shame, Guilt, Embarrassment, and Pride*, ed. June Price Tangney and Kurt W. Fischer (New York: Guilford Press, 1995), 255–73.

19. Felton Earls and Mary Carlson, "Towards Sustainable Development for American Families," *Daedalus* 122, 1 (1993): 93–122.

20. Erikson, *Childhood and Society*.

21. See Clifford Geertz, *The Interpretation of Cultures: Selected Essays* (New York: Basic Books, 1973).

22. Dana Wilde, "Problems at the English Department," *CEA Critic* (Winter/Spring 2000): 11; C. Eric Lincoln, *Race, Religion, and the Continuing American Dilemma* (New York: Hill and Wang, 1999), 9; Erikson, *Childhood and Society*.

23. On this point see Karen Horney, *The Neurotic Personality of Our Time* (New York: Norton, 1937), and *Neurosis and Human Growth* (New York: Norton, 1950).

24. On this point see Robert Nozick, *The Examined Life: Philosophical Meditations* (New York: Simon and Schuster, 1989).

25. J. C. Nyri cited in David M. Steiner, introduction to *Proceedings of the Twentieth World Congress of Philosophy*, Philosophy Documentation Center, Bowling Green State University, 1999, xxiii.

26. See Minuchin, *Families and Family Therapy*.

27. On this point see Louis Breger, *From Instinct to Identity* (Englewood Cliffs, N.J. Prentice-Hall, 1974).

28. Sigmund Freud, *A General Introduction to Psychoanalysis*, trans. G. Stanley Hall (New York: Liveright, 1935).

29. Charles J. Rzepka, *The Self as Mind: Vision and Identity in Wordsworth, Coleridge, and Keats* (Cambridge: Harvard University Press, 1986), 27.

30. Augustus Y. Napier and Carl A. Whitaker, *The Family Crucible: The Intense Experience of Family Therapy* (New York: Harper Perennial, 1978).

31. Kegan, *Evolving Self*, chap. 7.

32. Theodore Roszak, "On the Contemporary Hunger for Wonders," in *Seasonal Performance*, ed. Laurence Goldstein (Ann Arbor: University of Michigan Press, 1991), 72.

33. Steiner, introduction to *Proceedings*, xxi.

34. Alan Young, "Suffering and the Origins of Traumatic Memory," *Daedalus* 125, 1 (1996): 245–60.

35. Gitta Sereny, *Why Children Kill: The Story of Mary Bell* (New York: Henry Holt, 1999).

36. Alexander Garcia-Duettmann, " 'What Is Called Love in All the Languages and Silences of the World': Nietzsche, Genealogy, Contingency," *American Imago* 50, 3 (1993): 277–323.

37. Erikson, *Childhood and Society*, cited in Jesse Hollander, "Identity Formation and the Aetiology of Neurosis," unpublished manuscript, Boston University, 2001.

38. Jean Piaget, *The Language and Thought of the Child* (London: Routledge and Kegan Paul, 1932).

39. Ibid., and Piaget, *Six Psychological Studies*.

40. Pablo Neruda, "Sonnet XVII," in *One Hundred Love Sonnets*, trans. Stephen Tapscott (Austin: University of Texas Press, 1986).

41. Minuchin, *Families and Family Therapy*.

42. David Steiner, "Levinas' Ethical Interruption of Reciprocity," *Salmagundi*, nos. 130–31 (2001): 121.

43. On this point of change and transition, see William Bridges, *The Way of Transition: Embracing Life's Most Difficult Moments* (Cambridge, Mass.: Perseus, 2001).

44. Murray Bowen, *Family Therapy in Clinical Practice* (New York: Jason Aronson, 1978).

45. Rzepka, *Self as Mind*, 27.

46. Thomas J. Cottle, *Mind Fields: Adolescent Consciousness in a Culture of Distraction* (New York: Peter Lang, 2001).

47. Paul Tillich, *The Courage to Be* (New Haven: Yale University Press, 1952).

48. Adriaan T. Peperzak, *To the Other: An Introduction to the Philosophy of Emmanuel Levinas* (West Lafayette: Purdue University Press, 1993); Kegan *Evolving Self*, 19.

49. Brian Hall, *Madeline's World: A Child's Journey from Birth to Age 3* (Boston: Houghton Mifflin, 1997), 7.

50. See George Lakoff and Mark Johnson, *Metaphors We Live By* (Chicago: University of Chicago Press, 1980).

51. "I love my child," the comedian Jerry Seinfeld remarked, "she's so sweet. And I didn't know I would, because I hate children. But that baby comes along and you get *blindsided*. You can't reject that experience." Cited in the *Boston Globe*, May 25, 2001, D3; emphasis added. On Levinas, see Peperzak, *To the Other*.

52. On this point see Denis Donoghue, *Adam's Curse: Reflections on Religion and Literature* (Notre Dame: University of Notre Dame Press, 2001), esp. chap. 4.

53. Burton Blatt, *The Conquest of Mental Retardation* (Austin, Tex.: PRO-ED, 1987).

54. On this point see Jonathan Schiff, *Ashes to Ashes: Mourning and Social Dif-*

ferences in F. Scott Fitzgerald's Fiction (Selinsgrove, Pa.: Susquehanna University Press, 2001).

55. Carol Gilligan, *In a Different Voice* (Cambridge: Harvard University Press, 1982).

56. See Gerald S. Fain, "Special Education: Justice, Tolerance, and Beneficence as Duty," *Journal of Education* 180, (1998) 2: 41–56.

57. Levinas, "Philosophy and the Idea of the Infinite," 96.

58. Eli Hirsch claims that identity involves internal consistency accomplished by having the various stages of development held together. He calls the stages "sortals," which he defines as "a conceptual truth (a rule of language) that any spatio-temporally and qualitatively continuous succession of [stages] corresponds to (what counts as) stages in the career of a single persisting [thing]." See Hirsch, *The Concept of Identity* (New York: Oxford University Press, 1982), 38, cited in Christopher C. Phillips, "Don Juan: A Study in Identity Development," unpublished manuscript, Boston University, 2001, 1–2.

59. Levinas, "Philosophy and the Idea of the Infinite," 92.

60. A. S. Byatt, *On Histories and Stories* (Cambridge: Harvard University Press, 2001).

61. Friedrich Nietzsche, *Schopenhauer as Educator*, trans. James W. Hillesheim and Malcolm R. Simpson (South Bend, Ind.: Gateway Editions, 1965).

62. Kegan, *Evolving Self*, 16.

63. On this point see James A. Schinneller, *Art, Search, and Self-Discovery* (Scranton, Pa.: International Textbook, 1968).

64. Lee Siegel, "A Defense of Serious Fiction," *Los Angeles Times Book Review*, August 5, 2001, 10; emphasis added.

65. Oscar Wilde, *The Picture of Dorian Gray*, ed. Donald L. Lawler (New York: Norton, 1988), 84.

66. Stephanie Z. Dudek, "The Morality of Twentieth-Century Transgressive Art," *Creativity Research Journal* 6, 1–2 (1993): 145–52.

67. Michel Foucault, *The Birth of the Clinic: An Archaeology of Medical Perception* (New York: Random House, 1973).

68. Erich Fromm, *Escape from Freedom* (New York: Farrar and Rinehart, 1941); Erikson, *Childhood and Society*.

69. See Gunnar Karlsson, "Beyond the Pleasure Principle: The Affirmation of Existence," *Scandinavian Psychoanalytic Review* 21, 1 (1998) 37–52. See also Sigmund Freud, *Civilization and Its Discontents*, trans. Joan Riviere (London: Hogarth, 1930).

70. Margaret Mahler, *The Psychological Birth of the Human Infant* (Franklin Lakes, N.J.: Mahler Research Foundation Library, 1985).

71. See Fred Weinstein, *Freud, Psychoanalysis, Social Theory: The Unfulfilled Promise* (Albany: State University of New York Press, 2001), chap. 1.

CHAPTER 5. THE CONSTRUCTION OF AFFIRMATION

1. For material here and below from Erich Fromm, see *Escape from Freedom* (New York: Farrar and Rinehart, 1941); Erik H. Erikson, *Young Man Luther* (New York: Norton, 1962).

2. Elizabeth Young-Bruehl and Faith Bethelard, *Cherishment: A Psychology of the Heart* (New York: Free Press, 2000).

3. John Rawls, *A Theory of Justice* (Cambridge: Harvard University Press, Belknap Press, 1971).

4. Jean-Paul Sartre, *Existentialism and Human Emotions* (New York: Kensington Publishing, 1957), 23.

5. R. E. H. Muuss, *Theories of Adolescence* (New York: Random House, 1968).

6. See Bruno Bettelheim, *The Uses of Enchantment: The Meaning and Importance of Fairy Tales* (New York: Vintage Books, 1976).

7. Cited in Michael Tolkin, "The Loneliness of the Long-Distance Writer," review of *Chester Himes: A Life*, by James Sallis, *Los Angeles Times Book Review*, March 18, 2001, 2.

8. Diane Ackerman, *Deep Play* (New York: Vintage Books, 1999).

9. See Urie Bronfenbrenner, *The Ecology of Human Development* (Cambridge: Harvard University Press, 1979).

10. Rebecca Walker, *Black, White, and Jewish: The Autobiography of a Shifting Self* (New York: Riverhead Books, 2001), cited in the *Boston Globe*, March 19, 2001, B8.

11. See especially Erik H. Erikson, *Identity, Youth, and Crisis* (New York: Norton, 1968).

12. Rollo May, *The Discovery of Being: Writings in Existential Psychology* (New York: Norton, 1983); John Dewey, *Theory of the Moral Life* (New York: Irvington Publishers, 1960), 109. I am grateful to Gerald Fain for the Dewey reference.

13. Howard Gardner, *Frames of Mind: The Theory of Multiple Intelligences* (New York: Basic Books, 1983); Robert Kegan, *The Evolving Self* (Cambridge: Harvard University Press, 1982).

14. Kegan, *Evolving Self*.

15. Erikson, *Young Man Luther*, cited in Jonathan Kozol, foreword to *Will Standards Save Public Education?* by Deborah Meier (Boston: Beacon Press, 2000) viii, ix.

16. In a different context, Parker Palmer wrote, "Objectivism, fearful of both the knowing self and the thing known, distances self from the world and deforms our relationships with our subjects, our students and ourselves." See his *The Courage to Teach: Exploring the Inner Landscape of a Teacher's Life* (San Francisco: Jossey-Bass, 1998), 54.

17. See Ellen J. Langer, *Mindfulness* (Reading, Mass.: Addison-Wesley, 1989), and *The Power of Mindful Learning* (Reading, Mass.: Perseus, 1997).

18. See Stanley Coopersmith, *The Antecedents of Self-Esteem* (San Francisco: W. H. Freeman, 1967), and E. D. Hirsch, *The Schools We Need and Why We Don't Have Them* (New York: Doubleday, 1996).

19. Hirsch, *In the Schools We Need*; John Santrock, *Adolescence*, 8th ed. (New York: McGraw Hill, 2001), 302.

20. See Thomas J. Cottle *Intimate Appraisals: The Social Writings of Thomas J. Cottle* (Hanover, N.H.: University Press of New England, 2002).

21. C. Eric Lincoln, *Race, Religion, and the Continuing American Dilemma* (New York: Hill and Wang, 1999), 17.

22. Paul R. Gross and Norman Levitt, *Higher Superstition: The Academic Left and Its Quarrels with Science* (Baltimore: Johns Hopkins University Press, 1998).

23. On this point see Marcellus Andrews, *The Political Economy of Hope and Fear* (New York: New York University Press, 1999).

24. William Shakespeare, *Romeo and Juliet*, in *The Complete Works of William Shakespeare*, Shakespeare Head Press Edition (New York: Barnes and Noble, 1994), 275.

25. Rawls, *Theory of Justice*.

26. Kegan, *Evolving Self*.

27. See Arthur T. Jersild, "Social and Individual Origins of the Self," in *Relevant Readings in Human Development*, ed. John J. Mitchell (Berkeley, Calif.: McCutchan Publishing, 1971), 115.

28. Erik H. Erikson, *Childhood and Society* (New York: Norton, 1950).

29. Arnold H. Modell, *The Private Self* (Cambridge: Harvard University Press, 1993).

30. Modell argues that the public (sense of) self normally remains secondary to the private (sense of) self.

31. Lincoln, *Race, Religion, and the Continuing American Dilemma*, 13.

32. See John Dewey, *How We Think* (Amherst, N.Y.: Prometheus Press, 1991). See also Stephen J. Kemmis, "Action Research and the Politics of Reflection," in *Reflection: Turning Experience into Learning*, ed. D. Boud, R. Keogh, and D. Walker (London: Kogan Page, 1985), 139–64.

33. C. Gilligan, J. V. Ward, J. M. Taylor, and B. Bardige, *Mapping the Moral Domain: A Contribution of Women's Thinking to Psychological Theory and Education* (Cambridge: Harvard University Press, 1988), xii.

34. G. W. F. Hegel, *The Phenomenology of Mind*, trans. J. Baillie (New York: Harper and Row, 1967), 229.

35. On this point see Anthony Storr, *Solitude: A Return to the Self* (New York: Balantine Books, 1988).

36. Ernest Schachtel, *Metamorphosis: On the Development of Affect, Perception, Attention, and Memory* (New York: Basic Books, 1959). On "psychological numbing" and abuse see Judith Herman, *Trauma and Recovery* (New York: Basic Books, 1992).

37. See Armando R. Favazza, *Bodies under Siege: Self-Mutilation in Culture and Psychiatry* (Baltimore: Johns Hopkins University Press, 1987), and Derek Miller, with the assistance of Barry Carlton, *Attack on the Self: Adolescent Behavioral Disturbances and Their Treatment* (Northvale, N.J.: Aronson, 1986).

38. Erikson, *Identity, Youth, and Crisis.*

39. See James Gilligan, *Violence: Our Deadly Epidemic and Its Causes* (New York: G. P. Putnam's Sons, 1996).

40. Muuss, *Theories of Adolescence,* 64.

41. Stephen Tigner, "Harry Potter and the Good Life," unpublished manuscript, Center for Character Education, Boston University, 2001.

42. See, for example, Nina Bernstein, *The Lost Children of Wilder: The Epic Struggle to Change Foster Care* (New York: Pantheon Books, 2001).

43. See T. R. Nansel, M. Overpeck, and R. S. Pilla, "Bullying Behaviors among U.S. Youth: Prevalence and Association with Psychosocial Adjustment," *Journal of the American Medical Association* 285, 16 (2001): 2094–2100.

44. Tigner, "Harry Potter and the Good Life."

45. See Thomas J. Cottle, *Mind Fields: Adolescent Consciousness in a Culture of Distraction* (New York: Peter Lang, 2001).

46. Howard F. Stein, "Disposable Youth: The 1999 Columbine High School Massacre as American Metaphor," *Journal for the Psychoanalysis of Culture and Society* 5, 2 (2000): 224.

47. M. Bai, "Anatomy of a Massacre," *Newsweek,* May 3, 1999, 25.

48. Kegan, *Evolving Self.*

49. Jean-Paul Sartre, *The Words,* trans. Bernard Frechtman (New York: G. Braziller, 1964).

50. Walt Whitman, "To a Pupil," in *Complete Poetry and Selected Prose,* ed. James E. Miller (Boston: Houghton Mifflin, 1959), 275; Ralph Waldo Emerson, *Self-Reliance and Other Essays* (New York: Dover, 1993), 22.

51. Joseph Goldstein, Anna Freud, and Albert J. Solnit, *Before the Best Interests of the Child* (New York: Free Press, 1979).

52. Sigmund Freud, The Complete *Introductory Lectures on Psychoanalysis,* trans. and ed. James Strachey (New York: Norton, 1966). See also his *Inhibitions, Symptoms, and Anxiety,* trans. James Strachey (New York: Norton 1977).

53. Robert Karen, "Shame," *Atlantic,* February 1992, 40–70, and G. Thrane, "Shame and the Construction of the Self," *Annual Review of Psychoanalysis* 7 (1979): 321–41.

54. See Thomas J. Cottle and Daniel B. Frank, "Beware the Result of a Child Shamed, *Baltimore Sun,* September 14, 2000, 19A.

55. See Erving Goffman, *Stigma: Notes on the Management of Spoiled Identity* (Englewood Cliffs, N.J.: Prentice-Hall, 1963).

56. See D. A. Brent, "Suicide and Suicidal Behavior in Children and Adolescents," *Pediatrics in Review* 10 (1989): 269–75, and Jack Novick, "Attempted Suicide

in Adolescence: The Suicide Sequence," in *Essential Papers on Suicide*, ed. John T. Mattsberger and Mark J. Goldblatt (New York: New York University Press, 1996), 524–48.

57. See I. W. Borowsky, M. Ireland, and M. D. Resnick, "Adolescent Suicide Attempts: Risks and Protectors," *Pediatrics* 107, 3 (2001): 485–93.

58. Emmanuel Levinas, *Ethics and Identity: Conversations with Philippe Nemo*, trans. Richard A. Cohen (Pittsburgh: Duquesne University Press, 1982).

59. MacDaniel and Marcella Bombardieri, "Friends Tell of a Private but Giving Couple," *Boston Globe*, January 30, 2001, A8.

60. Jeff Jacoby, "McVeigh's Execution Should Be Televised," *Boston Globe*, March 12, 2001, A11.

61. See Sara Lawrence-Lightfoot and Jessica Hoffman Davis, *The Art and Science of Portraiture* (San Francisco: Jossey-Bass, 1997).

62. See Robert Coles, *The Moral Life of Children* (Boston: Atlantic Monthly Press, 1986).

63. Susan Reynolds, review of *I Cannot Tell a Lie, Exactly*, by Mary Ladd Gavell, *Los Angeles Times Book Review*, August 19, 2001, 11.

64. Tigner, "Harry Potter and the Good Life."

65. Ibid.

Chapter 6. Average, Expectable Environments

1. See Neal Gabler, *Life the Movie: How Entertainment Conquered Reality* (New York: Knopf, 1998), and Sven Birkerts, *Readings* (St. Paul, Minn.: Graywolf Press, 1999).

2. Salman Rushdie, *Fury* (New York: Random House, 2001).

3. Gabler, *Life*, and Birkerts, *Readings*.

4. Neal Postman, *Amusing Ourselves to Death: Public Discourse in the Age of Show Business* (New York: Penguin, 1986).

5. Thomas J. Cottle, *At Peril: Stories of Injustice* (Amherst: University of Massachusetts Press, 2001).

6. Thomas J. Cottle, *Mind Fields: Adolescent Consciousness in a Culture of Distraction* (New York: Peter Lang, 2001).

7. Cottle, *At Peril*, 24–25.

8. Statistics presented here and in following four paragraphs are from Samantha Stuart and Thomas J. Cottle, cited in "Money Doesn't Buy Everything," *Children First* 5 (June/July 2001): 22–23.

9. Burton Blatt, "The Monolith and the Promise," *Therapeutic Recreation Journal* 7, 4 (1973): 4. I am grateful to Professor Gerald S. Fain for this reference.

10. Erik H. Erikson, *Youth, Change, and Challenge* (New York: Basic Books, 1963), 9.

11. Christopher Lasch, *The Culture of Narcissism: American Life in an Age of*

Diminishing Expectations (New York: Norton, 1978). See also Efrain Bleiberg, "Normal and Pathological Narcissism in Adolescence," *American Journal of Psychotherapy* 48, 1 (1994): 30–51, and Ivan J. Miller, "Interpersonal Vulnerability and Narcissism: A Conceptual Continuum for Understanding and Treating Narcissistic Psychopathology," *Psychotherapy* 29, 2 (1992): 216–24.

12. Felton Earls and Mary Carlson, "Towards Sustainable Development for American Families," *Daedalus* 122, 1 (1993): 93–122. On a related point see Thomas M. Brinthaupt and Richard P. Lipka, eds., *Changing the Self: Philosophies, Techniques, and Experiences* (Albany: State University of New York Press, 1994).

13. John Bowlby cited in *Readings*, December 1991, 5.

14. Bruno Bettelheim, *A Good Enough Parent: A Book on Child Rearing* (New York: Knopf, 1987); D. W. Winnicott, *Mother and Child: A Primer of First Relationships* (New York: Basic Books, 1957); Thomas Maeder, *Children of Psychiatrists and Other Psychotherapists* (New York: Harper and Row, 1989).

15. See David Elkind, *The Hurried Child: Growing Up Too Fast Too Soon* (Reading, Mass.: Addison-Wesley, 1981).

16. Jean Paul Sartre, *The Words*, trans. Bernard Frechtman (New York: G. Braziller, 1964), 7.

17. On this point see Barbara Dafoe Whitehead, *The Divorce Culture* New York: Alfred Knopf, 1996).

18. Marian Wright Edelman, *Families in Peril: An Agenda for Social Change* (Cambridge: Harvard University Press, 1987).

19. See K. M. Pirke and D. Ploog, eds., *The Psychobiology of Anorexia Nervosa* (Berlin, N.Y.: Springer, 1984), and A. Rumney, *Dying to Please: Anorexia Nervosa and Its Cure* (Jefferson, N.C.: McFarland, 1983).

20. R. E. H. Muuss, *Theories of Adolescence* (New York: Random House, 1968), 65.

21. The notion puts me in mind of walking in the park one afternoon, several years ago, and meeting a woman who recognized me from a television appearance. "You know," she said, with a lilt in her voice, "you're a lot taller in real life than you are in person."

22. Erik H. Erikson, *Childhood and Society* (New York: Norton, 1950).

23. William Pollock, *Real Boys: Rescuing Our Sons from the Myths of Boyhood* (New York: Random House, 1998).

24. See K. W. Allison and R. M. Lerner, "Adolescents and the Family," in *Early Adolescence* ed. R. M. Lerner (Hillsdale, N.J.: Erlbaum, 1993), and S. A. Beebe and J. T. Masterson, *Family Talk* (New York: Random House, 1986).

25. Salvador Minuchin, *Families and Family Therapy* (Cambridge: Harvard University Press, 1974).

26. Erich Fromm, *Escape from Freedom* (New York: Farrar and Rinehart, 1941).

27. John Rawls, *A Theory of Justice* (Cambridge: Harvard University Press, Belknap Press, 1971).

28. On a related point see G. Armsden and M. T. Greenberg, "The Inventory of Parents and Peer Attachment: Individual Differences and Their Relationship to Psychological Well-Being in Adolescence," *Journal of Youth and Adolescence* 16 (1987): 427–54.

29. See E. M. Berscheid, M. Snyder, and A. M. Omoto, "Issues in Studying Close Relationships," in *Close Relationships*, ed. C. Hendrick (Newbury Park, Calif.: Sage, 1989).

30. On this point see Elkind, *Hurried Child*.

31. See Edwin J. Delattre, "The Test of Intimacy: Living Up to Love and Duty," unpublished manuscript, Boston University, 2000.

32. See F. Scott Peck, *The Road Less Traveled: A New Psychology of Love, Traditional Values, and Spiritual Growth* (New York: Simon and Schuster, 1978).

33. See David Bakan, *The Duality of Human Existence: An Essay on Psychology and Religion* (Chicago: Rand McNally, 1966).

34. See Thomas J. Cottle, *Hardest Times: The Trauma of Long Term Unemployment* (Westport, Conn.: Praeger, 2001).

35. See A. Strachen and D. Jones, "Changes in Identification during Adolescence: A Personal Construct Theory Approach," *Journal of Personality Assessment* 46 (1982): 139–48.

36. In a similar vein see M. C. Bateson, *Full Circles, Overlapping Lives: Culture and Generation in Transition* (New York: Random House, 2000).

37. See M. H. Bornstein, ed., *Children and Parenting*, vol. 3 (Hillsdale, N.J.: Erlbaum, 1995).

38. See S. Dowrick, *Intimacy and Solitude: Balancing Closeness and Independence* (New York: Norton, 1991).

39. See P. R. Silverman, *Never Too Young to Know: Death in Children's Lives* (New York: Oxford University Press, 1999).

CHAPTER 7. THE AFFIRMATION CURRICULUM

1. Deborah Meier, *Will Standards Save Public Education?* (Boston: Beacon Press, 2000).

2. Jean-Jacques Rousseau, cited in Larry C. Jensen and Richard S. Knight, *Moral Education: Historical Perspectives* (New York: New York University Press, 1981), 89.

3. See Hervé Varenne and Ray McDermott, with Shelley Goldman, Merry Naddeo, and Rosemarie Rizzo-Tolle, *Successful Failure: The School America Builds* (Boulder, Colo.: Westview, 1998).

4. Jonathan Kozol, *Savage Inequalities: Children in America's Schools* (New York: Crown, 1991), and Marian Wright Edelman, *Families in Peril: An Agenda for Social Change* (Cambridge: Harvard University Press, 1987).

5. Emmanuel Levinas, *Ethics and Identity: Conversations with Phillipe Nemo*, trans. Richard A. Cohen (Pittsburgh: Duquesne University Press, 1982), and Adriaan T. Peperzak, *To the Other: An Introduction to the Philosophy of Emmanuel Levinas* (West Lafayette: Purdue University Press, 1993). See also Alexander M. Sidorkin, *Beyond Discourse: Education, the Self, and Dialogue* (Albany: State University of New York Press, 1999), and Mier, *Will Standards Save Public Education?* I am grateful to Professor David Steiner for these references.

6. See K. W. Allison and R. M. Lerner, "Adolescents and the Family," in *Early Adolescence: Perspectives on Research, Policy, and Intervention*, ed. R. M. Lerner: Hillsdale, N.J.: Erlbaum, 1993).

7. "Study Details Teens' Troubles," *Boston Globe*, November 13, 1998, A7.

8. The A+ grade reminds me of the famous novelist who graduated from an esteemed American university with the highest grade point average that ever would be achieved since the school discarded the A+ grade soon after his graduation. Shortly after fulfilling his dream of writing a best-selling novel, he committed suicide.

9. See R. Slavin, "Cooperative Learning and Student Achievement," *Educational Leadership* 46, 2 (1988): 31–33.

10. On a related point, see M. Stein, *Transformation: Emergence of the Self* (College Station: Texas A&M University Press, 1998).

11. See B. A. Christiansen, M. S. Goldman, and A. Inn, "The Development of Alcohol-Related Expectancies in Adolescents: Separating Pharmacological from Social-Learning Influences," *Journal of Consulting and Clinical Psychology* 50, 3 (1982): 336–44.

12. I often think that this is a problem confronted frequently by President Clinton, whose popularity ratings even at the conclusion of his term in office presented a complicated picture. Many Americans apparently believed he wanted good for all citizens. But some opined that in trying to please everyone, he often failed to complete the job at hand and hence had no choice but to move on to the next project.

13. Leonard Nimoy, interview with the author.

14. Tom Rusk and Randy Read, *I Want to Change but I Don't Know How* (Los Angeles: Price/Stern/Sloan, 1986) 223–24). I am indebted to Professor Anita Scott Read for this reference.

15. See Alice Miller, *The Drama of the Gifted Child*, trans. Ruth Ward (New York: Basic Books, 1981).

16. Harris Sussman, conversation with the author.

17. Erik H. Erikson, *Childhood and Society* (New York: Norton, 1950).

18. See Phillip Zimbardo, *Shyness: What It Is, What to Do about It* (Reading, Mass.: Addison-Wesley, 1977). See also Jerome Kagan, *The Second Year: The Emergence of Self-Awareness* (Cambridge: Harvard University Press, 1981), and *The Nature of the Child* (New York: Basic Books, 1984).

19. Martin Heidegger, *Being and Time*, trans. Joan Stambaugh (Albany: State University of New York Press, 1966), and Rollo May, *The Discovery of Being: Writings in Existential Psychology* (New York: Norton, 1983).

20. On a similar point, see P. Watzlawick, J. H. Weakland, and R. Fisch, *Change: Principles of Problem Formation and Problem Resolution* (New York: Norton, 1974).

21. John Dewey, *How We Think: A Restatement of the Relation of Reflective Thinking to the Educative Process* (Lexington, Mass.: Heath, 1933).

22. See B. U. Wilhelmsen, S. Laberg, and H. Aas, "Alcohol Outcome Expectancies in Adolescence," *Psychology and Health*, November 6, 1998, 1037–44.

23. See Seán Desmond Healy, *Boredom, Self, and Culture* (Rutherford, N.J.: Fairleigh Dickinson University Press, 1984).

24. See D. B. Kandel, "Socialization and Adolescent Drinking," in *Alcohol and Youth*, vol. 2 of *Child Health and Development*, ed. O. Jeanneret (Basel: Karger, 1983), 66–75.

25. Heinz Kohut, *The Search for the Self*, vol. 2, ed. Paul Ornstein (New York: International Universities Press, 1978).

26. Thomas J. Cottle, *Mind Fields: Adolescent Consciousness in a Culture of Distraction* (New York: Peter Lang, 2001).

27. Erich Fromm, *Escape from Freedom* (New York: Farrar and Rinehart, 1941).

28. See Sara Lawrence-Lightfoot, *Respect* (Reading, Mass.: Perseus, 1999).

29. Edelman, *Families in Peril.*

30. John Updike, *Bech: A Book* (New York: Knopf, 1970).

31. See Thomas J. Cottle, "Shaming Children on Television," *Television Quarterly*, no. 1 (Spring 2002): 70–73.

References

Ackerman, Diane. *Deep Play*. New York: Vintage Books, 1999.

Adelson, Joseph, and Elizabeth Douvan. *The Adolescent Experience*. New York: John Wiley, 1966.

Ainsworth, Mary. "Deprivation of Maternal Care: A Reassessment of Its Effects." In *Maternal Care and Mental Health*, by John Bowlby. New York: Schocken Books, 1966.

Akhtar, Salman. "The Distinction between Needs and Wishes: Implications for Psychoanalytic Theory and Technique." *Journal of the American Psychoanalytic Association* 47, 1 (1999): 114–51.

Allen, James B., and Jennifer L. Ferrand. "Environmental Locus of Control, Sympathy, and Proenvironmental Behavior: A Test of Geller's Actively, Caring Hypothesis." *Environment and Behavior* 31, 3 (1999): 338–53.

Allison, K. W., and R. M. Lerner. "Adolescents and the Family." In *Perspectives on Research, Policy, and Intervention*, ed., R. M. Lerner. *Early Adolescence*: Hillsdale, N.I.: Erlbaum, 1993.

Andrews, Marcellus. *The Political Economy of Hope and Fear*. New York: New York University Press. 1999.

Armsden, G., and M. T. Greenberg. "The Inventory of Parents and Peer Attachment: Individual Differences and Their Relationship to Psychological Well-Being in Adolescence." *Journal of Youth and Adolescence* 16 (1987): 427–54.

Aronson, Joshua, Hart Blanton, and Joel Cooper. "From Dissonance to Disidentification: Selectivity in the Self-Affirmation Process." *Journal of Personality and Social Psychology* 68, 6 (1995): 986–96.

Asper, Kathrin. *Being-in-Oneself, Being-in-the-World: Finding a Home and Regaining Self-Worth*. London: Guild of Pastoral Psychology, 1994.

Bai, M. "Anatomy of a Massacre." *Newsweek*, May 3, 1999, 25–31.

Bakan, David. *The Duality of Human Existence: An Essay on Psychology and Religion*. Chicago: Rand McNally, 1966.

Basch, Michael F. *Doing Psychotherapy*. New York: Basic Books, 1980.

———. *Understanding Psychotherapy: The Science behind the Art*. New York: Basic Books, 1988.

Bateson, M. C. *Full Circles, Overlapping Lives: Culture and Generation in Transition*. New York: Random House, 2000.

Baumeister, Roy., Arlene M. Stillwell, and Todd F. Heatherton. "Interpersonal Aspects of Guilt: Evidence from Narrative Studies." In *Self-Conscious Emotions:*

The Psychology of Shame, Guilt, Embarrassment, and Pride, ed. June Price Tangney and Kurt W. Fischer, 255–73.

Beauregard, Keith S., and David Dunning. "Turning up the Contrast: Self-Enhancement Motives Prompt Egocentric Contrast Effects in Social Judgments." *Journal of Personality and Social Psychology* 74, 3 (1998): 606–21.

Beebe, S. A., and J. T. Masterson. *Family Talk.* New York: Random House, 1986.

Benjamin, Lorna Smith. "Good Defenses Make Good Neighbors." In *Ego Defenses: Theory and Measurement*, ed. Hope R. Conte and Robert Plutchik, 53–78. Publication series of the Department of Psychiatry of Albert Einstein College of Medicine of Yeshiva University, no. 10. New York: John Wiley, 1995.

Berens Ann E. "Search-for-Meaning Groups for the Homeless." *International Forum for Logotherapy* 15, 1 (1992): 46–49.

Bernstein, Nina. *The Lost Children of Wilder: The Epic Struggle to Change Foster Care.* New York: Pantheon Books, 2001.

Berscheid, E. M., M. Snyder, and A. M. Omoto. "Issues in Studying Close Relationships." In *Close Relationships*, ed. C. Hendrick. Newbury Park, Calif.: Sage, 1989.

Bettelheim, Bruno. *A Good Enough Parent: A Book on Child Rearing.* New York: Knopf, 1987.

———. *On Learning to Read: The Child's Fascination with Meaning.* New York: Knopf, 1981.

———. *The Uses of Enchantment: The Meaning and Importance of Fairy Tales.* New York: Vintage Books, 1976.

Birchler, Gary R., Diana M. Doumas, and William S. Fals-Stewart. "The Seven C's: A Behavioral Systems Framework for Evaluating Marital Distress." *Family Journal of Counseling and Therapy for Couples and Families* 7, 3 (1999): 253–64.

Birkerts, Sven. *Readings.* St. Paul, Minn.: Graywolf Press, 1999.

Blakeslee, Thomas R. *Beyond the Conscious Mind: Unlocking the Secrets of the Self.* New York: Plenum Press, 1996.

Blasi, A. "Identity and the Development of the Self." In *Self, Ego, and Identity: Integrative Approaches*, ed. D. Lapsley and F. C. Power. New York: Springer-Verlag, 1988.

Blatt, Burton. *The Conquest of Mental Retardation.* Austin, Tex.: PRO-ED, 1987.

———. "The Monolith and the Promise." *Therapeutic Recreation Journal* 7, 4 (1973): 4–32.

Bleiberg, Efrain. "Normal and Pathological Narcissism in Adolescence." *American Journal of Psychotherapy* 48, 1 (1994): 30–51.

Bok, Sissela. *Lying: Moral Choice in Public and Private Life.* New York: Pantheon, 1978.

Bornstein, M. H., ed. *Children and Parenting.* Vol. 3. Hillsdale, N.J.: Erlbaum, 1995.

Borowsky, I. W., M. Ireland, and M. D. Resnick. "Adolescent Suicide Attempts: Risks and Protectors." *Pediatrics* 107, 3 (2001): 485–93.

Bowen, Murray. *Family Therapy in Clinical Practice*. New York: Jason Aronson, 1978.

Bowlby, John. *Loss, Sadness, and Depression*. Vol. 3 of *Attachment and Loss*. New York: Basic Books, 1980.

Breger, Louis. *From Instinct to Identity* (Englewood Cliffs, N.J.: Prentice-Hall, 1974.

Brent, D. A. "Suicide and Suicidal Behavior in Children and Adolescents." *Pediatrics in Review* 10 (1989): 269–75.

Bridges, William. *The Way of Transition: Embracing Life's Most Difficult Moments*. Cambridge, Mass.: Perseus, 2001.

Brinthaupt, Thomas M., and Richard P. Lipka, eds. *Changing the Self: Philosophies, Techniques, and Experiences*. Albany: State University of New York Press, 1994.

Broer, Lawrence R. "Images of the Shaman in the Works of Kurt Vonnegut." In *Dionysus in Literature: Essays on Literary Madness*, ed. Branimir R. Rieger, 197–208. Bowling Green: Bowling Green State University Press, 1994.

Bronfenbrenner, Urie. *The Ecology of Human Development*. Cambridge: Harvard University Press, 1979.

Bruch, Hilde. *The Golden Cage: The Enigma of Anorexia Nervosa*. Cambridge: Harvard University Press, 1978.

Brumberg, Joan Jacobs. *Fasting Girls: The Emergence of Anorexia Nervosa as a Modern Disease*. Cambridge: Harvard University Press, 1988.

Bruner, Jerome. *Actual Minds, Possible Worlds*. Cambridge: Harvard University Press, 1986.

———. *On Knowing*. Cambridge: Harvard University Press, 1979.

Buber, Martin. *I and Thou*. Translated by Ronald Gregor Smith. New York: Scribner, 1958.

Byatt, A. S. *On Histories and Stories*. Cambridge: Harvard University Press, 2001.

Cameron, Patricia A., Carol J. Mills, and Thomas E. Heinzen. "The Social Context and Developmental Patterns of Crystallizing Experiences among Academically Talented Youth." *Roeper Review* 17, 3 (1995): 197–200.

Carroll, James. "Books Make Us Free and Also Human." *Boston Globe*, June 19, 2001, A15.

Christiansen, B. A., M. S. Goldman, and A. Inn. "The Development of Alcohol-Related Expectancies in Adolescents: Separating Pharmacological from Social-Learning Influences." *Journal of Consulting and Clinical Psychology* 50, 3 (1982): 50, 336–44.

Cohen, Richard, ed. *Face to Face with Levinas*. Albany: State University of New York Press, 1986.

Coles, R. *The Moral Life of Children*. Boston: Atlantic Monthly Press, 1986.

Cooley, Charles H. *Sociological Theory and Social Research*. New York: A. M. Kelly, 1969.

Cooney, William. "The Death Poetry of Emily Dickinson." *Omega: Journal of Death and Dying* 37, 3 (1998): 241–49.

Coopersmith, Stanley. *The Antecedents of Self-Esteem*. San Francisco: W. H. Freeman, 1967.

Cottle, Thomas J. *At Peril: Stories of Injustice*. Amherst: University of Massachusetts
Press, 2001.

———. *Hardest Times: The Trauma of Long Term Unemployment*. Westport, Conn.:
Praeger, 2001.

———. *Intimate Appraisals: The Social Writings of Thomas J. Cottle*. Hanover,
N.H.: University Press of New England, 2002.

———. *Mind Fields: Adolescent Consciousness in a Culture of Distraction*. New York:
Peter Lang, 2001.

———. "Shaming Children on Television." *Television Quarterly*, no. 1 (Spring
2002): 70–75.

Cottle, Thomas J., and Daniel B. Frank. "Beware the Result of a Child Shamed."
Baltimore Sun, September 14, 2000, 19A.

Csikszentmihalyi, Mihaly. *Educating for the Good Society*. New York: HarperCollins,
1993.

Damon, William. *The Moral Child*. New York: Free Press, 1988.

Delattre, Elwin J. "The Test of Intimacy: Living Up to Love and Duty." Unpublished manuscript, Boston University, 2000.

Deresiewicz, William. "The Radical Imagination. Review of *Where the Stress Falls*,
by Susan Sontag." *New York Times Book Review*, November 4, 2001, 7.

Derrida, Jacques. "The Other Heading." *PMLA* 108 (1990): 89–93.

Descartes, René. *Philosophical Works*. Translated by Elizabeth S. Haldane and
G. R. T. Ross. Cambridge: Cambridge University Press, 1911.

Des-Rosiers, Nathalie, Bruce Feldthusen, and Oleana A. R. Hankivsky. "Legal
Compensation for Sexual Violence: Therapeutic Consequences and Consequences for the Judicial System." *Psychology, Public Policy, and Law* 4, 1–2 (1998):
433–51.

Dewey, John. *How We Think*. Amherst, N.Y.: Prometheus Press, 1991.

———. *How We Think: A Restatement of the Relation of Reflective Thinking to the
Educative Process*. Lexington, Mass.: Heath, 1933.

———. *Theory of the Moral Life*. New York: Irvington Publishers, 1960.

Dinkmeyer, Don C. *Child Development: The Emerging Self*. Englewood Cliffs, N.J.:
Prentice-Hall, 1965.

Donoghue, Denis. *Adam's Curse: Reflections on Religion and Literature*. Notre
Dame: University of Notre Dame Press, 2001.

Dore, Martha M., Lani Nelson Zlupko, and Ela Kaufmann. "'Friends in Need':
Designing and Implementing a Psychoeducational Group for School Children
from Drug-Involved Families." *Social Work* 44, 2 (1999): 179–190.

Dowrick, S. *Intimacy and Solitude: Balancing Closeness and Independence*. New York:
Norton, 1991.

Drigotas, Stephen M., Caryl E. Rusbult, Jennifer Wieselquist, and Sarah W. Whitton. "Close Partner as Sculptor of the Ideal Self: Behavioral Affirmation and the Michelangelo Phenomenon." *Journal of Personality and Social Psychology* 77, 2 (1999): 293–323.

Dryfoos, J. G. *Safe Passage: Making It Through Adolescence in a Risky Society*. New York: Oxford University Press, 1998.

Dudek, Stephanie Z. "The Morality of Twentieth-Century Transgressive Art." *Creativity Research Journal* 6, 1–2 (1993): 145–152.

Earls, Felton, and Mary Carlson. "Towards Sustainable Development for American Families." *Daedalus* 122, 1 (1993): 93–122.

Edelman, Marian Wright. *Families in Peril: An Agenda for Social Change*. Cambridge: Harvard University Press, 1987.

Elbaz, R. *The Changing Nature of the Self: A Critical Study of the Autobiographic Discourse*. Iowa City: University of Iowa Press, 1987.

Eliade, Mircea. *The Sacred and the Profane: The Nature of Religion*. Translated by William R. Trask. New York: Harcourt Brace, 1959.

Elkind, David. *The Hurried Child: Growing Up Too Fast Too Soon*. Reading, Mass.: Addison-Wesley, 1981.

Emerson, Ralph Waldo. *Self-Reliance and Other Essays*. New York: Dover, 1993.

Epstein, Mark. *Going on Being: Buddhism and the Way of Change*. New York: Broadway Books, 2001.

Erchak, Gerald Michael. *The Anthropology of Self and Behavior*. New Brunswick, N.J.: Rutgers University Press, 1992.

Erikson, Erik H. *Childhood and Society*. New York: Norton, 1950.

———. *Identity, Youth, and Crisis*. New York: Norton, 1968.

———. *Young Man Luther*. New York: Norton, 1962.

———. *Youth, Change, and Challenge*. New York: Basic Books, 1963.

Evans, Richard I. *Dialogue with Erik Erikson*. New York: Harper and Row, 1967.

Fain, Gerald S. "Special Education: Justice, Tolerance, and Beneficence as Duty." *Journal of Education* 180, 2 (1998): 41–56.

Favazza, Armando R. *Bodies under Siege: Self-Mutilation in Culture and Psychiatry*. Baltimore: Johns Hopkins University Press, 1987.

Fein, Steven, and Steven J. Spencer. "Prejudice as Self-Image Maintenance: Affirming the Self through Derogating Others." *Journal of Personality and Social Psychology* 73, 1 (1997): 31–44.

Festinger, Leon, with Vernon Allen. *Conflict, Decision, and Dissonance*. Stanford: Stanford University Press, 1964.

Flannery, D. J., M. I. Singer, and K. Wester. "Violence Exposure, Psychological Trauma, and Suicide Risk in a Community Sample of Dangerously Violent Adolescents." *Journal of the American Academy of Child and Adolescent Psychiatry* 40, 4 (2001): 435–42.

Fosshage, James L. "Self-Psychology and Its Contributions to Psychoanalysis: An Overview." *Journal of Analytic Social Work* 5, 2 (1998): 1–17.

Foucault, Michel. *The Birth of the Clinic: An Archaeology of Medical Perception.* New York: Random House, 1973.

Fraiberg, Selma H. *The Magic Years: Understanding and Handling the Problems of Early Childhood.* New York: Scribner's, 1959.

Frankl, Viktor E. *Man's Search for Meaning: An Introduction to Logotherapy.* Translated by Ilse Lasch. Boston: Beacon, 1963.

———. *Psychotherapy and Existentialism: Selected Papers on Logotherapy.* New York: Washington Square Press, 1967.

———. *The Will to Meaning: Foundations and Applications of Logotherapy.* New York: New American Library, 1970.

Freud, Anna. *The Ego and the Mechanisms of Defense.* New York: International Universities Press, 1946.

Freud, Sigmund. *The Basic Writings of Sigmund Freud.* Translated and edited by A. A. Brill. New York: Modern Library, 1938.

———. *The Complete Introductory Lectures on Psychoanalysis.* Translated and edited by James Strachey. New York: Norton, 1966.

———. *Beyond the Pleasure Principle, Group Psychology, and Other Works.* Translated by James Strachey. London: Hogarth, 1955.

———. *Civilization and Its Discontents.* Translated by Joan Rivière. London: Hogarth, 1930.

———. "The Ego and the Id." In *The Standard Edition of the Complete Psychological Works of Sigmund Freud,* translated by James Strachey, 19; 58. New York: Norton, 1962.

———. *A General Introduction to Psychoanalysis.* Translated by G. Stanley Hall. New York: Liveright, 1935.

———. *Inhibitions, Symptoms, and Anxiety.* Translated by Alix Strachey. New York: Norton, 1977.

Fromm, Erich. *Escape from Freedom.* New York: Farrar and Rinehart, 1941.

———. *The Sane Society.* New York: Holt, Rinehart and Winston, 1955.

Gabler, Neal. *Life the Movie: How Entertainment Conquered Reality.* New York: Knopf, 1998.

Garcia-Duettmann, Alexander. "'What Is Called Love in All the Languages and Silences of the World': Nietzsche, Genealogy, Contingency." *American Imago* 50, 3 (1993): 277–323.

Gardner, Howard. *Frames of Mind: The Theory of Multiple Intelligences.* New York: Basic Books, 1983.

Gattengo, Caleb. *The Adolescent and His Will.* New York: Outerbridge and Dienstfrey, 1971.

Geertz, Clifford. *The Interpretation of Cultures: Selected Essays.* New York: Basic Books, 1973.

Gilligan, Carol. *In a Different Voice.* Cambridge: Harvard University Press, 1982.

Gilligan, C., J. V. Ward, J. M. Taylor, and B. Bardige. *Mapping the Moral Domain:*

A Contribution of Women's Thinking to Psychological Theory and Education. Cambridge: Harvard University Press, 1988.

Gilligan, James. *Violence: Our Deadly Epidemic and Its Causes.* New York: G. P. Putnam's Sons, 1996.

Glauber, Peter I. "Federn's Annotation of Freud's Theory of Anxiety." *Journal of the American Psychoanalytic Association* 11, 1 (1963): 84–96.

Goffman, Erving. *Stigma: Notes on the Management of Spoiled Identity.* Englewood Cliffs, N.J.: Prentice-Hall, 1963.

———. *The Presentation of Self in Everyday Life.* Garden City, N.Y.: Anchor Books, 1959.

Gold, Adam. "Affirmation and the Concept of the Gaze in Psychosocial Identity Formation." Unpublished manuscript, Boston University, 2001.

Goldberg, Arnold, ed. *Advances in Self Psychology.* With summarizing reflections by Heinz Kohut. New York: International Universities Press, 1980.

Goldstein, Joseph, Anna Freud, and Albert J. Solnit. *Before the Best Interests of the Child.* New York: Free Press, 1979.

Gould, William Blair. "Boundaries and Meaning." *International Forum for Logotherapy* 18, 1 (1995): 49–52.

Greenberg, Leslie S., and Sandra C. Paivio. "Allowing and Accepting Painful Emotional Experiences." *International Journal of Action Methods* 51, 2 (1998): 47–61.

Griffin, David Ray. ed. *Archetypal Process: Self and Divine in Whitehead, Jung, and Hillman.* Evanston, Il.: Northwestern University Press, 1989.

Groopman, J. *Measure of Our Days: New Beginnings at Life's End.* New York: Viking, 1997.

Gross, Paul R., and Norman Levitt. *Higher Superstition: The Academic Left and Its Quarrels with Science.* Baltimore: Johns Hopkins University Press, 1998.

Gundrum, Monica, Germain Lietaer, and Christiane Matthijssen Van-Hees. "Carl Rogers' Responses in the Seventeenth Session with Miss Mun: Comments from a Process-Experiential and Psychoanalytic Perspective." *British Journal of Guidance and Counseling* 27, 4 (1999): 461–82.

Gunzburg, John C. " 'What Works?' Therapeutic Experience with Grieving Clients." *Journal of Family Therapy* 16, 2 (1994): 159–71.

Hall, Brian. *Madeline's World: A Child's Journey from Birth to Age 3.* Boston: Houghton Mifflin, 1997.

Hand, Sean, ed. *The Levinas Reader.* Oxford: Basil Blackwell, 1989.

Hansot, Elisabeth. "Civic Friendship: An Aristotelian Perspective." In *Reconstructing the Common Good in Education,* ed. L. Cuban and D. Shipps 173–85. Stanford: Stanford University Press, 2000.

Healy, Seán Desmond. *Boredom, Self, and Culture.* Rutherford, N.I.: Fairleigh Dickinson University Press, 1984.

Hegel, G. W. F. *The Phenomenology of Mind.* Translated by J. Baillie. New York: Harper and Row, 1967.

Heidegger, Martin. *Being and Time*. Translated by Joan Stambaugh. Albany: State University of New York Press, 1966.

Heller, Caroline E. *Until We Are Strong Together: Women Writers in the Tenderloin*. New York: Teachers College Press, 1997.

Herman, Judith. *Trauma and Recovery*. New York: Basic Books, 1992.

Hermanowicz, Joseph C., and Harriet P. Morgan. "Ritualizing the Routine: Collective Identity Affirmation." *Sociological Forum* 14, 2 (1999): 197–214.

Hill, Susann R., and Toni R. Tollerud. "Restoring Dignity in At-Risk Students." *School Counselor* 44, 2 (1996): 122–32.

Hirsch, E. D. *The Schools We Need and Why We Don't Have Them*. New York: Doubleday, 1996.

Hirsch, Eli. *The Concept of Identity*. New York: Oxford University Press, 1982.

Hirsch, Kathleen. "Circle of Friends." *Boston Globe Magazine*, March 11, 2001; 14–15.

Hollander, Jesse. "Identity Formation and the Aetiology of Neurosis." Unpublished manuscript, Boston University, 2001.

Horney, Karen. *Neurosis and Human Growth*. New York: Norton, 1950.

———. *The Neurotic Personality of Our Time*. New York: Norton, 1937.

Humes, Dusty Lee, and Laura Lynn Humphrey. "A Multimethod Analysis of Families with a Polydrug-Dependent or Normal Adolescent Daughter." *Journal of Abnormal Psychology* 103, 4 (1994): 676–85.

Jacoby, Jeff. "McVeigh's Execution Should Be Televised." *Boston Globe*, March 12, 2001; A11.

James, William. *Principles of Psychology*. New York: Dover, 1950.

Jefferson, Margo. "The Critic in Time of War." *New York Times Book Review*, October 28, 2001, 35.

Jensen, Larry C., and Richard S. Knight. *Moral Education: Historical Perspectives*. New York: New York University Press, 1981.

Jensma, Jeanne L. "Kohut's Tragic Man and Imago Dei: Human Relational Needs in Creation, the Fall, and Redemption." *Journal of Psychology and Theology* 21, 4 (1993): 288–96.

Jersild, Arthur T. "Social and Individual Origins of the Self." In *Relevant Readings in Human Development*, ed. John J. Mitchell. Berkeley, Calif.: McCutchan Publishing, 1971.

Jung, Carl G. *Basic Writings*. Edited with an introduction by Violet Staub de Lazlo. New York: Modern Library, 1959.

Kagan, Jerome. *The First Two Years*. Cambridge: Harvard University Press, 1981.

———. *The Nature of the Child*. New York: Basic Books, 1984.

———. *The Second Year: The Emergence of Self-Awareness*. Cambridge: Harvard University Press, 1981.

Kandel, Denise B. "Socialization and Adolescent Drinking." In *Alcohol and Youth*. Vol. 2 of *Child Health and Development*, ed. O. Jeanneret, 66–75. Basel: Karger, 1983.

Kant, Immanuel. *The Critique of Pure Reason.* Translated by Norman Kent Smith. New York: St. Martin's Press, 1965.

Karen, Robert. "Shame." *Atlantic,* February 1992, 40–70.

Karlsson, Gunnar. "Beyond the Pleasure Principle: The Affirmation of existence." *Scandinavian Psychoanalytic Review* 21, 1 (1998): 37–52.

Kegan, Robert. *The Evolving Self.* Cambridge: Harvard University Press, 1982.

———. *In Over Our Heads: The Mental Demands of Modern Life.* Cambridge: Harvard University Press, 1994.

Kemmis, Stephen J. "Action Research and the Politics of Reflection." In *Reflection: Turning Experience into Learning,* ed. D. Boyd, R. Keogh, and D. Walker, 139–64. London: Kogan, Page, 1985.

Killingmo, Byron. "Affirmation in Psychoanalysis." *International Journal of Psychoanalysis* 76, 3 (1995): 503–18.

Kleinplatz, Peggy J. "The Erotic Encounter." *Journal of Humanistic Psychology* 36, 3 (1996): 105–23.

Kohut, Heinz. *The Analysis of the Self: A Systematic Approach to the Psychoanalytic Treatment of Narcissistic Personality.* New York: International Universities Press, 1971.

———. *The Kohut Seminars: On Self Psychology and Psychotherapy with Adolescents and Young Adults.* New York: Norton, 1987.

———. *The Search for the Self.* Vol. 2. Edited by Paul Ornstein. New York: International Universities Press, 1978.

Kovel, Joel. *White Racism: A Psychohistory.* New York: Vintage Books, 1979.

Kozol, Jonathan. Foreword to *Will Standards Save Public Education?* by Deborah Meier. Boston: Beacon Press, 2000.

———. *Savage Inequalities: Children in America's Schools.* New York: Crown, 1991.

Krueger, David. "Food as Selfobject in Eating Disorder Patients." *Psychoanalytic Review* 84, 4 (1997): 617–30.

Lacan, Jacques. *Language of the Self: The Function of Language in Psychoanalysis.* Translated by Anthony Wilden. Baltimore: Johns Hopkins University Press 1968.

Laing, R. D. *The Divided Self.* Baltimore: Penguin, 1965.

———. *Reason and Violence: A Decade of Sartre's Philosophy, 1950–1960.* New York: Pantheon, 1964.

Lakoff, George, and Mark Johnson. *Metaphors We Live By.* Chicago: University of Chicago Press, 1980.

Langer, Ellen J. *Mindfulness.* Reading, Mass.: Addison-Wesley, 1989.

———. *The Power of Mindful Learning.* Reading, Mass.: Perseus, 1997.

Lasch, Christopher. *The Culture of Narcissism: American Life in an Age of Diminishing Expectations.* New York: Norton, 1978.

Lawrence, Lauren. *Dream Keys for Love: Unlocking the Secrets of Your Own Heart.* New York: Dell, 1999.

Lawrence-Lightfoot, Sara. *Respect*. Reading, Mass.: Perseus, 1999.

Lawrence-Lightfoot, Sara, and Jessica Hoffman Davis. *The Art and Science of Portraiture*. San Francisco: Jossey-Bass, 1997.

Levin, Jack, and Arnold Arluke, *Gossip: The Inside Scoop*. New York: Plenum Press, 1987.

Levinas, Emmanuel. *Ethics and Infinity: Conversations with Philippe Nemo*. Translated by Richard A. Cohen. Pittsburgh: Duquesne University Press, 1985.

———. *The Levinas Reader*. Edited by Seán Hand. Cambridge, Mass.: Basil Blackwell, 1989.

———. *Otherwise than Being, or Beyond Essense*. Translated by Alphonso Lingis. Boston: Martinus Nijhoff, 1981.

———. "Philosophy and the Idea of the Infinite." *Revue Philosophique de la France et de l'Etranger* 147 (1957) 7, 9: 241–54.

———. *Totality and Infinity: An Essay on Exteriority*. Translated by Alphonso Lingis. Pittsburgh: Duquesne University Press, 1969.

Lincoln, C. Eric. *Race, Religion, and the Continuing American Dilemma*. New York: Hill and Wang, 1999.

Lionnet, F. *Autobiographical Voices: Race, Gender, Self-Portraiture*. Ithaca: Cornell University Press, 1989.

Loewald, Hans W. "Ego and Reality." *International Journal of Psychoanalysis* 32 (1951): 10–18.

———. "Instinct Theory, Object Relations, and Psychic Structure Formation." *Journal of the American Psychoanalytic Association* 26, 3 (1978); 493–506.

Mack, John. *Nightmares and Human Conflict*. Boston: Little, Brown, 1970.

Maeder, Thomas. *Children of Psychiatrists and Other Psychotherapists*. New York: Harper and Row, 1989.

Maguire, John. *The Power of Personal Story Telling: Spinning Tales to Connect with Others*. New York: Jeremy P. Tarcher/Putnam, 1998.

Mahler, Margaret. *The Psychological Birth of the Human Infant*. Franklin Lakes, N.J.: Mahler Research Foundation Library, 1985.

Mair, M. "Psychology as Story Telling." *International Journal of Construct Psychology* 1, 2 (1988): 125–37.

Marcuse, Herbert. *One Dimensional Man: Studies in the Ideology of Advanced Industrial Society*. Boston: Beacon Press, 1964.

Markus, Hazel. "Self-Knowledge: An Expanded View." *Journal of Personality* 51, 3 (1983): 543–65.

Marris, Peter. "Holding on to Meaning through the Life-Cycle." In *Challenges of the Third Age: Meaning and Purpose in Later Life*, ed. Robert S. Weiss and Scott A. Bass, 13–28. New York: Oxford University Press, 2001.

May, Rollo. *The Discovery of Being: Writings in Existential Psychology*. New York: Norton, 1983.

Mays, Gloria Denise, and Carole Holden Lund. "Male Caregivers of Mentally Ill Relatives." *Perspectives in Psychiatric Care* 35, 2 (1999): 19–28.

Mead, George Herbert. *Mind, Self, and Society from the Standpoint of a Social Behaviorist.* Chicago: University of Chicago Press, 1934.

Meier, Deborah. *Will Standards Save Public Education?* Boston: Beacon Press, 2000.

Melson, Gail. *Why the Wild Things Are.* Cambridge: Harvard University Press, 2001.

Merleau-Ponty, Maurice. "The Child's Relations with Others." Translated by W. Cobb. In *The Primacy of Perception.* Edited by J. M. Edie, 96–155. Evanston, Ill.: Northwestern University Press, 1964.

Miller, Alice. *The Drama of the Gifted Child.* Translated by Ruth Ward. New York: Basic Books, 1981.

Miller, Derek, with the assistance of Barry Carlton. *Attack on the Self: Adolescent Behavioral Disturbances and Their Treatment.* Northvale, N.J.: Aronson, 1986.

Miller, Ivan J. "Interpersonal Vulnerability and Narcissism: A Conceptual Continuum for Understanding and Treating Narcissistic Psychopathology." *Psychotherapy* 29, 2 (1992): 216–24.

Minuchin, Salvador. *Families and Family Therapy.* Cambridge: Harvard University Press, 1974.

Modell, Arnold H. *The Private Self.* Cambridge: Harvard University Press, 1993.

Moody, Harry R. "Why Dignity in Old Age Matters." *Journal of Gerontological Social Work* 29, 2–3 (1997): 13–38.

Murray, Sandra L., John G. Holmes, Geoff MacDonald, and Phoebe C. Ellsworth. "Through the Looking Glass Darkly? When Self-Doubts Turn into Relationship Insecurities." *Journal of Personality and Social Psychology* 75, 6 (1998): 1459–80.

Muuss, Rolf E. H. *Theories of Adolescence.* New York: Random House, 1968.

Naipul, V. S. *Half a Life.* New York: Knopf, 2001.

Nansel, T. R., M. Overpeck, and R. S. Pilla. "Bullying Behaviors among U.S. Youth: Prevalence and Association with Psychosocial Adjustment." *Journal of the American Medical Association* 285, 16 (2001): 2094–2100.

Napier, Augustus Y., and Carl A. Whitaker. *The Family Crucible: The Intense Experience of Family Therapy.* New York: Harper and Row, 1978.

Narramore, Bruce. "Serving Two Masters? Commentary on 'Dealing with religious resistance in psychotherapy': Reply." *Journal of Psychology and Theology* 22, 4 (1994): 261–63.

Naus, Peter J. and John P. Theis. "The Significance of Fatherly Affirmation for a Man's Psychological Well-Being: A Comparison of Canadian and Dutch University Students." *Canadian Journal of Human Sexuality* 4, 4 (1995): 237–45.

Neruda, Pablo. "Sonnet XVII." In *One Hundred Love Sonnets.* Translated by Stephen Tapscott. Austin: University of Texas Press, 1986.

Newberger, Eli H. "Treating This Heavy Mid-Life of Men." *American Journal of Orthopsychiatry* 71 (July 2001): 278–80.

Nietzsche, Friedrich. *Schopenhauer as Educator.* Translated by James W. Hillesheim and Malcolm R. Simpson. South Bend, Ind.: Gateway Editions, 1965.

———. *The Will to Power.* Translated by Walter Kaufman and R. J. Hollingdale. New York: Vintage Books, 1968.

Novak, Michael. *Belief and Unbelief: A Philosophy of Self-Knowledge.* New York: Macmillan, 1965.

Novick, Jack. "Attempted Suicide in Adolescence: The Suicide Sequence." In *Essential Papers on Suicide,* ed. John T. Mattsberger and Mark J. Goldblatt, 524–98. New York: New York University Press, 1996.

Nozick, Robert. *The Examined Life: Philosophical Meditations.* New York: Simon and Schuster, 1989.

Ornstein, Anna. "A Developmental Perspective on the Sense of Power, Self-Esteem, and Destructive Aggression. *Annual Review of Psychoanalysis* 25 (1997): 145–54.

Palladino, Donald, Jr. "Poets to Come: Walt Whitman, Self Psychology, and the Readers of the Future." Unpublished manuscript, 2000.

Palmer, Parker J. *The Courage to Teach: Exploring the Inner Landscape of a Teacher's Life.* San Francisco, Jossey-Bass, 1998.

Pardeck, John, T. *Social Work Practice: An Ecological Approach.* Westport, Conn.: Auburn House/Greenwood Publishing Group, 1996.

Parry, A. "Universe of Stories." *Family Process* 30 (1991): 37–54.

Peck, F. Scott. *The Road Less Traveled: A New Psychology of Love, Traditional Values, and Spiritual Growth.* New York: Simon and Schuster, 1978.

Peperzak, Adriaan T. *To the Other: An Introduction to the Philosophy of Emmanuel Levinas.* West Lafayette: Purdue University Press, 1993.

Phillips, Christopher C. "Don Juan: A Study in Identity Development." Unpublished manuscript, Boston University, 2001.

Piaget, Jean. *The Language and Thought of the Child.* London: Routledge and Kegan Paul, 1932.

———. *Six Psychological Studies.* New York: Random House, 1967.

Pines, M. "The Universality of Shame: A Psychoanalytic Approach." *British Journal of Psychotherapy* 11, (1995): 346–87.

Pirke, K. M., and D. Ploog, eds. *The Psychobiology of Anorexia Nervosa.* Berlin, N.Y.: Springer, 1984.

Pollock, William. *Real Boys: Rescuing Our Sons from the Myths of Boyhood.* New York: Random House, 1998.

Postman, Neal. *Amusing Ourselves to Death: Public Discourse in the Age of Show Business.* New York: Penguin, 1986.

Pretat, Jane R. *Coming to Age: The Croning Years and Late-Life Transformation.* Toronto: Inner City Books, 1994.

Quinn, William H. "The Client Speaks Out: Three Domains of Meaning." *Journal of Family Psychotherapy* 7, 2 (1996): 71–93.

Rawls, John. *A Theory of Justice*. Cambridge: Harvard University Press, Belknap Press, 1971.

Remen, Rachel Naomi. *My Grandfather's Blessings: Stories of Strength, Refuge, and Belonging*. New York: Riverhead, 2000.

Reynolds, Susan. Review of *I Cannot Tell a Lie, Exactly*, by Mary Ladd Gavell. *Los Angeles Times Book Review*, August 19, 2001, 11.

Ricoeur, Paul. *The Conflict of Interpretations*. Evanston, Ill.: Northwestern University Press, 1974.

Robbins, Michael. "Therapeutic Presence in Holistic Psychotherapy." In *Therapeutic Presence: Bridging Expression and Form*, ed. Arthur Robbins, 153–81. London: Jessica Kingsley Publishers, 1998.

Rogers, Carl. *Client-Centered Therapy: Its Current Practice, Implications, and Theory*. Boston: Houghton Mifflin, 1965.

———. *Counseling and Psychotherapy: New Concepts in Practice*. Boston: Houghton Mifflin, 1942.

Rooke, Constance. "Old Age in Contemporary Fiction: A New Paradigm of Hope." In *Handbook of the Humanities and Aging*, ed. Thomas R. Cole and David Dirck Van Tassel, 241–57. New York: Springer, 1992.

Rose, M. *Industrial Behavior*. London: Allen Lane, 1975.

Rosenberg, M. *Conceiving the Self*. New York: Basic Books, 1979.

Roszak, Theodore. "On the Contemporary Hunger for Wonders." In *Seasonal Performances*, ed. Laurence Goldstein, 63–78. Ann Arbor: University of Michigan Press, 1991.

Rubin, Theodore Isaac, with Eleanor Rubin. *Compassion and Self-Hate: An Alternative to Despair*. New York: D. McKay, 1975.

Rumney, A. *Dying to Please: Anorexia Nervosa and Its Cure*. Jefferson, N.C.: McFarland, 1983.

Rushdie, Salman. *Fury*. New York: Random House, 2001.

Rusk, Tom, and Randy Read. *I Want to Change but I Don't Know How*. Los Angeles: Price/Stern/Sloan, 1986.

Rzepka, Charles. J. *The Self as Mind: Visions and Identity in Wordsworth, Coleridge, and Keats*. Cambridge: Harvard University Press, 1986.

Sable, Pat. "Attachment, Detachment, and Borderline Personality Disorder," *Psychotherapy* 34, 2 (1997): 171–81.

Santrock, John. *Adolescence*. 8th ed., New York: McGraw Hill, 2001.

Sartre, Jean-Paul. *Existentialism and Human Emotions*. New York: Kensington Publishing, 1957.

———. *The Words*. Translated by Bernard Frechtman. New York: G. Braziller, 1964.

Sasso, Gary M. "The Retreat from Inquiry and Knowledge in Special Education." *Journal of Special Education* 34, 4 (2001): 178–93.

Schachtel, Ernest. *Metamorphosis: On the Development of Affect, Perception, Attention, and Memory.* New York: Basic Books, 1959.

Scheffler, Tanya S. and Peter J. Naus. "The Relationship between Fatherly Affirmation and a Woman's Self-Esteem, Fear of Intimacy, Comfort with Womanhood, and Comfort with Sexuality." *Canadian Journal of Human Sexuality* 8, 1 (1999): 39–45.

Schiff, Jonathan. *Ashes to Ashes: Mourning and Social Differences in F. Scott Fitzgerald's Fiction.* Selinsgrove, Pa.: Susquehanna University Press, 2001.

Schinneller, James A. *Art, Search, and Self-Discovery.* Scranton, Pa.: International Textbook, 1968.

Schwarzenbach, Sibly A. "On Civic Friendship." *Ethics 107,* 1 (1996): 97–128.

Sears, Douglas. "A Message from Douglas Sears." In *Update,* 1. Boston: Boston University, School of Education, September 2001, page 1.

Sehl, Mark. "Stalemates in Therapy and the Notion of Gratification." *Psychoanalytic Review* 81, 2 (1994): 301–21.

Selzer, Richard. *Letters to a Young Doctor.* New York: Simon and Schuster, 1983.

Sereny, Gitta. *Why Children Kill: The Story of Mary Bell.* New York: Henry Holt, 1999.

Shakespeare, William. *Romeo and Juliet. In The Complete Works of William Shakespeare.* Shakespeare Head Press Edition. New York: Barnes and Noble, 1994.

Sidorkin, Alexander M. *Beyond Discourse: Education, the Self, and Dialogue.* Albany: State University of New York Press, 1999.

Siegel, Lee. "A Defense of Serious Fiction." *Los Angeles Times Book Review*, August 5, 2001, 8–10.

Silverman, P. R. *Never Too Young to Know: Death in Children's Lives.* New York: Oxford University Press, 1999.

Simpson, Jeffry A., and W. Steven Rholes, eds. *Attachment Theory and Close Relationships.* New York: Guilford Press, 1998.

Slavin, R. "Cooperative Learning and Student Achievement." *Educational Leadership* 46, 2 (1988): 31–33.

States, Bert O. *Dreaming and Story Telling.* Ithaca: Cornell University Press, 1993.

Stein, Howard F. "Disposable Youth: The 1999 Columbine High School Massacre as American Metaphor." *Journal for the Psychoanalysis of Culture and Society* 5, 2 (2000): 217–36.

Stein, Murray. *Transformation: Emergence of the Self.* College Station: Texas A&M University Press, 1998.

Steiner, David. Introduction to *Proceedings of the Twentieth World Congress of Philosophy.* Philosophy Documentation Center, Bowling Green State University, 1999.

———. "Levinas' Ethical Interruption of Reciprocity." *Salmagundi*, nos. 130–31 (2001): 120–42.

Stelzig, Eugene L. *All Shades of Consciousness: Wordsworth's Poetry and the Self in Time*. The Hague: Mouton, 1975.

Stevens, Anthony. *Archetypes: A Natural History of the Self*. New York: Morrow, 1982.

Stevens, Richard. *Erik Erikson*. New York: St. Martin's Press, 1983.

Stone, Jeff. "What Exactly Have I Done? The Role of Self-Attribute Accessibility in Dissonance." In *Cognitive Dissonance: Progress on a Pivotal Theory in Social Psychology*, ed. Eddie Harmon-Jones and Judson Mills, 175–200. Science Conference Series. Washington, D.C.: American Psychological Association, 1999.

Storr, Anthony. *Solitude: A Return to the Self*. New York: Balantine Books, 1988.

Strachen, A., and D. Jones. "Changes in Identification during Adolescence: A Personal Construct Theory Approach." *Journal of Personality Assessment* 46 (1982): 139–48.

Straus, Martha B. *No Talk Therapy*. New York: Norton, 1999.

Stryk, Lucien. *The Awakened Self: Encounters with Zen*. New York: Kodansha International, 1995.

Stuart, Samantha, and Thomas J. Cottle. "Money Doesn't Buy Everything." *Children First* 5 (June/July 2001): 22–23.

"Study Details Teens' Troubles," *Boston Globe*, November 13, 1998, A7.

Suler, John R., and Anthony Molino, eds. *The Couch and the Tree: Dialogues in Psychoanalysis and Buddhism*. New York: North Point Press, 1998.

Summers, Randall W., ed. *Teen Violence: A Global View*. Westport, Conn.: Greenwood, 2000.

Sved-Williams, Anne. "A Group for the Adult Daughters of Mentally Ill Mothers: Looking Backwards and Forwards." *British Journal of Medical Psychology* 71, 1 (1998): 73–83.

Teicholz, Judith Guss. "Loewald's 'Positive Neutrality' and the Affirmative Potential of Psychoanalytic Interventions." In *The Psychoanalytic Study of the Child*, 50:48–75. New York: International Universities Press, 1995.

Thoreau, Henry David. "Life without Principle." In *The Norton Anthology of American Literature*, 5th ed., ed. Nina Baym et al. New York: Norton, 1998.

Thornton, Bill, and Jason Maurice. "Physique Contrast Effect: Adverse Impact of Idealized Body Images for Women." *Sex Roles* 37, 5–6 (1997): 433–39.

Thrane, G. "Shame and the Construction of the Self." *Annual Review of Psychoanalysis* 7 (1979): 321–41.

Tigner, Stephen. "Harry Potter and the Good Life." Unpublished manuscript, Center for Character Education, Boston University, 2001.

Tillich, Paul. *The Courage to Be*. New Haven: Yale University Press, 1952.

Tolkin, Michael. "The Loneliness of the Long-Distance Writer." Review of *Chester Himes: A Life*, by James Sallis. *Los Angeles Times Book Review*, March 18, 2001, 2.

Turiel, Eliot. "The Development of Social-Convention and Moral Concepts." In *Fundamental Research in Moral Development: A Compendium*, ed. Bill Puka, 2: 255–92. New York: Garland, 1994.

Underwood, Geoffrey, and Robin Stevens, eds. *Aspects of Consciousness*. New York: Academic Press, 1979.

Updike, John. *Bech: A Book*. New York: Knopf, 1970.

Valois, R. F., K. J. Zullig, E. S. Huebner, and W. Drane. "Relationship between Life Satisfaction and Violent Behaviors among Adolescents. *American Journal of Health Behavior* 25, 4 (2001): 353–66.

Varenne, Hervé, and Ray McDermott, with Shelley Goldman, Mervy Naddeo, and Rosemarie Rizzo-Tolk. *Successful Failure: The School America Builds*. Boulder, Colo.: Westview, 1998.

Veroff, Joseph, Elizabeth Douvan, Terri L. Orbuch, and Linda K. Acitelli. "Happiness in Stable Marriages: The Early Years." In *The Developmental Course of Marital Dysfunction*, ed. Thomas N. Bradbury, 152–79. Cambridge: Cambridge University Press, 1998.

von Franz, Marie-Louise, *Archetypal Dimensions of the Psyche*. Boston: Shambhala Publications, 1994.

Vygotsky, Lev. *Mind in Society*. Cambridge, MA: Harvard University Press, 1978.

Walen, Susan R., Raymond DiGiuseppe, and Richard L. Wessler. *A Practitioner's Guide to Rational-Emotive Therapy*. 2d ed. New York: Oxford University Press, 1980.

Walker, Rebecca. *Black, White, and Jewish: The Autobiography of a Shifting Self.* New York: Riverhead Books, 2001.

Warton, B. "The Hidden Face of Shame: The Shadow, Shame, and Separation." *Journal of Analytical Psychology* 35, 3 (1990): 279–99.

Watzlawick, P., J. H. Weakland, and R. Fisch. *Change: Principles of Problem Formation and Problem Resolution*. New York: Norton, 1974.

Weinstein, Fred. *Freud, Psychoanalysis, Social Theory: The Unfulfilled Promise*. Albany: State University of New York Press, 2001.

West, Cornel. *Race Matters*. New York: Vintage Books, 1994.

Whitehead, Barbara Dafoe. *The Divorce Culture*. New York: Alfred Knopf, 1996.

Whitman Walt. "Song of Myself." In *Leaves of Grass*. Garden City, N.Y.: Doubleday, 1926.

———. "To a Pupil." In *Complete Poetry and Selected Prose*. Edited by James E. Miller. Boston: Houghton Mifflin, 1959.

Wilde, Dana. "Problems at the English Department." *CEA Critic* 62 (Winter/ Spring 2000): 1–18.

Wilde, Oscar. *The Picture of Dorian Gray*. Edited by Donald L. Lawler. New York: Norton, 1988.

Wilhelmsen, B. U., S. Laberg, and H. Aas. "Alcohol Outcome Expectancies in Adolescence." *Psychology and Health* 13 (November 6, 1998): 1037–44.

Willis, Albert, and Robert A. Harper. *A New Guide to Rational Living*. Englewood-Cliffs, N.J.: Prentice-Hall, 1975.

Wilson, Terence G. "Acceptance and Change in the Treatment of Eating Disorders and Obesity." *Behavior Therapy* 27, 3 (1996): 417–39.

Winnicott, D. W. *Mother and Child: A Primer of First Relationships*. New York: Basic Books, 1957.

Wood, Joanne V., Maria Giordano Beech, and Mary-Jo Ducharme. "Compensating for Failure through Social Comparison." *Personality and Social Psychology Bulletin* 25, 11 (1999): 1370–86.

Wright, Andrew G. "American Teenagers Distracted," unpublished manuscript, Boston University, 2001.

Wright, Eugene J. *Erikson: Identity and Religion*. New York: Seabury Press, 1982.

Wurmser, L. *The Mask of Shame*. Baltimore: Johns Hopkins University Press, 1981.

Young, Alan. "Suffering and the Origins of Traumatic Memory." *Daedalus* 125, 1 (1996): 245–60.

Young-Bruehl, Elizabeth, and Faith Bethelard. *Cherishment: A Psychology of the Heart*. New York: Free Press, 2000.

Zimbardo, Phillip. *Shyness: What It Is, What to Do about It*. Reading, Mass.: Addison-Wesley, 1977.

Zuckerman, Barry. "Read to Your Child Every Day: An Rx for Dads Everywhere. *Boston Globe*, June 17, 2001, F7.

A SOCIOLOGIST and licensed clinical psychologist, THOMAS J. COTTLE is professor of education at Boston University. He received his B.A. degree from Harvard University, his M.A. and Ph.D. degrees from the University of Chicago, and an L.H.D. degree from Lesley University, Cambridge, Massachusetts.

Professor Cottle is the author of almost thirty books and more than five hundred and fifty articles, essays, and reviews. His most recent book titles include *Hardest Times: The Trauma of Long Term Unemployment*, *At Peril: Stories of Injustice*, and the forthcoming *When the Music Stopped: Discovering My Mother*.

Professor Cottle is married to Kay Mikkelsen Cottle, a high school history teacher. They are the parents of three children and the grandparents of three children.